Improving Spoken English

Improving Spoken English

An Intensive Personalized Program in Perception, Pronunciation, Practice in Context

Joan Morley

Ann Arbor   The University of Michigan Press

Acknowledgments

Many colleagues and many students have been most generous in contributing their time and their suggestions during the preparation of *Improving Spoken English*. My sincere appreciation to Ronald Wardhaugh·and H. Douglas Brown for their personal as well as administrative support of the project and to Bradford Arthur, H. Douglas Brown, Sandra C. Browne, William W. Crawford, and Carlos A. Yorio for their reading of portions of the manuscript. Special acknowledgment to James L. Bixler, broadcast engineer, for his painstaking recording of the entire text; to Albert Davis, ELI Language Laboratory coordinator for his laboratory management of the experimental materials; and to Eleanor Foster, administrative assistant, for her attention to the preparation and office management of the materials. Special thanks to Sandra C. Browne and Larry Nessly who served in research posts on the project and to William R. Acton, E. Margaret Baudoin, Sandra C. Browne, William W. Crawford, Beverly S. Fried, Adelaide W. Heyde, and Wayne Lord for their enthusiastic participation in the establishment of special pronunciation lab/classes as an extension of the listening/speaking curriculum at the English Language Institute.

Particular appreciation to Thomas B. Coates, director, University of Michigan Television Center, and Erwin M. Hamson, director, Modern Language Laboratory, for the interdepartmental support and assistance accorded to me and to the English Language Institute.

Joan Morley

Preface

Improving Spoken English is a pronunciation program written for English as a second language (ESL) students and for their ESL teachers.

The Students

One of the primary concerns of *Improving Spoken English* is to involve students, consciously, in their own learning process as they work to improve their spoken English. Each part of each lesson focuses students' attention on *what* they are doing and *why* they are doing it. The intent is to help students to develop: (1) an awareness of and an interest in language learning, (2) a sense of personal responsibility for their own learning, and (3) a feeling of pride in their own accomplishments.

To meet the above goals, two kinds of material have been written—practice activities and explanations. *Practice activities* in listening and in speaking are directed toward the gradual development of an auditory base and a physical base for improving spoken English. The lessons present activities designed to guide students toward making use of auditory distinctions and articulatory patterns which are important for English pronunciation. *Explanations* are included to give students sufficient speech awareness to enable them to monitor and to control their pronunciation for increased intelligibility both during the instructional period and beyond.

Acoustic information, physiological information, and linguistic information have been expressed in straight-forward lay terminology. Explanations throughout are simplified for the sake of clarity.

The Teachers

Another primary objective of *Improving Spoken English* is to aid teachers in their role as facilitator of learning. To avoid a separate teachers' book, section notes and resource materials have been included in the students' workbook. These are directed toward assisting teachers in presenting the lessons easily and effectively.

To reach the above objective, two kinds of material have been written—methodological notes and informational notes. *Methodological notes* are included so that teachers do not have to guess at the intended use of lessons and parts of lessons. *Informational notes* provide a ready reference on points of English phonology. Resource pages provide materials for supplementary work. Footnotes include both methodological and informational material. Some of the information provided is rather detailed. The teacher can determine whether it is appropriate to discuss this material with students.

The explanatory material in *Improving Spoken English*, whether directed to students or to teachers, is intended not as an instructional end in itself, but as an aid to learning. The annotating is thorough, in order to provide ready access to additional material to aid in answering unexpected student questions or to give a student further production cues, when necessary. This has been done in the belief that it can be a convenience both to experienced teachers and to novices.

The Program

Improving Spoken English is subtitled *An Intensive Personalized Program in Perception, Pronunciation, Practice in Context.* Each word in the subtitle has been chosen to reflect the content of the book. The content of the book, in turn, reflects basic assumptions about: (*a*) language and language learning, and (*b*) the cognitive and affective aspects of learner processes. Seven key concepts in the title are:

1. *Improving.* The lesson material is planned for adult and high school ESL students who already speak some English; it is not a book for absolute beginners. Lesson flexibility, however, permits use by high-beginning, intermediate, and low-advanced classes.
2. *Intensive.* The lesson activities are carefully focused and concentrated.

3. *Personalized.* Presenting a positive attitude, the lessons encourage personal involvement by providing students with *ways and means* (*a*) to take responsibility for their own work and (*b*) to take a personal pride in their many small accomplishments along the way toward improved spoken English; and with *tools and techniques* with which (*a*) to monitor others and themselves, (*b*) to modify their spoken English—in bits and pieces—toward an increasingly closer match with the model, and (*c*) to continue to improve their spoken English when they leave the formal classroom and language laboratory.

4. *Program.* The workbook presents carefully arranged sequences of basic material in two units—(1) stress, rhythm, and intonation, and (2) vowels—and additional sequences of supplementary lessons which provide a variety of options to meet individual student needs.

5. *Perception.* The program is designed to develop students' auditory sensitivity as a perceptual base for improving spoken English.

6. *Pronunciation.* The program is designed to develop students' oral-tactile and oral-kinesthetic sensitivity as a physical base for improving spoken English.

7. *Practice in Context.* Supplements A and B contain short exercises which provide interesting and meaningful practice opportunities beyond those presented in the fundamental perception and pronunciation work of Unit 1 and Unit 2.

The Purposes and the Presentation

Some ESL students do not seem to enjoy the pronunciation class. They look upon it as a pain not as a pleasure. No other language area seems to generate more self-deprecation on the one hand, or more denial of need for improvement on the other. Some students are shy and embarrassed and appear to be threatened by attention to their spoken English. Others use the world's oldest self-protection device, professing not to care (although sometimes admitting privately that they have a bad accent or terrible pronunciation). With these concerns in mind, the goals of *Improving Spoken English* are to help students to accomplish four things:

1. to increase their self-confidence in speaking English and in listening to English;
2. to increase their level of intelligibility in speaking English and their level of aural comprehension in listening to English;
3. to increase their fluency in speaking English;
4. to increase their accuracy in speaking English.

Improving Spoken English attempts to emphasize the positive in several ways. It looks upon improvement as a gradual process, not as an overnight phenomenon. It is concerned with gradual modification of pronunciation toward a closer match with the abstract notion of model pronunciation, rather than with good or bad, correct or incorrect. It presents relatively easy selections on the self-evaluative tests, and it encourages personal pride in small accomplishments.

Above all, *Improving Spoken English* promotes *self-monitoring* and self-comparison, not student-to-student comparisons. This is an important point to emphasize, for there always will be those students for whom pronunciation improvements come rapidly and easily and those for whom pronunciation improvements come slowly and with great difficulty.

The pronunciation lessons and the recordings of *Improving Spoken English* are based on General American English. *A Pronouncing Dictionary of American English*, by John S. Kenyon and Thomas A. Knott (Springfield, Mass.: G. and C. Merriam Company, 1953), was used as a reference guide.

Some of the spelling information contained in Unit 2 was compiled using material presented in "English Orthography: Its Graphical Structure and Its Relation to Sound," by Richard L. Venezky (in *Reading Research Quarterly* 2, no. 3 [1976]); *Annotated Spelling-to-Sound Correspondence Rules*, by Bruce Cronnell (Southwest Regional Laboratory Technical Report, 32 [1971]); and *Phoneme-Grapheme Correspondences as Cues to Spelling Improvement*, by Paul R. Hanna, Jean S. Hanna, Richard E. Hodges, and Edwin H. Rudorf, Jr. (Washington, D.C.: Department of Health, Education, and Welfare, Office of Education, 1966).

Medical anatomy references and direct observation were used to prepare the descriptions of articulatory positions and movements in *Improving Spoken English*. Facial diagrams in the text are based on cinefluorographic frames of the author filmed by the University of Michigan Television Center in the X-ray department of the University of Michigan Medical Center. Explanations and illustrations throughout are simplified and stylized for the sake of clarity.

The phonetic notations in *Improving Spoken English* employ forms of the International Phonetic Alphabet with the following adaptations.

1. The symbol /a/ is used, rather than /ɑ/, for the first vowel sound in *father*.
2. The symbol /y/ is used, rather than /j/, for the first sound in *yes*.
3. The following have a second component added to the symbol as an aid to the learner of English as a second language.
   /iʸ/ is used for /i/, as in *see*
   /eⁱ/ is used for /e/, as in *say*
   /uʷ/ is used for /u/, as in *two*
   /oᵘ/ is used for /o/, as in *no*
4. The symbols /i/ and /u/, rather than /ɪ/ and /ʊ/, are used for the diphthongs in /ai/, /au/, and /ɔi/.

Contents

For Teachers

Improving Spoken English is in student workbook form. It includes six segments.

1. Unit 1: Stress, Rhythm, and Intonation
2. Unit 2: Vowels
3. Supplement A: Practice in Context for Unit 1
4. Supplement B: Practice in Context for Unit 2
5. Supplement C: Vowel Contrasts for Unit 2
6. Answer Key/Teacher Script

Teachers may wish to use the lessons in consecutive order as they occur in the text. They may wish to complete Unit 1 before going on to Unit 2, using materials from the supplements wherever appropriate.

However, in an alternative format of usage, Units 1 and 2 (and their supplementary materials) may be used together. The text is planned so that the presentation of Unit 2 may be instituted as soon as the work in Unit 1 has progressed through section C (lessons 6 and 7). At that point, work on Unit 2 may be used in either an alternating or a simultaneous program of study. A simultaneous usage plan such as the following might be appropriate for high-beginning or intermediate classes.

Unit 1	Supplement A	Unit 2	Supplement B	Supplement C
Section A				
Section B				
Section C	Section B	Section A		
Section D	Section C	Section B		Contrasts
Section E	Section D	Section C	Section B	Contrasts
Section F	Section E	Section D	Section C	Contrasts
Section G	Section F	Section E	Section D	Contrasts
		Section F	Section E	Contrasts

The entire series of *Improving Spoken English* lessons is available on tape. The tapes for each basic unit (Units 1 and 2) are intended for teacher-controlled use in a pronunciation laboratory class or in a regular pronunciation class setting. They are *not* intended for individual student self-help use *except* as a follow-up after teacher/class presentation. The tapes for the supplementary lessons in Supplements A, B, and C may be used in a pronunciation laboratory class *or* as individual student self-help use, at the discretion of the teacher.

If the taped lessons are not available, the lessons may be presented live by the teacher, using the appended Answer Key/Teacher Script (AK/TS).

Unit 1

The twenty lessons in Unit 1 have been designed to provide ESL students with a systematic and sequential introduction to selected features of English stress, rhythm, and intonation, and to include first steps toward improvement of these features in spoken English. Attention to prosodic elements is presented at the beginning of *Improving Spoken English* for one primary purpose. It is judged to be of fundamental importance to build a base of experience with some of the synthesizing aspects of the prosodic structure of spoken English at the outset, before work with individual sound segments is taken up in order to:

1. orient students to the dynamic nature of "pronunciation"—speech as a moving process, not a series of isolated postures; prepare them for immediate participation in contextual practice (Supplement A presents samples) and communicative speech activities (which can be provided only within the milieu of each unique classroom situation);
2. allow the individual sound segments (in Unit 2) to be presented and practiced within a natural prosodic environment which already is familiar to students; permit study of the changes which

take place within the rhythmic patterns of connected speech and the ways sounds influence the sounds around them;

3. permit the twenty-four vowel lessons in Unit 2 to serve as additional practice opportunities for reinforcement of the features of stress, rhythm, and intonation studied in Unit 1.

It is important to note here, that students are *not expected to master* these features of stress, rhythm, and intonation in a few short lessons. The lessons in Unit 1 are intended to begin a gradual process of improvement with review and reinforcement throughout the remainder of the program.

The graphic notations used in the text of Unit 1 do not come from one source. They are symbols which have been adapted from a number of sources and modified over an extended period of experimental use with ESL students. They are a combination of concrete notational forms which has been found to be successful in enhancing students' understanding of some of the most abstract phenomena of spoken English.

Unit 1 has seven sections. Each section begins with section notes.

Section A presents two introductory lessons to English stress, rhythm, and intonation, and introduces chart 1, Key Sentences for Stress, Rhythm, and Intonation.

Sections B, C, D, E, and F present fourteen intensive lessons including special test sentences for self-monitoring and self-testing. (See page 8 of Unit 1 for notes on using the intensive lessons.)

Section G presents four rapid-review-and-testing lessons.

Unit 2

The twenty-four lessons in Unit 2 have been designed to provide ESL students with a systematic introduction to the fifteen vowel sounds of General American English and to include first steps toward improving these sounds in spoken English.

Unit 2 is constructed with a whole/parts orientation. The introductory lesson builds on knowledge which most ESL students have already—knowledge of a five-sound vowel system of /i/, /e/, /a/, /o/, /u/. The additional ten vowels of English then are mapped onto the vowel chart relative to these five. Each vowel is assigned a *key word* as a mnemonic aid to the study of the vowel system and as a device later for self-monitoring. The fifteen key words combine into seven short phrases. Students are urged to practice these key words concentrating on memorizing each one—the "sound" of it and the "feel" of it. This is described fully on pages 123 and 125.

Working from the whole system, where each sound is an integral part of a total pattern, each vowel then is singled out from the others for its own intensive perception, pronunciation, and sound/spelling study. The five vowels /i/, /e/, /a/, /o/, and /u/ may seem too easy for students, inasmuch as students already "have" these vowels. In fact, what students "have" is a pronunciation of these sounds which is unique to their first languages, and in many cases it is more difficult for students to modify these five "old" sounds to their uniquely American English pronunciation, than it is to learn sounds which are "new" to them. Page 118 summarizes some possible sources of ESL pronunciation interference/learning problems.

The intensive work with a particular vowel sound can be followed up whenever necessary by contrastive work with two vowels of the system. Supplement C presents pronunciation and perception work with selected vowel contrasts.

As in Unit 1, it is important to note here that students are *not expected to master* each and every vowel in a few short lessons. The lessons in Unit 2 are intended to begin a gradual process of improvement with review and reinforcement throughout the remainder of the program.

Unit 2 has six sections. Each section begins with section notes.

Section A presents two introductory lessons on the English vowel system and introduces the Vowel Chart and the key words.

Sections B, C, D, and E present nineteen intensive lessons and tests. (See page 126 of Unit 2 for notes on using the intensive lessons.)

Section F presents three rapid-review-and-testing lessons.

For Students

The Purpose of the Lessons

The only way ESL students can improve their pronunciation of spoken English is to spend many hours listening to English and many hours speaking English. However, a directed program of speaking and listening can shorten the time. The workbook lessons, the tapes, and the explanations in *Improving Spoken English* provide the first part of such a program.

It is the purpose of this workbook to provide carefully planned speaking and listening lessons to help students to accomplish four things:

1. to increase self-confidence in speaking English and in listening to English;
2. to increase intelligibility in speaking English and in listening to English;
3. to increase fluency in speaking English;
4. to increase accuracy in speaking English.

This series of lessons in speaking and listening is intended for use by adults and teenagers who are studying English as a second language. It is not for beginners; it is for students who already speak at least a little English but who now need to *improve* their spoken English. Lesson flexibility permits high-beginning, intermediate, and low-advanced students to use this book to improve their spoken English.

Using the Lessons and Learning to Self-Monitor

The lessons in *Improving Spoken English* can be used in two ways.

1. They can be used in an ESL class and language laboratory with an ESL teacher.
2. Each lesson can be repeated and reviewed using the recorded tape for the lesson.

The real goal of this book is to *help students* to *help themselves* in improving their spoken English. The lessons are designed to help ESL students:

1. to develop speech awareness;
2. to learn to self-monitor and to "correct" their own pronunciation;
3. to continue to improve their spoken English beyond the formal instruction of the classroom and laboratory.

This takes time and practice. Each lesson is planned carefully to move toward these goals. However, the directions given in the book and those given on the tape must be followed *exactly*. There is no way to improve spoken English except to *concentrate*, to *practice*, and to *monitor* pronunciation. The most important thing in this pronunciation work is for students to learn to *monitor* their own speech.

Unit 1
Stress, Rhythm, and Intonation

Section A—Introduction

Section Notes

Section A has two lessons.

Lesson 1 is a sentence dictation exercise with fourteen sentences. Each of these sentences is a key sentence which focuses on one feature of stress, rhythm, or intonation. The sentences to be dictated are on page 315 in the Answer Key/Teacher Script (AK/TS).

Lesson 2 presents chart 1, Key Sentences for Stress, Rhythm, and Intonation. Students are asked to practice these sentences carefully and to memorize them.

These two lessons provide an introduction and a framework within which the remaining lessons in Unit 1 will be studied. Subsequent lessons will isolate each item and give it brief but intensive perceptual and productive attention.

In particular, chart 1 is important as a graphic representation of some of the most vital features of English pronunciation which are much more abstract and difficult to isolate than the vowel and consonant sounds. The chart is a valuable classroom tool; it can serve as a reference source for teachers and students in fostering monitoring of pronunciation during classroom speaking activities.

Lesson 1

Introduction to Stress, Rhythm, and Intonation

Directions: Read and discuss with your teacher. Write the sentences as they are dictated. (AK/TS p. 315)

Part 1—Accented and Unaccented Syllables

Three sentences will be dictated. Listen and repeat. Listen and write. Listen and check. Practice the sentences. Notice the accented syllables.

1. _____ (4 words)

2. _____ (3 words)

3. _____ (5 words)

(Lab: Stop the tape. Write the sentences on the chalkboard. Practice.)

Part 2—Syllables and Suffixes

Two sentences will be dictated. Listen and repeat. Listen and write. Listen and check. Practice the sentences. Notice the plural and past tense suffixes.

4. _____

_____ (9 words)

5. _____

_____ (8 words)

(Lab: Stop the tape. Write the sentences on the chalkboard. Practice.)

Part 3—Sentence Rhythm and Stress

Three sentences will be dictated. Listen and repeat. Listen and write. Listen and check. Practice the sentences. Notice the rhythm and stress of each sentence.

6. _____ (6 words)

7. _____ (6 words)

8. _____ (7 words)

(Lab: Stop the tape. Write the sentences on the chalkboard. Practice.)

Part 4—Contractions and Sound Changes

Three sentences will be dictated. Listen and repeat. Listen and write. Listen and check. Practice the sentences. Notice the contractions.

9. _____ (3 words)
    (The second word is *isn't*, a contraction.)

10. _____ (6 words)
    (The third word is *(n)*, a spoken contraction of the word *and*.)

11. _____ (6 words)
    (The first word is *I'm*, a contraction. The second word is *gonna*, a special contracted spoken form of *going to*.)

(Lab: Stop the tape. Write the sentences on the chalkboard. Practice.)

Part 5—Intonation

Three sentences will be dictated. Listen and repeat. Listen and write. Listen and check. Practice the sentences. Notice the intonation.

12. _____ (2 words)
    (The first word is *I'm*, a contraction.)

13. _____ (3 words)

14. _____

    _____ (8 words)

(Lab: Stop the tape. Write the sentences on the chalkboard. Practice.)

Turn to lesson 2 for practice with these sentences.

Lesson 2

Key Sentences for Stress, Rhythm, and Intonation

Part 1—The Chart of Key Sentences

In Lesson 1, which you have just completed, you wrote fourteen dictated sentences. Look at chart 1. These are the same fourteen sentences. Each sentence is a *key sentence* for stress, rhythm, and intonation. Follow the directions in part 2 and practice each sentence.

Part 2—Practicing the Key Sentences

Look at chart 1 on page 7. Listen, repeat, and practice. Memorize each key sentence.

1. *Two-Syllable Words*[1]   I forgót my péncil.
                             1 2   1 2

2. *Three-Syllable Words*   Tomórrow is Sáturday.
                            1 2 3   1 2 3

3. *Reduced Syllables and Schwa*[2]   Call me tonight aróund séven.
                                         x   x   x

4. *Past Tense*   I closed the door and wáited for the bus.
                     1   1 2

5. *Plural*   I bought four books for my two clásses.
                 1   1 2

6. *Rhythm and Sentence Stresses*   I ate a <u>chick</u>en-salad <u>sand</u>wich.

7. *Rhythm and Reduced Words*   T̶h̶e̶ students a̶r̶e̶ going t̶o̶ Chicago.

8. *Rhythm and Linking*   He‿was‿waiting‿at‿the‿bus : stop.

9. *Two-Word Contractions*   He isn't coming.

10. *One-Word Contractions and Linking*[3]   The boys ('n') girls were late.

11. *Contractions and Sound Changes*   I'm (gonna) study at the lab.

12. *Rising/Falling Intonation (Final)*   ₂I'm hun͞gry.

13. *Rising Intonation (Final)*   ₂Am I láte?

14. *Nonfinal Intonation*[4]   ₂I bought <u>hotdogs</u>, ₂<u>French fries</u>, ₂<u>apples</u>, ₂<u>and</u> candy.

---

1. Primary stress, only, is marked in this text.
2. The × indicates that the syllable is re<u>duce</u>d and the vowel neutralizes toward schwa.
3. In sentences 10 and 11, the ('n') and (gonna) are spoken contracted forms.
4. The dotted portion of the int<u>onation</u> line indicates an alternative tone pattern.

6

Chart 1
KEY SENTENCES FOR STRESS, RHYTHM, AND INTONATION

Accented/Unaccented Syllables

1. I forgót my péncil.   *Two-Syllable Words*
     1 2   1 2

---

2. Tomórrow is Sáturday.   *Three-Syllable Words*
     1 2 3   1 2 3

---

3. Call me toníght aróund séven.   *Reduced Syllables and Schwa*
     x   x   x

Syllables and Suffixes

4. I closed the door and wáited for the bus.   *Past Tense*
     1   1 2

---

5. I bought four books for my two clásses.   *Plural*
          1   1 2

Sentence Sense: Rhythm and Stress

6. I ate a chicken-salad sandwich.   *Rhythm and Sentence Stresses*

---

7. The students are going to Chicago.   *Rhythm and Reduced Words*

---

8. He was waiting at the bus : stop.   *Rhythm and Linking*

Elisions and Assimilations

9. He isn't coming.   *Two-Word Contractions*

---

10. The boys ('n') girls were late.   *One-Word Contractions and Linking*

---

11. I'm (gonna) study at the lab.   *Contractions and Sound Changes*

Intonation

12. ₂I'm hungry.   *Rising/Falling Intonation (Final)*

---

13. ₂Am I late?   *Rising Intonation (Final)*

---

14. ₂I bought hotdogs, ₂French fries, ₂apples, ₂and candy.   *Nonfinal Intonation*

7

Using the Intensive Lessons in Sections B, C, D, E, and F

Each of lessons 3 through 16 provides brief, but intensive, perception and pronunciation work with one feature of stress, rhythm, or intonation. Lessons 3, 4, and 5 also contain dictionary homework. Activities in each lesson are varied, involve active student participation, provide for feedback and self-evaluation, and encourage speech awareness and self-monitoring.

Each part of each lesson has a specific function. In general, the parts of each lesson are:

Information
    a. presents brief explanatory notes and gives examples
    b. although students may not understand the entire explanation at the outset, the subsequent practice should clarify the nature of the specific feature
Pronunciation Practice
    a. presents a few practice items for rapid vigorous oral practice; uses graphic notations to aid the students in understanding the nature of the specific feature; suggests a second cycle of practice with the items with attention to natural speed and rhythm
    b. asks students to practice vigorously in order to develop an oral-tactile and oral-kinesthetic "feel" for English stress, rhythm, and intonation; encourages students to monitor themselves
Listening Practice
    a. presents items and asks for an active student response, usually in the form of marking items in response to information received aurally; in lessons 14, 15, and 16, the active student response takes the form of echoing
    b. asks students to give the answers and to check their own work immediately; asks students to practice the items
Listening and Writing Practice
    a. presents items and asks for a written response to information received aurally
    b. asks students to give the answers and to check their own work immediately; asks students to practice the items orally
Test Sentences for Self-Monitoring and Self-Testing
    a. presents four sentences for oral practice, recording, and self-analysis
    b. encourages students to use these sentences to check on their pronunciation of a specific feature of stress, rhythm, or intonation

Following each lesson is resource material to use as supplementary practice. Many lessons contain a few short practice-in-context selections similar to those in Supplement A.

Section B—Accented/Unaccented Syllables

Section Notes

Section B presents three lessons. Resource material for additional practice is included at the end of each lesson.

Lesson 3 presents intensive listening/speaking practice with syllable accent in two-syllable words. With this first substantive lesson, attention is directed to the importance of self-monitoring.

Lesson 4 presents similar practice with syllable accent in three-syllable words.

Lesson 5 focuses on reduced syllables and the neutral vowel sound schwa, /ə/. This is a new concept for many students. It is taken up here, early in the program, for two reasons. First, it can help students in making an aural comprehension breakthrough as they encounter native speakers who are using the natural conversational fast speech of English, in which reduced syllables play a key role. Second, it can help reduce pronunciations which come from sound/symbol interpretations from the students' first languages.

Work with a vowel box such as the following may help students in locating the neutral vowel. (See Unit 2, page 117.)

[1] s<u>ee</u>		[8] tw<u>o</u>
[3] s<u>ay</u>	/ə/	[10] n<u>o</u>
	[7] st<u>o</u>p	

One caution is suggested. In presenting sentence practice, avoid overaccenting. Those syllable accents which are not also sentence stresses are somewhat muted; that is, they are not pronounced with as much accent as when they are pronounced as isolated words.

Teachers may wish to discuss chart 2 with students for an overview, or as a review, of this section.

Chart 2
ACCENTED/UNACCENTED SYLLABLES

I forgót my péncil.
1 2   1 2

Two-Syllable Words
In two-syllable words, one syllable is accented; that is, it is pronounced with more strength than the other one.

Tomórrow is Sáturday.
1 2 3   1 2 3

Three-Syllable Words
In three-syllable words, one syllable is accented; that is, it is pronounced with more strength than the other two.

Call me tonight aróund séven.
    x   x   x

Reduced Syllables and Schwa
Many unaccented syllables do not have a strong *a, e, i, o,* or *u* vowel but are pronounced with the neutral vowel schwa, /ə/.

9

Lesson 3
Two-Syllable Words

I forgót my péncil.
1   2   1   2

Part 1—Accented Syllables

Words of *one* syllable have *one* spoken part. Repeat.

we	come	add	want	stop
1	1	1	1	1

Words of two syllables have *two* spoken parts. In English one of the two parts is *accented* and one is *unaccented*. Accented means:

1. the vowel in the syllable is l o n g e r;
2. the syllable is a little **stronger**;
3. the syllable often is a little ↗higher↘ in tone.[1]

Repeat.

First Syllable Accent[2]	*Second Syllable Accent*[3]
sándwich Énglish páper	believe acróss begín
1 2 1 2 1 2	1 2 1 2 1 2

Unaccented means:

1. the vowel in the syllable is shorter;
2. the syllable is a little weaker;
3. the syllable often is a little ↘lower↗ in tone.

This is different from many languages of the world in which syllable strength is equal (or nearly equal) for all syllables (parts) of a word. Repeat the above words again. Notice this mark (´) is written over the *first vowel letter* in the accented syllable.

---

1. The words presented to illustrate syllable accent are spoken in isolation; they are shown with an intonation graphic representing a higher tone on the accented syllable. In connected speech, however, accented syllables are not necessarily higher in tone. See Unit 1, lesson 16.
2. If the syllable accent is on the next-to-the-last syllable or earlier, the falling pattern of the tone is shown as *step-down* between the two syllables.
3. If the syllable accent is on the last syllable, the falling pattern of the tone is shown as *glide-down* on the vowel of the last syllable.

10

Part 2—Pronunciation Practice

Listen and repeat the words below. Give more strength to the accented syllables. Listen to yourself as you practice. Pronunciation practice is the time for you to *talk* to yourself and to *listen* to yourself.

First Syllable Accent		*Second Syllable Accent*	

1. táble
   1 2
	3. áfter
	   1 2
		1. toníght
		     1 2
			3. arríve
			    1 2

2. háppy
   1 2
	4. síster
	   1 2
		2. retúrn
		    1 2
			4. asléep
			    1 2

(Lab: Stop the tape. Allow a few minutes for individual practice.)

Listen and repeat the following words and sentences.[4] Give more strength to the accented syllables. This mark (´) shows an accented syllable. *Talk* to yourself and *listen* to yourself as you practice. Talking to yourself and listening to yourself are ways to *self-monitor*.

1. péncil   I need a péncil and some páper.   3. belíeve   I belíeve the class begíns at ten.
   páper   begíns

2. nótebook I gave my nótebook to the téacher. 4. todáy   Todáy is the fourth of Julý.
   téacher   Julý

(Lab: Stop the tape. Allow a few minutes for individual practice and self-monitoring.)

Part 3 — Listening and Marking Accented Syllables (AK/TS)

Listen and repeat. Listen and put an accent mark over each accented syllable. The accent mark (´) must be written over the *first vowel letter* in the accented syllable.

Examples: stúdy   arríve   belíeve
                 1 2   1 2   1 2

1. because
   1 2
	4. myself
	   1 2
		7. asleep
		   1 2

2. today
   1 2
	5. never
	   1 2
		8. kitchen
		   1 2

3. brother
   1 2
	6. arrive
	   1 2
		9. sandwich
		   1 2

(Lab: Stop the tape and ask students to give the answers. Start the tape and have students check their work as the accents are given.)

Listen and repeat the following sentences. Listen and put an accent mark over the accented syllable in each two-syllable word.

1. The téacher was late.   3. The báby was asléep.
       1 2   1 2   1 2

2. He arríved at ten.   4. Perháps I should do it mysélf.
     1 2   1 2   1 2

(Lab: Stop the tape and ask students to give the answers. Start the tape and have students check their work as the accents are given.)

---

4. See the section notes for a caution in avoiding overaccenting during sentence practice.

Practice each sentence again using natural speed. Exaggerate the accented syllables slightly.[5]

(Lab: Stop the tape and allow a few minutes for individual practice and self-monitoring.)

Part 4—Writing Sentences from Dictation and Marking Accents (AK/TS)

Four sentences will be dictated. Listen and repeat. Listen and write. Listen and check. Mark the accented syllables. Practice each sentence.

1. _____ (3 words)

2. _____ (5 words)

3. _____ (4 words)

4. _____ (5 words)

(Lab: Stop the tape and ask students to read their sentences and to give the accents. Start the tape and have students check their work as the accents are given.)

Practice the sentences again using natural speed.

Part 5—Test Sentences for Self-Monitoring and Self-Testing

Self-monitoring means talking to yourself and listening to yourself as you practice. Practice the following sentences using natural speed. Record. Listen and monitor your pronunciation.

1. My bróther is cóming on Fríday.
2. I belíeve the class begíns at ten.
3. I was asléep when they arríved.
4. Todáy is the fourth of Julý.

Part 6—Dictionary Homework

Look up the following words in your dictionary. Copy the pronunciation exactly. Include the syllable accent marks.

1. correct _____   3. lazy _____

2. between _____   4. reason _____

---

5. Following these two self-test exercises for recognition of syllable accent, try the following rapid pronunciation work. Write a list of two-syllable words on the chalkboard; mark the accented syllables. (Use the resource materials for this lesson.) Point to words rapidly in random order; ask individuals, or the group, to pronounce the words.

Resource Material

This list is provided as a resource for supplementary work for lesson 3.[6] It can be used for listening practice activities, such as those in part 3 of this lesson. It can be used for pronunciation practice, such as that outlined in footnote 5 on page 12. Material for study by advanced classes is indicated in the notes.

Part 1—Second Syllable Accent

Fewer than 20 percent of high frequency two-syllable words are accented on the second syllable. Six of the word groups in this category contain prefixed words.

Verbs		Nouns	Adjectives		Adverbs	Prepositions		Conjunctions
agrée	forgét	alárm	afráid	alíve	agáin	abóut	befóre	althóugh
arríve	enjóy	degrée	asléep	alóne	ahéad	acróss	behínd	becáuse
begín	invíte	evént	enóugh	entíre	apárt	agáinst	belów	unléss
belíeve	prepáre	expénse		awáke	awáy	alóng	besíde	untíl
compléte	suggést	succéss			perháps	amóng		
decíde		escápe				aróund		

Additional word groups in this category are: reflexive/intensive pronouns, teen numbers, compound verbs, and a miscellaneous group made up primarily of borrowed words including some proper names.

Reflexive/Intensive Pronouns		Numbers*		Compound Verbs	Miscellaneous		
mysélf	yoursélf	thirtéen	sixtéen	outsmárt	caréer	hotél	Julý
himsélf	yoursélves	fourtéen	eightéen	outlíve	café	políce	Eugéne
hersélf	oursélves	fiftéen	ninetéen	outdó	ballóon	machíne	Eláine
itsélf	themsélves				garáge	políte	Suzánne
					guitár	matúre	Joánne

*Alternative accenting will be studied later in the program.

---

6. Students find it useful to practice these words in sentences and/or conversational dialogues. Ask students to look for these words in daily classwork activities, and encourage them to monitor themselves and others on syllable accents.

Part 2—First Syllable Accent

Over 80 percent of high frequency two-syllable words are accented on the first syllable. The following are examples from four word groups: base words (i.e., nonprefixed nouns, verbs, adjectives, etc.), compounds, suffixed words, and proper names.

Base Words			Compounds		Suffixed Words		Names
vísit	lánguage	báby	Mónday	ráilroad	twénty	lóvely	Jóhnson
hábit	cóurage	háppy	Túesday	súnshine	thírty	úseful	Míller
mínute	cóllege	húngry	Wédnesday	máybe	fórty	cáreful	Dávis
tícket	hándsome	móney	Thúrsday	thérefore	fífty	dríven	Wílson
pócket	wélcome	jóurney	Fríday	méanwhile	sáfety	wrítten	Táylor
sálad	próblem	qúestion*	áirplane	sómebody	cóming	dríver	Mártin
trável	scíence	pátient*	bédroom	sómehow	góing	léader	Thómpson
péncil	dístance	spécial*	báthroom	sómeone	réading	téacher	Máry
líttle	óffice	sócial*	bóokcase	sómewhere	spéaking	áctor	Jánet
báttle	fámous	sóldier*	bréakfast	fórward	wríting	sáfer	Bétty
táble	óver	précious*	hótdog	báckward	ártist	sáfest	Hélen
wóman	áfter	mótion*	mídnight	álways	chémist	kíndest	Ríchard
cóusin	bróther	vísion*	nótebook	álso	sóftly	páyment	Róbert
lésson	dóllar	míllion*	pássport		qúickly	kíndness	Árthur
lísten	stránger	ónion*	pópcorn		fríendly		Thómas

*Call students' attention to these words. The letter *i* is not pronounced as an extra syllable. The sound before the letter *i* in each of these words is a palatal sound: /ʃ/, /ʒ/, /tʃ/, /dʒ/, or /y/.

Part 3—Listening/Speaking Practice with Two-Syllable Words

As a class activity, ask students to listen as each group of words is read. Ask students to put an accent mark over the accented syllable in each word; ask them to draw a line under the one word in each group which has an accent different from the other three. Then ask individuals to pronounce the words in one of the groups and to monitor themselves on syllable accents.

Example:	táble	forgét	péncil	móther
Group 1.	afraid	Monday	myself	decide
Group 2.	dollar	midnight	guitar	softly
Group 3.	thirteen	balloon	science	agree
Group 4.	herself	cousin	maybe	visit
Group 5.	soldier	artist	money	escape
Group 6.	polite	across	popcorn	expense

Part 4

As an individualized activity, ask students to fill in the blanks below with the correct words from the list at the right of each sentence. Ask students to practice the sentences and to monitor themselves on syllable accents.

1. I _____ to set my _____ .   alárm   forgót

2. My _____ is a _____ _____ .   bróther fámous dóctor

3. I bought a _____ and some _____ .   hótdog pópcorn

4. The _____ was _____ and _____ .   húngry thírsty púppy

5. The _____ had a new _____ .   guitár sínger

15

Lesson 4

Three-Syllable Words[7]

> **Tomórrow is Sáturday.**
> 1 2 3   1 2 3

Part 1—Accented Syllables

Words of *three* syllables have *three* spoken parts. In English one of the three parts is *accented*:

1. the vowel in the syllable is l o n g e r;
2. the syllable is a little **stronger**;
3. the syllable often is a little ↗higher↘ in tone.[8]

Repeat.

First Syllable Accent		*Second Syllable Accent*		*Third Syllable Accent*	
fúrniture	áccident	discóver	contínue	understánd	afternóon
1 2 3	1 2 3	1 2 3	1 2 3	1 2 3	1 2 3

Part 2—Pronunciation Practice

Listen and repeat the following words and sentences. Give more strength to the accented syllables. This mark (´) shows an accented syllable. *Talk* to yourself as you practice and *listen* to yourself as you practice.

1. afternóon — Good afternóon.
   1 2 3
2. médical — He's in médical school.
   1 2 3
3. understánd — I don't understánd.
   1 2 3
4. président — We have a new président.
   1 2 3
5. Septémber — Today is Septémber tenth.
   1 2 3
6. remémber — I can't remémber.
   1 2 3

Practice the sentences again using natural speed.

(Lab: Stop the tape and allow a few minutes for individual practice and self-monitoring.)

Part 3—Listening and Marking Accented Syllables (AK/TS)

Listen and repeat the following sentences. Listen and put an accent mark over the accented syllable in each three-syllable word. The accent mark (´) must be written over the *first vowel letter* in the accented syllable.

Examples: Novémber   afternóon   yésterday
            1 2 3   1 2 3   1 2 3

---

7. If this lesson is not done on the same day as lesson 3, do a few minutes of review work using rapid pronunciation work as outlined in footnote 5 on page 12.
8. For notes on tone and the intonation graphic, see footnotes 1, 2, and 3 on page 10.

1. Somebody took my overcoat.
   1   2 3   1 2 3

2. She's a wonderful musician.
            1   2   3   1 2 3

3. We bought some beautiful furniture.
                   1   2 3 1 2 3

4. We can buy the medicine at the hospital.
                     1 2 3   1   2 3

(Lab: Stop the tape and ask students to give the answers. Start the tape and have students check their work as the accents are given.)

Practice each sentence again using natural speed.

(Lab: Stop the tape and allow a few minutes for individual practice and self-monitoring.)

Part 4—Writing Sentences from Dictation and Marking Accents (AK/TS)

Four sentences will be dictated. Listen and repeat. Listen and write. Listen and check. Mark the accented syllables. Practice the sentences.

1. _____ (5 words)

2. _____ (5 words)

3. _____ (5 words)

4. _____ (5 words)

(Lab: Stop the tape and ask students to read their sentences and to give the accents. Start the tape and have students check their work as the accents are given.)

Practice the sentences again using natural speed.

Part 5—Test Sentences for Self-Monitoring and Self-Testing

Self-monitoring means talking to yourself and listening to yourself as you practice. Practice the following sentences using natural speed. Record. Listen and monitor your pronunciation. Notice these sentences contain both two-syllable and three-syllable words.

1. The stúdents are góing to Chicágo.

2. He wants a hámburger and a cup of cóffee.

3. Todáy is Julý sevénteenth.

4. The président was elécted in Novémber.

Part 6—Dictionary Homework

Look up the following words in your dictionary. Copy the pronunciation exactly. Include the syllable accent marks.

1. gentleman _____

2. successful _____

3. possibly _____

4. happiness _____

Resource Material

This list is provided as a resource for supplementary work for lesson 4.[9] It can be used for listening practice activities, such as those in part 3 of this lesson. It can be used for pronunciation practice activities, such as that outlined in footnote 5 on page 12. Material for study by advanced classes is indicated in the notes.

Part 1—First Syllable Accent

áccident	cítizen	hóspital	térrible	fávorite*	Cánada
ánimal	ávenue	médicine	póssible	mýstery*	México
cápital	cómpany*	président	pópular	réally*	Flórida
fámily*	mémory*	nátural*	régular	víctory*	

*In Kenyon and Knott alternative two-syllable pronunciations are given for these words. The middle syllables are deleted. These are examples of syncope, which will be studied specifically later in the program.

Part 2—Second Syllable Accent

tomáto	Chicágo	idéa	apártment	impórtant
volcáno	tomórrow	aréna	depártment	accóuntant
potáto	mosquíto	banána	arrángement	exámple
Ohío	Hawáii	Aláska	advénture	

Part 3—Third Syllable Accent

enginéer	understánd	underpáid	disappóint
afternóon	overlóok	disappéar	disagrée

Part 4—First or Third Syllable Accent

Many dictionaries list these words as correctly accented on *either* the first *or* third syllable.

mágazine	gásoline	cígarette	magazíne	gasolíne	cigarétte

---

9. Students find it useful to practice these words in sentences and/or conversational dialogues. Ask students to look for these words in daily classwork activities, and encourage them to monitor themselves and others on syllable accents.

Part 5—Second Syllable Accent: Special Attention to the Letter *i*[10]

The words in this word group each have the letter *i* in the last syllable. The *i* is not pronounced as an extra syllable. The sound before the letter *i* in each of these words is a palatal sound: /ʃ/, /ʒ/, /tʃ/, /dʒ/, or /y/. The accent is on the middle (next to the last) syllable.

offícial	occásion	suggéstion	relígion	famíliar	opínion
commércial	divísion		relígious	pecúliar	compánion
fináncial				Itálian	
physícian					
suffícient					

Part 6—First Syllable Accent: Special Attention to the letter *i*

The words in this word group each have the letter *i* in the last syllable. As an optional pronunciation, the letter *i* does not have to be pronounced as an extra syllable. This reduces the word from three to two syllables. If the word is pronounced as two syllables, the second syllable begins with the palatal sound, /y/. Ask students to pronounce these words in both ways, with two syllables and with three syllables.

périod	sérious	várious	glórious	brílliant	áudience

Part 7—Listening/Speaking Practice with Three-Syllable Words

As a class activity, ask students to listen as each group of words is read. Ask students to put an accent mark over the accented syllable in each word; ask them to draw a line under the one word in each group which has an accent different from the other three. Then ask individuals to pronounce the words in one of the groups and to monitor themselves on syllable accents.

Example:	ávenue	hóspital	<u>tomáto</u>	cítizen
Group 1.	president	reduction	appearance	important
Group 2.	accident	hospital	tomorrow	enemy
Group 3.	engineer	afternoon	capital	overlook
Group 4.	tomato	Canada	Chicago	Ohio
Group 5.	animal	Florida	avenue	example
Group 6.	adventure	potato	idea	underpaid

---

10. Attention to the letter *i* and palatals is given here and in part 6, early in the course, both for the specific words included in this lesson and in lesson 3, and to prepare students for more complex word stress study later.

Part 8

As an individualized activity, ask students to fill in the blanks below with the correct words from the list at the right of each sentence. Ask students to practice the sentences and to monitor themselves on syllable accents.

1. I _____ that _____ is very _____.   expénsive
   gasolíne
   understánd

2. The _____ gave us the _____ report.   accóuntant
   futuráncial

3. I flew from _____ to _____ and then to   Chicágo
   Flórida
   _____ City.   México

4. My _____ is near the _____.   apártment
   hóspital

5. _____ they will visit the _____ in _____.   cápital
   tomórrow
   Wáshington

Lesson 5

Reduced Syllables and Schwa

> **Call me tonight around séven.**
>   x   x   x

Part 1—Unaccented Syllables and the Use of Schwa

English has five vowel letters, with the names *a, e, i, o,* and *u.* A *sixth* vowel letter has the name *schwa.* The letter for schwa is the phonetic symbol /ə/.[11] Schwa is pronounced like the first sound in *upón.*

Many unaccented syllables do not have a strong vowel sound of *a, e, i, o,* or *u.* Instead they are pronounced with schwa, /ə/.[12] Schwa is called the neutral or *reduced* vowel because it is formed with the tongue in the neutral or *rest* position. In the following words, the *a* in the unaccented syllable is pronounced /ə/. Notice the mark (x) under the *a.* Repeat.

---

aróund   agrée   agó   abóut
x   x   x   x

Many languages of the world do *not* have vowel reduction in unaccented syllables. Sometimes ESL students believe that vowel reduction is poor speech or careless speech. The opposite is true. In both British and American dialects of English, reduced vowels are both natural and correct.

Part 2—Pronunciation Practice

Listen and repeat the following words and sentences. The mark (x) has been placed under the vowel in the unaccented syllable. The following words are pronounced according to *A Pronouncing Dictionary of American English*, by Kenyon and Knott.[13] Repeat.

1. tonight   I'll see you tonight.
      x
                      (The vowel sound in the first syllable of the word *tonight* is reduced. Repeat.)

2. aróund   I walked aróund the house.
      x
                      (The vowel sound in the first syllable of the word *aróund* is reduced. Repeat.)

3. séven   I'll call you at séven.
      x
                      (The vowel sound in the second syllable of the word *séven* is reduced. Repeat.)

---

11. Phonetic symbols are enclosed in slash marks, / /.
12. This one symbol, /ə/, is used here to cover a range of variants in the pronunciation of vowels in reduced syllables; these include a short *i* sound (similar to the /ɪ/ sound in *it*), and a short *ŭ* sound (similar to the /ʊ/ sound in *books*). Teachers may wish to discuss these variations with advanced classes.
13. All example words in this lesson are listed in Kenyon and Knott with the neutral vowel, /ə/. However, with *l, m,* and *n,* some speakers use an alternative pronunciation with the vowel deleted and the consonant, syllabic. In this program syllabic consonants will not be studied until later; teachers with advanced classes may wish to discuss them at this time.

21

4. télephone   I heard the télephone.
    x   x

                    (The vowel sound in the second syllable of the word *télephone* is reduced. Repeat.)

5. suppóse   I suppóse we should wait.
    x

                    (The vowel sound in the first syllable of the word *suppóse* is reduced. Repeat.)

6. fámous   I met a fámous man.
    x   x

                    (The vowel sound in the second syllable of the word *fámous* is reduced. Repeat.)

Practice the sentences again using natural speed.

(Lab: Stop the tape and allow a few minutes for individual practice and self-monitoring.)

Part 3—Listening and Marking Reduced Syllables[14] (AK/TS)

Listen and repeat the following words. One syllable in each word is reduced. Listen and place the mark (x) under the vowel in the reduced syllable. Listen and check. Notice that the accented syllable in each word has been marked with an accent mark (´) over the first vowel in the accented syllable.

    1. todáy   2. toníght   3. agáin   4. tomórrow   5. télegram   6. disappéar

       1 2   1 2   1 2   1 2 3   1 2 3   1 2 3

(Lab: Stop the tape and ask students to give the answers. Start the tape and have students check the reduced syllables as they are given.)

Practice the words again using natural speed. Notice the reduced syllable is *never* the accented syllable.

(Lab: Stop the tape and allow time for individual practice and self-monitoring.)

Part 4—Test Sentences for Self-Monitoring and Self-Testing

Practice the following sentences using natural speed. Record. Listen and monitor your pronunciation.

    1. He sent a télegram.   3. I came aróund ten.
                 x   x

    2. I'll see you toníght.   4. I heard the télephone.
               x   x

Part 5—Dictionary Homework

Look up the following words in your dictionary. Copy the pronunciation exactly.[15]

    1. afraid   _____   4. tonight   _____

    2. along   _____   5. accident   _____

    3. disappear _____   6. medicine   _____

---

14. Following this self-test exercise for recognition of reduced syllables, do a few minutes of rapid pronunciation work, as outlined in footnote 5 on page 12.
15. Many dictionaries indicate the reduced vowel in a syllable by using the /ə/ symbol. Encourage students to check for a reduced vowel in the unaccented syllables of new vocabulary items.

Resource Material

This list is provided as a resource for supplementary work for lesson 5. It can be used for listening practice activities, such as those in part 3 of this lesson. It can be used for pronunciation practice activities, such as that outlined in footnote 5 on page 12. Material for study by advanced classes is indicated in the notes.

Part 1—First Syllable Reduced/Second Syllable Accented

In the following words the accent is on the *second* syllable. The *first* syllable is reduced.

a-	*to-*	*col-,* *com-, con-*	*po-*	*sub-, sus-,* *suc-, sug-, sup-*
agrée	todáy	colléct	políte	succéss
afráid	toníght	compáre	políce	suggést
arríve	tomórrow	compléte	potáto	suppóse
asléep	tomáto	connéct		suppórt
aróund				subtráct
awáy				suspéct (verb)

Part 2—Last Syllable Reduced/First Syllable Accented

In the following words the accent is on the *first* syllable. The *last* syllable is reduced. A slash mark (/) through a letter indicates a silent letter.

-m, -em, -om, -ome	*-ment*	*-ful*	*-man*	*-en**	*-ace, -ose, -uce, -ous,* *-as, -fast, -ence, -mas*
rhýthm	góvernment	hélpful	wóman	séven	súrface
sýstem	páyment	cáreful	húman	héaven	púrpose
próblem	móvement	úseful	wórkman	léngthen	léttuce
cústom	tréatment		póstman	stréngthen	fámous
séldom				háppen	Téxas
hándsome				óf/en	Chrís/mas
wélcome				dríven	bréakfast
				gíven	séntence

*Sometimes, in fast speech, in words ending in *-ven*, *-fen*, *-ben*, or *-pen*, the alveolar *n* undergoes assimilation resulting in a syllabic labial *m* and deletion of the /ə/. Notice the absence here of alveolars before *-en*. When another alveolar consonant (i.e., homorganic) precedes final *-en*, Kenyon and Knott often give the pronunciation of the last syllable as syllabic *n* with deletion of the /ə/.

Part 3—Middle Syllable Reduced/First or Third Syllable Accented

In the following words the accent is on the *first* or the *third* of the three syllables. The *middle* syllable is reduced.

-a-		-e-	-i-		
disappéar	disagrée	énemy	áccident	médicine*	cápital*
disappóint	cómpany	télephone	président	térrible*	ánimal*
sýllable*	réalize	télegram	hóliday	póssible*	cítizen*

*In Kenyon and Knott these words are given with a syllabic consonant in the last syllable.

Part 4—First and Last Syllables Reduced/Middle Syllable Accented

appéarance	colléction	posítion	pollútion
arrángement	complétion	posséssion	suggéstion

Part 5

As an individualized activity, ask students to fill in the blanks below with the correct words from the list. Ask students to practice the sentences as a group or individually and to monitor their pronunciation of both accented and unaccented syllables.

áccident	góvernment	páyment	sálad	sýllable	Téxas
bréakfast	hóliday	pówerful	séntence	télegram	tomáto
collécts	léttuce	président	séven	térrible	tomórrow

1. I eat _____ at _____ o'clock every morning.

2. The first word in the _____ is accented on the last _____.

3. I sent a _____ to the _____.

4. He ate a _____ and _____ _____ for lunch.

5. There are no classes _____ because it's a _____.

6. The state _____ of _____ is very _____.

7. My landlord _____ the rent _____ on the first of the month.

8. There was a _____ car _____ on the corner.

Section C—Syllables and Suffixes

Section Notes

Section C has two lessons. There is resource material for additional practice at the end of each lesson.

Lesson 6 presents intensive listening/writing/speaking practice with the regular past tense forms of English. The three phonologically based rules for the pronunciation of regular past tense are presented in chart 4 on page 29. All voiceless and voiced consonants are presented, with examples.

Lesson 7 presents similar practice with the regular plural forms of English. The three phonologically based rules for the pronunciation of regular plural are presented in chart 5 on page 35. All voiceless and voiced consonants are presented, with examples.

These two lessons on the pronunciation/grammar rules for regular past tense and plural suffixing are presented at this point in the text for two reasons. First, they are predictable pronunciation problems for many ESL students and need to be emphasized early and reinforced continuously. Second, the *-ed* pronunciation of /əd/ or /ɪd/ and the *-es* pronunciation of /əz/ or /ɪz/ can be related meaningfully to the preceding lesson on reduced syllables and schwa.

Teachers may wish to discuss chart 3 with students for an overview, or as a review, of this section.

Chart 3
SYLLABLES AND SUFFIXES

I closed the door and wáited for the bus.
   1   1 2

Past Tense
The regular past tense is formed by adding *-ed* to the verb. If the verb ends in *t* or *d*, it is pronounced as an extra syllable, /əd/ or /ɪd/; if the verb ends in any other sound, it is pronounced only as the added sound of /t/ or /d/.

I bought four books for my two clásses.
          1   1 2

Plural
The regular plural is formed by adding *-s* or *-es* to the noun. If the noun ends in one of the six sibilant or affricate consonants, *s*, *z*, *sh*, *zh*, *ch*, or *j*, it is pronounced as an extra syllable, /əz/ or /ɪz/. If it ends in any other sound, it is pronounced only as the added sound of /s/ or /z/.

Lesson 6

Past Tense

I closed the door and wáited for the bus.[1]
   1   1   2

Part 1—Three Pronunciations of the Past Tense -ed

Past tense forms of regular verbs are pronounced in the following ways.[2]

    1. If the verb ends in *t* or *d* the *-ed* suffix is pronounced as an extra syllable. Repeat.

---

wait	wáited	need	néeded
1	1 2	1	1 2

The vowel sound in the unaccented syllable, *-ed*, is a reduced vowel. It is pronounced either as /əd/ (with the schwa sound, /ə/, as in the first syllable of *upón*) or as /ɪd/ (similar to the /ɪ/ sound in *it*).

    2. If the verb ends in any *voiceless* consonant, except *t*, the past tense is not pronounced as an extra *syllable*. It is pronounced only as the extra voiceless *sound* /t/. The *e* is silent (ȩ). Repeat.

---

wash	washȩd (wash + /t/)	laugh	laughȩd (laugh + /t/)
1	1	1	1

---

    3. If the verb ends in any *vowel sound* or any *voiced* consonant, except *d*, the past tense is not pronounced as an extra *syllable*. It is pronounced only as the extra voiced *sound* /d/. The *e* is silent (ȩ). Repeat.

---

wave	wavȩd (wave + /d/)	rain	rainȩd (rain +/d/)
1	1	1	1

Part 2—Pronunciation Practice

Listen and repeat the following words and sentences. Pronounce the past tense forms carefully.

    Group 1: The past tense is pronounced as an *extra syllable* in these words.

        1. decíded   I decided to go.
              1 2 3
        2. wáited   I waited for the bus.
              1 2
        3. néeded   I needed some money.
              1 2

---

1. This line (/) through a letter indicates that the letter is silent.
2. For a complete listing of the sounds in each of these three groups, see chart 4 on past tense pronunciation in the resource material for this lesson. Teachers may wish to spend extra time working with the groups of voiceless and voiced sounds helping students to understand this distinction.

Group 2: The past tense is *not* pronounced as an extra syllable in these words. Pronounce it only as the extra voiceless sound /t/. The *e* is silent.

1. watch¢d   I watch¢d a movie.   (watch + /t/)
   1
2. talk¢d   We talk¢d about it.   (talk + /t/)
   1
3. wash¢d   I wash¢d my sweater.   (wash + /t/)
   1

Group 3: The past tense is *not* pronounced as an extra syllable in these words. Pronounce it only as the extra voiced sound /d/. The *e* is silent.

1. clos¢d   She clos¢d her book.   (close + /d/)
   1
2. ópen¢d   I open¢d a window.   (open + /d/)
   1 2
3. seem¢d   He seem¢d unhappy.   (seem + /d/)
   1

Turn back to group 1. Practice the sentences in each group again using natural speed. Pronounce the past tense forms carefully. Monitor your pronunciation of the past tense forms.

Part 3—Listening Practice[3] (AK/TS)

Listen and repeat. Listen and draw a circle around the form you hear in the sentence. Listen and check.

	Column 1	Column 2	
1. I	(need	needed)	help.
2. I	(want	wanted)	to go.
3. I	(attend	attended)	class.
4. I	(talk	talked)	a lot.
5. I	(like	liked)	him.
6. I	(wash	washed)	the dishes.
7. I	(play	played)	a song.
8. I	(live	lived)	in Miami.
9. I	(study	studied)	in the lab.

(Lab: Stop the tape. Ask students to give their answers. Start the tape. Have students check their work as the answers are given.)

---

3. For more work of this kind, see the resource material for this lesson.

Part 4—Listening and Writing[4] (AK/TS)

Listen and repeat as each word from column 1 is read. Listen and repeat as the past tense is pronounced. Write the past tense of the word in the correct column: column 2, column 3, or column 4.

Column 1	Column 2	Column 3	Column 4
Examples:	/t/	/d/	/ɪd/ or /əd/
load call dance	*danced*	*called*	*loaded*

		Column 2	Column 3	Column 4
1. add	6. play	_____	_____	_____
2. work	7. need	_____	_____	_____
3. wish	8. like	_____	_____	_____
4. live	9. wait	_____	_____	_____
5. want	10. close			_____

(Lab: Stop the tape. Ask students to give their answers. Start the tape. Have students check their work as the past tense forms are given.)

Part 5—Dictation (AK/TS)

Four sentences will be dictated. Listen and repeat. Listen and write. Listen, check, and underline each past tense.

1. _____ (4 words)

2. _____ (4)

3. _____ (6)

4. _____ (8)

(Lab: Stop the tape. Ask students to read the past tense forms. Start the tape. Have students check their work as the past tense forms are given.)

Practice the sentences again using natural speed. Pronounce the past tense forms carefully.

(Lab: Stop the tape for individual practice.)

Part 6—Test Sentences for Self-Monitoring and Self-Testing

Practice the following sentences using natural speed. Pronounce the past tense forms carefully. Record. Listen and monitor your pronunciation.

1. I ordered a sandwich.   3. I waved at the children.

2. I opened a window.   4. I laughed at the clown.

---

4. For more work of this kind, see the resource material for this lesson.

Resource Material

Part 1—Past Tense Pronunciation Chart

As a class activity, ask students to practice the forms in columns 1, 2, and 3. As an individualized activity, ask one student to pronounce a word from the word list and its past tense form; ask another student to tell where it should be written on the chart. The word list is on page 30.

Chart 4
PAST TENSE PRONUNCIATION

		Column 1	Column 2	Column 3
Final Sound[5]		/t/	/d/	/ɪd/ or /əd/
Alveolar plosive consonants	t			waited
	d			needed
All other voiceless consonant sounds	p	stopped		
	k	kicked		
	f	laughed		
	s	kissed		
	sh /ʃ/	wished		
	ch /tʃ/	watched		
All other voiced consonant sounds (*Pronunciation note*: Vowel sounds *before* voiced consonant sounds are lengthened.)	b		robbed	
	g		dragged	
	v		waved	
	th /ð/		breathed	
	z		used (*s* = /z/)	
	j /dʒ/		judged (*dg* = /dʒ/)	
	m		slammed	
	n		burned	
	ng /ŋ/		banged	
	l		called	
	r		roared	
Vowels and diphthongs[6] (all voiced)	ay		played	
	oy		enjoyed	
	ie		died	
	ow		showed	
	ee		freed	
	aw		sawed	

---

5. No English words end in the consonant sound of /h/. No verbs end in the voiceless *th*, /θ/. Few verbs end in /ʒ/.
6. This list includes only a few vowels and diphthongs; it is not intended to be a complete listing.

Word List (AK/TS)

1. work	6. dance	11. like	16. wash
2. stay	7. open	12. want	17. talk
3. snow	8. decide	13. live	18. invite
4. rain	9. add	14. order	19. agree
5. call	10. close	15. load	20. test

Part 2

As a class activity, read one of the two sentences (a or b); ask the students to draw a circle around the form they hear. As an individualized activity, ask a student to read one of the two sentences; ask the class to tell which sentence the student has read (a or b).

1. a. We often   work   until after ten.

    b. We often   worked   until after ten.

2. a. They   live   at the dorm.

    b. They   lived   at the dorm.

3. a. The students   need   help.

    b. The students   needed   help.

4. a. Most of the stores   close   at eight-thirty.

    b. Most of the stores   closed   at eight-thirty.

5. a. They   talk   all the time.

    b. They   talked   all the time.

6. a. I   live   in Miami.

    b. I   lived   in Miami.

7. a. The students   study   every weekend.

    b. The students   studied   every weekend.

8. a. They   start   the movie at two o'clock.

    b. They   started   the movie at two o'clock.

9. a. They   want   to go to New York.

    b. They   wanted   to go to New York.

10. a. We usually   walk   on the beach.

    b. We usually   walked   on the beach.

11. a. They   attend   class every day.

    b. They   attended   class every day.

12. a. They   serve   lunch at twelve o'clock.

    b. They   served   lunch at twelve o'clock.

Lesson 7

Plural

> **I bought four books for my two clásses.**
>   1   1   2

Part 1—Three Pronunciations of the Plural Form[7]

Plural forms of regular nouns are pronounced in following ways:[8]

1. If the noun ends in one of the six sibilant or affricate consonants (*s, z, sh, zh, ch,* or *j*), the plural suffix is pronounced as an extra syllable. Repeat.

---

dish	díshes	judge	júdges
1	1 2	1	1 2

The vowel sound in the unaccented syllable, *-es,* is a reduced vowel. It is pronounced either as /əz/ (with the schwa sound, /ə/, as in the first syllable of *upón*) or as /ɪz/ (similar to the /ɪ/ sound in *it*).

2. If the noun ends in any *voiceless* consonant (except *s, sh,* or *ch* in number 1), the plural is not pronounced as an extra *syllable.* It is pronounced only as the extra voiceless *sound* /s/. The *e* is silent. Repeat.

---

lake	lak¢s (lake + /s/)	lamp	lamps (lamp + /s/)
1	1	1	1

---

3. If the noun ends in any vowel sound or any *voiced* consonant (except those in number 1), the plural is not pronounced as an extra *syllable.* It is pronounced only as the extra voiced *sound* /z/. The *e* is silent. Repeat.

---

name	dog
1	1
nam¢s (name + /z/)	dogs (dog + /z/)
1	1

---

7. Third person singular and possessives follow the same pronunciation pattern.
8. For a complete listing of the sounds in each of these three groups, see chart 5 on plural pronunciation in the resource material for this lesson. Teachers may wish to spend extra time working with the groups of voiceless and voiced sounds helping students to understand this distinction.

Part 2—Pronunciation Practice

Listen and repeat the following words and sentences. Pronounce the plural forms carefully.

Group 1: The plural is pronounced as an *extra syllable* in these words.

1. díshes   I broke some dishes.
   1   2
2. bóxes   The boxes were heavy.
   1   2
3. clásses   The classes begin on Monday.
   1   2

Group 2: The plural is not pronounced as an extra syllable in these words. Pronounce it only as the extra voiceless sound /s/. The *e* is silent.

1. books   The books were heavy.   (book + /s/)
2. lakǿs   Mountain lakǿs are beautiful. (lake + /s/)
3. stúdents   The students were early.   (student + /s/)

Group 3: The plural is not pronounced as an extra syllable in these words. Pronounce it only as the extra voiced sound /z/. The *e* is silent.

1. téachers   The teachers were early.   (teacher + /z/)
2. keys   I lost my keys.   (key + /z/)
3. glovǿs   I bought some glovǿs.   (glove + /z/)

Turn back to group 1. Practice the sentences in each group again using natural speed. Pronounce the plural forms carefully. Monitor your pronunciation of the plural forms.

Part 3—Listening Practice[9] (AK/TS)

Listen and repeat. Listen and draw a circle around the form you hear in the sentence.

	Column 1	Column 2	
1. I bought the	(rose	roses)	for a friend.
2. I packed my	(suitcase	suitcases).	
3. We were waiting for the	(bus	buses).	
4. I got the new	(book	books)	yesterday.
5. We met the	(student	students)	at the lab.
6. I wrote the	(note	notes)	on the chalkboard.
7. I saw the	(teacher	teachers)	in the hall.
8. I wrote the	(name	names)	in my notebook.
9. He closed the	(window	windows).	

(Lab: Stop the tape. Ask students to give their answers. Start the tape. Have students check their work, as the answers are given.)

---

9. For more work of this kind, see the resource material for this lesson.

Part 4—Listening and Writing[10] (AK/TS)

Listen and repeat as each word from column 1 is read. Listen and repeat as the plural form is pronounced. Write the plural of the word in the correct column: column 2, column 3, or column 4.

Column 1	*Column 2*	*Column 3*	*Column 4*
Examples:	/s/	/z/	/ɪz/ or /əz/
dish door lamp	*lamps*	*doors*	*dishes*

1. cat 6. lake	_____	_____	_____
2. class 7. box	_____	_____	_____
3. chair 8. key			
4. rose 9. rope	_____	_____	_____
5. name 10. watch			_____

(Lab: Stop the tape. Ask students to give their answers. Start the tape. Have students check their work as the plural forms are given.)

Part 5—Dictation (AK/TS)

Four sentences will be dictated. Listen and repeat. Listen and write. Listen, check, and underline each plural form.

1. _____ (5 words)

2. _____ (6)

3. _____ (6)

4. _____ (7)

(Lab: Stop the tape. Ask students to read the plural forms. Start the tape. Have students check their work as the plural forms are given.)

Practice the sentences again using natural speed. Pronounce the plural forms carefully.

(Lab: Stop the tape for individual practice.)

---

10. For more work of this kind, see the resource material for this lesson.

Part 6—Test Sentences for Self-Monitoring and Self-Testing

Practice the following sentences using natural speed. Pronounce the plural forms carefully. Record. Listen and monitor your pronunciation.

1. The books cost five dollars and twenty cents.
2. The boys and girls ate sixteen sandwiches.
3. The test took two hours and ten minutes.
4. I bought four books for my two classes.

Resource Material

Part 1—Plural Pronunciation Chart

As a class activity, ask students to practice the forms in columns 1, 2, and 3. As an individualized activity, ask one student to pronounce the singular and plural forms of a word from the word list; ask another student to tell where it should be written on the chart. The word list is on page 36.

Chart 5
PLURAL PRONUNCIATION

		Column 1	Column 2	Column 3
Final Sound[11]		/s/	/z/	/ɪz/ or /əz/
Sibilant and affricate consonants	s			buses
	z			roses (s = /z/)
	sh /ʃ/			wishes
	zh /ʒ/			garages
	ch /tʃ/			churches
	j /dʒ/			judges
All other voiceless consonant sounds	p	lamps		
	t	cats		
	k	socks		
	f	cuffs		
	th /θ/	fifths		
All other voiced consonant sounds (*Pronunciation note*: Vowel sounds *before* voiced consonant sounds are lengthened.)	b		cabs	
	d		roads	
	g		dogs	
	v		waves	
	m		dimes	
	n		pens	
	ng /ŋ/		rings	
	l		hills	
	r		cars	
Vowels and diphthongs[12] (all voiced)	aw		laws	
	ey		keys	
	ay		days	
	oe		toes	
	ie		pies	
	oy		boys	

---

11. No English words end in the consonant sound of /h/. No nouns end in the voiced *th*, /ð/. Irregular plural forms include words which end in voiceless *th* in the singular but change to voiced pronunciation in the plural, (mou<u>th</u>—mou<u>ths</u>) and words which end in *f* in the singular but change to *v* in the plural (knife—kni<u>v</u>es).
12. This list includes only a few vowels and diphthongs; it is not intended to be a complete listing.

Word List (AK/TS)

1. nurse	6. lake	11. window	16. corsage
2. book	7. student	12. watch	17. rope
3. table	8. teacher	13. dish	18. toy
4. buzz	9. glove	14. box	19. month
5. name	10. suitcase	15. class	20. language

Part 2

As a class activity read one of the two sentences (a or b); ask the students to draw a circle around the form they hear. As an individualized activity ask a student to read one of the two sentences; ask the class to tell which sentence the student has read (a or b).

1. a. The book cost five dollars.
   b. The books cost five dollars.
2. a. The judge came into the courtroom.
   b. The judges came into the courtroom.
3. a. The boy found twenty-five dollars.
   b. The boys found twenty-five dollars.
4. a. We met our friend at the restaurant.
   b. We met our friends at the restaurant.
5. a. I bought the chair on sale.
   b. I bought the chairs on sale.
6. a. The fox ran into the woods.
   b. The foxes ran into the woods.
7. a. We went to the movie on Saturday.
   b. We went to the movies on Saturday.
8. a. She put the rug on the porch.
   b. She put the rugs on the porch.
9. a. I didn't hear the bell ring.
   b. I didn't hear the bells ring.
10. a. He gave her the ring for her birthday.
    b. He gave her the rings for her birthday.
11. a. I watched the taxi cab drive away.
    b. I watched the taxi cabs drive away.
12. a. The fire burned all night.
    b. The fires burned all night.

As a homework or class project, ask students to make up a similar chart for third person singular forms and possessive forms, which follow the same pronunciation rules as regular plurals.

Section D—Sentence Sense: Rhythm and Stress

Section Notes

Section D has three lessons. There is resource material for additional practice at the end of each lesson.

Lesson 8 presents intensive listening/speaking practice with rhythm and sentence stresses. This lesson begins with a review of the stronger parts of *words* (accented syllables) versus the weaker parts (unaccented and sometimes reduced syllables). This, then, is compared to the stronger parts of *sentences* (sentences stresses) versus the weaker parts (reduced words).

Lesson 9 presents intensive listening/speaking practice with rhythm and reduced words. As with reduced *syllables*, this information and practice with reduced *words* is particularly important in order to help students to make an aural comprehension breakthrough in understanding the natural conversational fast speech of English.

Lesson 10 presents similar practice in rhythm and linking. The speaker links words together in groups as one of the ways to help the listener get the sense (or meaning) of the sentence.

The material presented in these three lessons—sentence stresses, reduced words, and linking—is some of the most important material in the whole area of stress, rhythm, and intonation. It is vital to the ESL student for both aural comprehension and production of spoken English.

Teachers may wish to discuss chart 6 with students for an overview, or as a review, of this section.

Chart 6
SENTENCE SENSE: RHYTHM AND STRESS

I ate a <u>chick</u>en-salad <u>sand</u>wich.

(la- la- la) (LA- la- la- la) (LA- la)

Rhythm and Sentence Stresses
Every sentence has one or more sentence stresses, or *strong* beats in the rhythm of the sentence.

~~The~~ students ~~are~~ going ~~to~~ Chicago.

Rhythm and Reduced Words
Sentence stresses are the *strong* parts in the sentence rhythm of English. Reduced words are the *weak* parts in the rhythm of the sentence.

He‿was‿waiting‿at‿the‿bus : stop.

Rhythm and Linking
In natural speech, words are linked together in groups. The speaker links words together in groups to help the listener get the sense, or meaning, of the sentence.

Lesson 8

Rhythm and Sentence Stresses

> **I ate a <u>chick</u>en-salad <u>sand</u>wich.**

Part 1—Sentence Stresses

In lessons 3, 4, and 5 we studied accented, unaccented, and reduced syllables. In lessons 6 and 7 we worked with past tense and plural suffixes. We noted that *words* have parts which are *strong* (accented syllables) and parts which are *weak* (unaccented, and sometimes reduced, syllables).

In the same way *sentences* have parts which are *strong* (sentence stresses) and parts which are *weak* (unstressed, and sometimes reduced, words). Sentence stresses are the strong parts in the rhythm of the sentence. The speaker gives more strength to certain parts to help the listener get the sense (or the meaning) of the sentence.

Part 2—Pronunciation Practice with Short Sentences

Look at the sentence in the box. Notice it has two strong sentence stresses.[1] The two stresses are:

1. on the <u>chick</u> in *chícken*;
2. on the <u>sand</u> in *sándwich*.

The last sentence stress, on the <u>sand</u> in sandwich, is a little stronger than the other one. Repeat several times. Imitate the rhythm exactly. Notice the patterns of la-LA-la's which are used to show the stronger parts (the LA's) and the weaker parts (the la's) of the sentence.

I ate a <u>chick</u>en-salad <u>sand</u>wich.
(la- la- la) (LA- la- la- la) (LA- la)

Repeat the following sentences. Listen to the rhythm. There is nearly equal time between the sentence stresses. The words between the strong stresses are lengthened or shortened to fit the rhythm pattern of spoken English. This means that some words (or parts of words) are longer and stronger while some words (or parts of words) are shorter and weaker. Repeat each sentence and the la-LA-la pattern of the rhythm. Feel the rhythm.[2]

1. The <u>stu</u>dents are <u>go</u>ing to Chicago.
   la- LA- la   la- LA-la la- la- LA-la

2. The <u>chil</u>dren <u>danced</u> and <u>sang</u>.
   la- LA- la   LA   la- LA

3. The <u>kit</u>ten was <u>hun</u>gry and <u>thirst</u>y.
   la- LA-la   la- LA-la   la- LA-la

4. The <u>clas</u>ses <u>start</u>ed on <u>Mon</u>day.
   la- LA-la LA-la la- LA- la

5. To<u>day</u> is the <u>sev</u>enth of <u>Aug</u>ust.
   la- LA la- la- LA- la la- LA- la

6. Get <u>read</u>y for the <u>test</u>.
   la- LA-la la- la- LA

---

1. Sometimes one-syllable words carry a sentence stress; in a word of two or more syllables the stress is on the accented syllable.
2. Encourage students to feel the rhythm by making a physical movement in time with the beat of the sentence. Some teachers have students follow the rhythmic beat by tapping the book with their hand or their pencil; some have students make a slight head movement in time with the rhythm. These motor responses seem to aid students both in perceiving and producing the rhythm and stress of English. The patterns of la-La-la's are used as a visual aid to perception and production of rhythm and stress patterns.

Repeat each sentence in part 2. Exaggerate the sentence stresses slightly. Feel the rhythm. Listen to yourself. Self-monitor your stress and rhythm pattern. Self-monitoring means talking to yourself and listening to yourself.

Part 3—Pronunciation Practice with Long Sentences

Longer sentences can be divided into parts with slight pauses between the groups of words. Repeat the following sentence in three parts. Make the *last* stress in each part a little *stronger*. Repeat each part three times. Feel the rhythm.

First I finished packing,   then I called a taxi,   and then I went outside.

LA la-LA-la   LA- la   LA la- LA la-LA-la   la- LA la- la- la- LA

Repeat the entire sentence with slight pauses between the parts. This symbol (|) is used to show a slight pause.

First I finished packing, | then I called a taxi, | and then I went outside.

Repeat each sentence in the following sequence. Reduce words and increase speed as the length of the sentence increases. Feel the rhythm. Listen to yourself.

1. I'd like a sandwich.
2. I'd like a chicken sandwich.
3. I'd like a chicken-salad sandwich.
4. I'd like a chicken-salad sandwich | and a cup of coffee.
5. I'd like a chicken-salad sandwich, | a cup of coffee, | and some ice cream.

Practice the sentences again using natural rhythm and stress.[3]

(Lab: Stop the tape for individual practice and self-monitoring.)

Part 4—Listening and Marking Sentence Stresses (AK/TS)

Read the first sentence silently. Draw a line under the sentence stress. Listen and check. Listen and repeat. Continue in this way.[4]

1. I'd like some popcorn. (Mark 1 sentence stress.)

2. I'd like some popcorn | and a Coke.[5] (Mark 2 sentence stresses.)

---

3. It is important to do the follow-up part of the exercises in this section. Its purpose is to encourage students to use rapid and natural rhythm and stress. This is essential in order to help students to develop a feel for the natural rhythm and stress of English.
4. This is the first lesson in which the students are asked to use their intuition and to guess where sentence stresses will fall. The tape gives them a few seconds to mark a sentence, then the sentence is pronounced so that they may check their intuition. Next the tape gives the answer so that they get immediate feedback on their guess. Finally the tape gives them an opportunity to repeat the sentence. The same procedure should be followed if this lesson is read live.
5. This mark (|) is used to indicate possible brief pause points in the sentence. It is used in this exercise to aid students in marking the stresses.

3. I'd like some popcorn, | a Coke, | and a candy bar. (Mark 3 sentence stresses.)

Practice the sentences again using natural rhythm and speed.

(Lab: Stop the tape for individual practice and self-monitoring.)

Part 5—Test Sentences for Self-Monitoring and Self-Testing

Practice the following sentences using natural rhythm and speed. Exaggerate the sentence stresses, slightly. Shorten the unstressed words and increase your speed as the length of the sentence increases.

Record. Listen and monitor your pronunciation, that is, *talk* to yourself and *listen* to yourself.

1. I'm going.
2. I'm going on Monday.
3. I'm going to New York on Monday.

Resource Material

Part 1

As a class activity, ask students to practice the following sequences of sentences. Encourage students to monitor their rhythm and sentence stresses. Each sentence stress has a line under it. This mark (|) indicates a pause.

A. 1. Take out a <u>pencil</u>.

2. Take out a <u>pencil</u> and some <u>paper</u>.

3. Take out your <u>dictionary</u>, | a <u>pencil</u>, | and some <u>paper</u>.

B. 1. She's <u>coming</u> on <u>Thursday</u>.

2. She's <u>coming</u> to <u>visit</u> on <u>Thursday</u>.

3. She's <u>coming</u> to <u>visit</u> the <u>classes</u> on <u>Thursday</u>.

C. 1. I'll <u>meet</u> you on <u>Friday</u>.

2. I'll <u>meet</u> you in <u>London</u> on <u>Friday</u>.

3. I'll <u>meet</u> you at the <u>airport</u> in <u>London</u> on <u>Friday</u>.

D. 1. I'd like a <u>salad</u>.

2. I'd like a bowl of <u>soup</u> | and a <u>salad</u>.

3. I'd like a bowl of <u>soup</u>, | some <u>crackers</u>, | and a <u>salad</u>.

4. I'd like a bowl of <u>soup</u>, | some <u>crackers</u>, | a <u>salad</u>, | and a <u>Coke</u>.

Part 2

Most ESL students have learned dialogues—short conversations—in their grammar classes. The two-line dialogues in the following section are called *rhymalogues*. These rhymalogues have a special rhythm and stress pattern. The last two words in each line rhyme and each receives a sentence stress. There is a pause before the last word, which is the name of the person being addressed. The second word in each line also receives stress.

Ask students to practice the rhymalogues imitating the rhythm and stress pattern exactly. Encourage students to monitor their rhythm and sentence stresses.

1. *Lee*: I'll <u>meet</u> you at the <u>bank</u>, | <u>Frank</u>.
   Frank: I'll <u>be</u> there at <u>three</u>, | <u>Lee</u>.

2. *Lou*: What <u>time</u> is the <u>show</u>, | <u>Joe</u>?
   Joe: I <u>think</u> it starts at <u>two</u>, | <u>Lou</u>.

3. *Ben*: What <u>time</u> shall we <u>eat</u>, | <u>Pete</u>?
   Pete: I'd <u>like</u> to eat at <u>ten</u>, | <u>Ben</u>.

4. *Kay*: I <u>heard</u> you lost your <u>cat</u>, | <u>Matt</u>.
   Matt: I <u>think</u> he ran a<u>way</u>, | <u>Kay</u>.

5. *Gail*: I <u>like</u> your new <u>hat</u>, | <u>Pat</u>.
   Pat: I <u>got</u> it on <u>sale</u>, | <u>Gail</u>.

Lesson 9

Rhythm and Reduced Words

> The students are going to Chicago.

Part 1—Review

Lessons 1 and 2 introduced this unit and the fourteen key sentences. In lessons 3 and 4 we worked with two-syllable and three-syllable words and accented syllables. Notice that this mark (´) has been written over the first vowel letter in the accented syllable. Repeat.

	Two-Syllable Words			*Three-Syllable Words*	
preténd	áccent	discúss	diréction	understánd	sýllable
1 2	1 2	1 2	1 2 3	1 2 3	1 2 3

In lesson 5 we practiced reduced syllables. In lessons 6 and 7 we studied reduced syllable pronunciation of past tense and plural suffixes. Notice that this mark (x) has been placed under the vowel in the reduced syllable. Repeat.

Reduced Syllables			*Past Tense Forms*			*Plural / Third Person Forms*		
toníght	télephone	áccident	néeded	wáited	decíded	wátches	róses	chánges
1 2	1 2 3	1 2 3	1 2	1 2	1 2 3	1 2	1 2	1 2

In lesson 8 we studied sentence stresses and sentence rhythm. Sentence stresses are the parts of sentences which are stronger. The speaker gives more strength to certain parts to help the listener get the sense (or meaning) of the sentence. Notice that each sentence stress is underlined. Repeat.

Rhythm and Sentence Stresses

I'd like a chicken-salad sandwich.

Get ready for the test.

Part 2—Reduced Words: Weak Forms of Words

In lesson 5 we studied reduced *syllables* in words; in this lesson we will study reduced *words* in sentences. We will work with one-syllable words of the kind listed below and in the resource material on page 46.

These words have *stronger*[6] forms when they are pronounced by themselves, but they have *weaker* (or reduced) forms used in the rhythm pattern of natural conversational English. Contrast the following strong and weak forms.[7]

Strong	*Weak*
and	'nd
to	t'
some	s'm'
are	're
an	'n
a	/ə/

Practice the following sentences using weak forms. Notice each weak form is marked by a line through it (—). Repeat.

1. I like cream and sugar.   /ənd/, /nd/, /n/
2. I went to class.   /tə/, /t/
3. I need some chalk.   /səm/, /sm/
4. The birds are singing.   /r/
5. She has an apple.   /ən/, /n/
6. I bought a book.   /ə/

Practice the sentences again. The weak forms may be reduced in two ways:

1. The schwa sound, /ə/, may be substituted, as for the *a* in *and*, for the *o* in *to*, for the *a* in *an*, and the *a* in *a*;
2. the vowel sound may be omitted, as in *some* (which is pronounced /sm/), or as in *are* (which is pronounced as syllabic /r/).[8]

Use natural rhythm and speed of spoken English.[9]

---

6. Strong forms are called *citation* forms in some books.
7. The weakness of weak forms and the strength of strong forms varies from speaker to speaker and according to the conditions in which the speaker is speaking. Each of these words also can be stressed for particular emphasis and particular meaning. When stressed the strong form is used.
8. The symbol /ɝ/ will be used for vocalic *r* in Unit 2.
9. See footnote 3 on page 39.

Part 3—Pronunciation Practice with Weak Forms

A range of weaker forms and stronger forms will be heard in natural spoken English. As an ESL student, you may prefer to use stronger forms in your own personal speech. However, train yourself to *hear* and to *understand* the weaker forms when they are used in the natural conversational "fast speech" of English. Listen carefully. Practice the weaker forms below. Practice them in order to experience the "feeling" of weaker forms, even though you may not wish to use them in your own spoken English. Weak forms (reduced words) are marked by a line through them; sentence stresses are underlined.

1. The boy ate the apple.[10]
2. I can come later.
3. I can come at three.
4. I can come from four to five.
5. I need eight or nine cups.
6. I'm as tall as John.
7. Can you come?
8. I like your hat.

Repeat the sentences again using natural rhythm and speed and reduced weak forms.

(Lab: Then stop the tape and allow time for individual practice and self-monitoring.)

Part 4—Listening and Marking Reduced Words (AK/TS)

Read the first sentence silently. Draw a line through each reduced word. Listen and check. Listen and repeat. Continue in this way.[11]

1. I was hungry and thirsty. (Draw a line through 2 words which are reduced.)
2. The students are going to class. (3 words)
3. Bill and Sam are from Chicago. (3 words)
4. I must go to class at two. (3 words)

(Lab: Stop the tape. Ask students to give the answers. Start the tape. Have students check their work as the reduced words are given.)

Practice the sentences again using natural rhythm, speed, and reduced weak forms.

---

10. The variations for *the* as /ə/ before consonants and /ɪ/ or /i/ before vowels may be studied as the teacher chooses.
11. Again in this lesson students are asked to use their intuition and to guess which words will be reduced. The tape gives students a few seconds to mark the reduced words; then the sentence is pronounced so that they may check their intuition. Next the tape gives the answer so that they may get immediate feedback on their guess. Finally, the tape gives them an opportunity to repeat the sentence. The same procedure should be followed if this lesson is read live.

Part 5—Test Sentences for Self-Monitoring and Self-Testing

Practice the following sentences using natural rhythm, stress, and reduced weak forms. Record. Listen and monitor your pronunciation.

1. I must go to class at ten.
2. I need some money to pay for the trip.
3. Get ready for the test.
4. The students are going to Chicago.

Part 6—Dictionary Homework

Look up the following words in your dictionary. Copy the pronunciation exactly. Copy all variations in pronunciation which are listed.

1. and _____   4. from _____

2. the _____   5. can _____

3. for _____

Resource Material

Part 1—Word List for Lessons 9 and 12

The following is a list of sixty-five high-frequency words. These words make up nearly 60 percent of the spoken English in daily use. Most of these words have stronger forms when they are pronounced in isolation and weaker forms when they are used in phrases and sentences in the natural rhythm of conversational speech. Many dictionaries give both the stronger and the weaker forms.

As an exercise to demonstrate the frequency of usage of these words, ask students to read this paragraph and the paragraph above. Ask them to draw a circle around every occurrence of every word which appears on the list below.

a	an	some	the			
did	do	does				
am	are	be	been	is	was	were
had	has	have				
and	but	or	just			
he	him	I	it	me	my	she
them	they	us	we	you		
as	at	by	for	from	in	of
on	to	than	with			
can	could	may	might	must	shall	
should	will	would				
her	his	its	our	their	your	mine
if	not					
this	that	there				

Part 2

Part 2 includes a few of the many phrases heard frequently in conversational speech. Each reduced word has a line through it. As a class activity, ask students to practice the following phrases. Encourage students to monitor their rhythm, stresses, and reductions. As a class activity, make up sentences with some of the phrases.

sooner or later	older than John	cream and sugar
to class	a box of candy	once in a while
back and forth	put it here	at the store
from time to time	some more coffee	as far as I know
at home	all but one	what did he want
like to see it	now and then	taller than Bill
one of the best	to work	a glass of milk

Part 3

Part 3 contains three short rhymes. In rhymes 1 and 2, the words at the ends of the second line and the fourth line rhyme. In rhyme 3, lines one and two rhyme and lines three and four rhyme. Ask students to practice these with attention to reduced words, rhythm, and stresses. Each reduced word has a line through it; each stress has a line under it. Discuss the meanings of the rhymes.

1. Roses are red;

   Violets are blue.

   Sugar is sweet,

   And so are you.

   (Either strong or weak forms of *is* in line three and *and* and *are* in line four may be used.)

2. Early to bed,

   Early to rise,

   Makes a man healthy,

   Wealthy, and wise.

3. Rainbow at night,

   Is the sailors' delight.

   Rainbow at morning,

   Sailors take warning!

   (Either the strong or weak form of *is* in line two may be used.)

Lesson 10
Rhythm and Linking

> He␣was␣waiting␣at␣the␣bus : stop.

Part 1—Linking Words

As you read this page of *printed* English notice the space between the words. It is easy to see where one word ends and the next word begins.

In *spoken* English, however, there is little or no space (or pause) between the words in phrases or short sentences. Words seem to run together. ESL students are not sure where one word ends and the next word begins as they listen to spoken English. The speaker links words together in groups to help the listener get the sense (or meaning) of the sentence. In short sentences, all words are linked together, with no pauses. In this lesson we will practice *linking* words.

Linking
In linking, the end of one word blends into the beginning of the next word with little or no pause. This mark (␣) is used to show linking. Repeat the following sentences. Link the words.[12]

    1. Who␣are␣you?   2. I'm␣ready␣for␣class.   3. My␣office␣is␣empty.

Part 2—Lengthening Sounds / Holding Sounds

Lengthening Continuant Sounds
In places where the same sound is at the *end* of one word and the *beginning* of the next word, the sound is not pronounced twice. It is pronounced only once but it is lengthened a little. This mark (:) is used to show *lengthening*.

Repeat the following sentences. Lengthen the marked sound very slightly.[13]

    1. I found some : money   3. I wish : she could come.

    2. We stayed one : night.   4. Meet me at the bus : stop.

Holding for Plosive Sounds
If the sounds are plosive sounds, /p/, /b/, /t/, /d/, /k/, or /g/, the sound is not pronounced twice, but it is formed and held for a brief time before it is released.[14]

---

12. Encourage students to link the words at each juncture point (i.e., the place where one word ends and the next word begins). The purpose here is to help students blend words together smoothly within short sentences and within phrases in longer sentences. Attention to linking will aid students who have a staccato-like syllable-by-syllable delivery (sometimes marked by glottal stops between syllables).
13. Contrast this portion of the lesson, which illustrates the manner in which doubled *continuant* sounds may be *lengthened*, with the following portion of the lesson in which doubled *plosive* sounds are preceded by a tiny *pause* before their release.
14. Contrast this portion of the lesson, which illustrates the manner in which doubled *plosive* sounds are preceded by a tiny *pause* before their release, with the preceding portion of the lesson in which doubled *continuant* sounds may be *lengthened*. The resource materials for this lesson give additional practice material for these two kinds of consonant sounds.

Repeat the following sentences.

1. He's a bad : dog.

2. What : time is it?

3. I like : candy.

4. We can help : Paul.

Repeat the sentences in part 2. Use natural speed and rhythm of spoken English.

Part 3—Pronunciation Practice with Linking and Lengthening / Holding

Listen and repeat these sentences. Follow the marks which show linking (‿) and lengthening / holding (‿:‿).

1. I won some : money and a car.

2. He's my favorite : teacher.

3. I should call : Lou.

4. My brother : ran away.

Repeat the sentences again. Use natural speed and rhythm of spoken English.[15]

(Lab: Stop the tape for individual practice and self-monitoring.)

Part 4—Dictation (AK/TS)

Four sentences will be dictated. Listen and repeat; listen and write; listen and check.

1. _____ (5 words)

2. _____ (4)

3. _____ (5)

4. _____ (5)

Now look at the sentences you have written. Draw lengthening/holding marks.[16]

(Lab: Then stop the tape and have students give their answers.)

Practice the sentences again using natural speed and rhythm.

(Lab: Then stop the tape for a few minutes of individual practice and self-monitoring.)

_____

15. See footnote 3 on page 39.

16. *Lab*: The tape repeats the sentences again allowing a few seconds for students to draw lengthening marks.

Part 5—Test Sentences for Self-Monitoring and Self-Testing[17]

Practice the following sentences using natural speed and rhythm. Record. Listen and monitor your pronunciation.

1. I wish : she would hurry.

2. The students : sang a sad song.

3. I must help : Paul.

4. I'll meet you at the bus : stop.

---

17. Later in the program attention will be given to juncture and redistribution of syllabic boundaries across word boundaries in relation to stress, rhythm, and intonation and in relation to distribution of plosive sounds which force a closure in the vocal tract. Examples:

    Pick it up.→ Pi cki tup.
    I bought a candied apple. → I bough ta can die da pple.

    Teachers of advanced classes may want to discuss it at this time.

Resource Material

Part 1—Linking Words and Lengthening Continuant Sounds

As a class activity, ask students to practice the following sentences, giving special attention to linking words and lengthening the continuant sounds slightly, as marked.

1. They gave : Victor the money.

2. More : rain is expected on Monday.

3. The teacher : read us a story.

4. I wish : she would hurry.

5. They stayed only one : night.

Ask students to make up sentences/dialogues using the following phrases.

1. _____ us : some _____.

2. _____ we'll : let _____.

3. _____ been : no _____.

4. _____ with : three _____.

Part 2—Linking Words and Holding Plosive Sounds

As a class activity, ask students to practice the following, giving special attention to linking words and holding the plosive sounds briefly, as marked. Notice that the two plosive sounds may be the same or different but the same brief pause is made before the second sound is pronounced. The first of the two sounds is formed but is not exploded.

1. We took : Kay to the game.

2. I need : time to finish my homework.

3. Don't : tell the teacher I was late.

4. I must help : Bob with his homework.

5. We didn't : take the bus.

Ask students to make up sentences/dialogues using the following phrases.

1. _____ next : Tuesday _____.

2. _____ back : tire _____.

3. _____ next : time _____.

4. _____ look : tired _____.

Part 3—Practice with Limericks

Part 3 contains two limericks. Limericks are a special kind of rhyme. They have five lines and a special rhythm and rhyme system. Lines one, two, and five have three sentence stresses and the last words in these lines rhyme. Lines three and four have two sentence stresses and the last words in these lines rhyme. Ask students to practice these limericks with attention to monitoring rhythm, stresses, and reductions.

1. There once was a woman named Bunny,
   Whose smile was so happy and sunny.
   People's names she forgot,
   But that worried her not.
   She simply called all of them, "Honey!"

2. There once was a fellow from Maine,
   Who couldn't go out in the rain.
   For he loaned his umbrella,
   To Aunt Isabella,
   Who lost it while travelling in Spain.

Section E—Elisions and Assimilations

Section Notes

Section E has three lessons on *elision*—the omission or dropping out of a sound or sounds resulting in a shortened speech form—and *assimilation*—the process by which sounds change phonetically to become more like neighboring sounds. There is resource material for additional practice at the end of each lesson.

Lesson 11 presents listening/speaking work with the standard contractions of English which ESL students study as they study English grammar.

Lesson 12 presents intensive listening/speaking practice with special one-word contractions and linkings characteristic of the natural conversational fast speech of informal English.

Lesson 13 goes one step beyond the contractions presented in lessons 11 and 12. It presents intensive listening/speaking practice with predictable sound changes (assimilations) which occur when sounds "touch" each other across word boundaries. It includes such items as *going + to* which becomes *gonna* and *meet + you* which becomes *meetcha*. Although ESL students may not wish to use these special pronunciations, they must train themselves to hear and to understand them in the natural conversational fast speech of informal English.

Teachers may wish to discuss chart 7 with students for an overview, or as a review of this section.

Chart 7
ELISIONS AND ASSIMILATIONS

He isn't coming.	*Two-Word Contractions* In two-word contractions, two words are combined into one word and one or two sounds are omitted.
The boys 'n' girls were late.	*One-Word Contractions and Linking* These contractions are like reductions of words but they also can have omissions of vowels or consonants or both; in addition, the remaining sounds *must* be linked to the words on one or both sides.
I'm gonna study at the lab.	*Contractions and Sound Changes* At the place where one word ends and another word begins, two sounds touch. Sometimes one of these two sounds forces the other sound to change.

Lesson 11

Two-Word Contractions

```
He isn't coming
```

Part 1—Two-word Contractions

ESL students study contractions as they study English grammar. The key sentence above has the contraction *isn't*. In this contraction the two words *is* and *not* are combined into one word, *isn't*. The letter *o* is omitted. This mark ('), the apostrophe, shows where the letter *o* has been omitted.

Practice the pronunciation of the following contractions. Give special attention to linking the sounds within a contraction wherever sounds have been omitted. Repeat, first the full form, then the contraction.[1]

Full Form	*Contraction*
1. I am happy.	I'm happy.
2. They have gone.	They've gone.
3. He would like to go.	He'd like to go.
4. I should have called him.	I should've called him.

Sometimes ESL students believe contractions are poor speech or sloppy speech. The *opposite* is true. The contractions in this lesson are both natural and correct in spoken English. They also may be used in informal written English.

Part 2—Pronunciation Practice with Forms of *Be*, *Have*, and Modals.

The following are two-word contractions with forms of *Be*, *Have*, and modals linked to pronouns and nouns. The resource materials for this lesson present additional contractions. Practice. Link the sounds within a contraction wherever sounds have been omitted. Repeat.

Be

1. *I'm*
   I'm waiting for the bus.
2. *she's*
   She's very pretty.
3. *Mary's*
   Mary's coming later.
4. *we're*
   We're late to class.

Have + Past Participle

5. *he's*
   He's worked for an hour.
6. *Bill's*
   Bill's studied all day.
7. *we've*
   We've finished our work.
8. *he'd*
   She told me he'd gone to Chicago.

---

1. The meaning contrast between full forms and contractions must be studied later.

53

Modals

9. *we'll*
   We'll see you tomorrow.

10. *John'll*
    John'll go with us.

11. *I'd*
    I'd like to go.

12. *boys'd*
    The boys'd like to go.

Modals + *Have* + Past Participle

13. *might've*
    He might've called me.

14. *should've*
    I should've asked him.

15. *must've*
    I must've seen him.

16. *could've*
    I could've gone with them.

(Lab: Stop the tape and have students give the full *forms for each contraction.)*

Part 3—Pronunciation Practice with Information Questions and *Be*, *Have*, and *Do*

The following are two-word contractions with forms of *Be*, *Have*, and *Do* linked to *information questions*, questions which begin with the *Wh* words (*who, when, where, which, why*) and *how*. Link the sounds within a contraction wherever sounds have been omitted. Repeat.

Be

1. *what's*
   What's your name?

2. *why're*
   Why're you crying?

3. *when're*
   When're you going?

4. *how's*
   How's your mother?

Have + Past Participle

5. *how've*
   How've you been?

6. *why's*
   Why's he waited so long?

7. *where've*
   Where've you been?

8. *who'd*
   Who'd stolen your books?

Do

9. *what'd*
   What'd he do?

10. *why'd*
    Why'd she wait so long?

11. *when'd*
    When'd he call?

12. *how'd*
    How'd she know?

(Lab: Stop the tape and have students give the full *forms for each contraction.)*

Part 4—Pronunciation Practice with *Not* and *Be*, *Have*, *Do*, and Modals

The following are two-word contractions with forms of *Be*, *Have*, *Do*, and modals linked to *not*. Link the sounds within a contraction where sounds have been omitted. Repeat.

Be

1. *isn't*
   He isn't coming to class.

2. *weren't*
   They weren't at the restaurant.

3. *wasn't*
   She wasn't invited.

Have + Past Participle

4. *haven't*
   I haven't seen him.

5. *hasn't*
   He hasn't called me.

6. *hadn't*[2]
   They hadn't finished their dinner.

Do

7. *don't*
   I don't know his name.

8. *doesn't*
   He doesn't work here.

9. *didn't*
   We didn't find it.

Modals

10. *shouldn't*
    I shouldn't leave until five.

11. *wouldn't*
    He wouldn't tell me his name.

12. *won't*
    She won't be back until five.

(*Lab: Stop the tape and have students give the* full *forms for each contraction.*)

Part 5—Pronunciation Practice with Negative Yes/No Questions[3]

The following are two-word contractions with forms of *not* linked to *Be, Have, Do,* and modals. Link the sounds within a contraction wherever sounds have been omitted. Repeat.[4]

Be

1. *isn't*
   Isn't he there?

2. *wasn't*
   Wasn't he ready?

3. *aren't*
   Aren't you coming?

Have + Past Participle

4. *hasn't*
   Hasn't he called?

5. *hadn't*
   Hadn't he told you?

6. *haven't*
   Haven't they come?

Do

7. *don't*
   Don't you want to come?

8. *doesn't*
   Doesn't he like it?

9. *didn't*
   Didn't he call you?

Modals

10. *can't*
    Can't you come?

11. *won't*
    Won't you ask him?

12. *shouldn't*
    Shouldn't we wait for him?

---

2. Give special help with pronunciation of the contraction *hadn't*. Alert students to the fact that the *d* is formed but exploded nasally, not orally, with the *n* which is pronounced as a syllabic *n*. This pronunciation pattern is the same for any word which ends in *d* contracted with *not*, as in *didn't, couldn't, wouldn't, shouldn't*.

3. The full forms of these contractions (i.e., the negative question forms of *not* linked to *Be, Have, Do,* and modals) are never used except to signal very special meanings.

4. Notice the rising intonation which signals a request for a *Yes/No* answer. See lesson 15 in this unit.

Part 6—Writing Sentences from Dictation (AK/TS)

Four sentences will be dictated. Listen and repeat. Listen and write. Listen and check. Write the *contracted* forms. (Contractions are counted as one word.)

1. _____ (4 words)

2. _____ (4)

3. _____ (3)

4. _____ (4)

(Lab: Stop the tape and ask students to read their sentences and to give the contractions. Start the tape and have students check their work. Then stop the tape for individual practice and self-monitoring.)

Practice the sentences again using natural rhythm, speed, and contractions.[5]

Part 7—Test Sentences for Self-Monitoring and Self-Testing

Practice the following sentences using natural rhythm, stress, reductions, and contractions. Record. Listen and monitor your pronunciation.

1. Can't you come or don't you want to?
2. His friends weren't at the restaurant.
3. They aren't here yet.
4. What's his name or didn't he tell you?

---

5. It is important to do the follow-up part of the exercises in this section. Its purpose is to encourage students to use natural rhythm in sentences with contractions. This is essential in order to help students to develop a feel for natural rhythm in the use of contractions in spoken English.

Resource Material

Part 1

The practice material for lesson 11 used only a few of the hundreds of contractions of spoken English. The contractions charts (charts 8 and 9) are a summary presentation of a few additional combinations. The listings are not intended to be complete. They present only a few of the more useful combinations.

When a line (across) and a column (down) meet, a dot indicates that the two items can be combined to form a contraction. As an individualized activity, ask one student to read a sentence from the list beside the chart; ask another student to locate the contraction on the chart by giving the numbers of the line (across) and the column (down).

In practicing contractions, alert students to the final sounds such as /m/ in *I'm*, /v/ in *I've*, /1/ in *we'll*, /d/ in *he'd*, /z/ in *she's*, /r/ in *they're*, and /nt/ in *can't*. These sounds must not be omitted. They must be pronounced and linked to the following word.

Discussion for Chart 8
Notice that the contractions for *I + had* and *I + would* are both spelled and pronounced *I'd*. Notice that the contractions for *he + is* and *he + has* are both spelled and pronounced *he's*. The words which follow the contractions indicate which contraction is intended. Discuss the grammar and the meaning of the following sentences.

1. I'd waited an hour. (I had waited an hour.)
2. I'd like to go. (I would like to go.)
3. He's late. (He is late.)
4. He's waited an hour. (He has waited for an hour.)

Sentences for Chart 8 (AK/TS)

1. I'm hungry.
2. He's waiting for his friends.
3. We're late.
4. I've been waiting for an hour.
5. We'll meet you at six.
6. They'd forgotten to call.
7. They said they'd like to go.
8. Bob's never late.
9. Jean'll be back in an hour.
10. We'd like to watch TV.
11. The program's at seven.
12. It'll be over about eight.
13. I wish you'd waited for me.
14. I wish you'd wait for me.
15. The teacher's never late.

Chart 8
CONTRACTIONS

	Be			Have			Will and Would	
	1	2	3	4	5	6	7	8
	am	are	is	has	have	had	will	would
1a. I	●				●	●	●	●
2a. we		●		●	●	●	●	●
3a. they		●		●	●	●	●	●
4a. you		●			●	●	●	●
5a. he			●	●		●	●	●
6a. she			●	●		●	●	●
7a. it			●	●		●	●	●
8a. Jean			●	●		●	●	●
9a. Bob			●	●		●	●	●

Discussion for Chart 9
The contractions formed by words marked by asterisks (*) have unusual spelling and/or pronunciation patterns.

do + *not*	becomes *don't* /dont/
will + *not*	becomes *won't* /wont/
shall + *not*	becomes *shan't* /ʃænt/

An (×) indicates contractions which are possible, but not in frequent use, particularly in writing.

Sentences for Chart 9 (AK/TS)

1. They must've forgotten.
2. They didn't remember.
3. The classes don't begin until ten.
4. We won't have time to go to the lab.
5. He wasn't hungry.
6. They weren't at the restaurant.
7. They shouldn't have waited.
8. Bob might've called after I left.
9. My watch doesn't work.
10. It isn't time for class.
11. I haven't done my homework.
12. I can't go until Sunday.
13. He should've waited for us.
14. I would've called you but I forgot your number.
15. It hasn't rained for a week.

Chart 9
CONTRACTIONS

	1	2
	not	*have*
1a. is	●	
2a. was	●	
3a. were	●	
4a. do*	●	
5a. does	●	
6a. did	●	
7a. have	●	
8a. has	●	
9a. had	●	
10a. can	●	×
11a. will*	●	●
12a. must	●	●
13a. could	●	●
14a. would	●	●
15a. should	●	●
16a. might	×	●
17a. shall*	×	×
18a. may	×	×

Part 2

As a class activity, ask students to pronounce these sets of rhyming words. Add to the lists.

I'm	dime	time	_____	what's	cuts	shuts	_____
she's	knees	skis	_____	why're	tire	choir	_____
Mary's	carries	berries	_____	how's	cows		_____
we're	near	dear	_____	why's	ties	buys	_____
Bill's	hills	fills	_____	don't	won't		_____
we've	leave	Steve	_____	who'd	food		_____
he'd	need	read	_____	when'd	send	mend	_____
we'll	he'll	feel	_____	how'd	loud	crowd	_____
I'd	tried	cried	_____				

Lesson 12

One-Word Contractions and Linking

The boys ('n') girls were late.

Part 1—Contractions in Single Words

In lesson 11 we practiced contractions in which two words were shortened and combined into one word. The contractions discussed in lesson 11 may be used in informal written English and are the contractions ESL students study as they study English grammar.

In this lesson we will look at a second group of contractions. In contrast to two-word contractions, the following contractions will not be found in grammar books, because they are *spoken* but never written.[6]

One-word contractions are like the reductions of lesson 9, but in addition to reduction of a vowel to schwa, /ə/, they can have *omissions* of consonants or vowels or both. The remaining sounds must be linked to the words on one or both sides.

Look at the following sentences. Apostrophes show where sounds have been omitted. These written forms would be incorrect in any other context. They are used here for the teaching purpose of helping ESL students study special one-word contractions and linking used in the natural conversational fast speech of English. Repeat, first the full form, then the contracted form.

Full Form		Contracted Form
1. I like her very much.	(like'er)	I like 'er very much.
2. I like him very much.	(like'im)	I like 'im very much.
3. I like them very much.	(like'em)	I like 'em very much.
4. I like them very much.	(like th'm)	I like th'm very much.
5. Was he happy?	(was'e)	Was 'e happy?

Part 2—Pronunciation Practice with Contractions

Both full forms and a range of contracted forms will be heard in natural spoken English.[7] As an ESL student, you may prefer to use less contracted forms in your personal speech. However, train yourself to hear and to understand these special contractions when they are used in the natural conversational fast speech of English. Listen carefully and practice the contracted forms listed below. Practice them in order to experience the feeling of this special kind of one-word contraction and linking. Repeat, first the contraction, then the sentence with the contraction.[8]

---

6. Written forms of these contractions will be found only in certain kinds of fiction writing, in comic strips, and in cartoons.
7. The spoken use of these contractions varies from speaker to speaker and according to the conditions in which the speaker is speaking.
8. Notice that the full form is printed to the right of the contracted forms and the sentences with contracted forms.

1. (Is'e)   Is'e coming?   (Is he coming?)
2. (I'_she)   I'_she coming?   (Is she coming?)
3. (saw 'er)   I saw 'er yesterday.   (I saw her yesterday.)
4. (took 'im)   We took 'im home at noon. (We took him home at noon.)
5. (cream 'n' sugar) I'd like cream 'n' sugar. (I'd like cream and sugar.)
6. ('s it)   's it a local call?   (Is it a local call?)
7. (D'you) (like 'im) D'you like 'im?   (Do you like him?)
8. (does 'e) (know 'er) Does 'e know 'er?   (Does he know her?)
9. (was 'e)   Was 'e waiting?   (Was he waiting?)
10. (ask 'er)   You can ask 'er later.   (You can ask her later.)
11. (when'd 'e)   When'd 'e come?   (When did he come?)
12. (where'd 'e)   Where'd 'e go?   (Where did he go?)
13. (what'd 'e)   What'd 'e want?   (What did he want?)
14. (how'd 'e)   How'd 'e do it?   (How did he do it?)
15. (why'd 'e)   Why'd 'e go?   (Why did he go?)

(Lab: Stop the tape for a few minutes of practice and self-monitoring.)

Part 3—Hearing Contractions / Writing Full Forms (AK/TS)

Listen and repeat. Rewrite each sentence. Write the full form of each word. Check.

1. What's y'r name?

_____

2. Where're y' from?

_____

3. 't 's time f'r lunch.

_____

4. 's 'e fr'm France 'r fr'm Spain?

_____

5. D' y' want tea 'r coffee?

_____

(Lab: Stop the tape and ask students to read their answers. Start the tape and have students check their work.)

Practice the sentences using natural rhythm, stress, and contractions.[9]

(Lab: Stop the tape for a few minutes of individual practice and self-monitoring.)

---

9. It is important to do this follow-up part of the exercises in this section in order to help students develop a better awareness of the use of these contractions in the informal speech of many speakers of English.

Part 4—Writing Sentences from Dictation:
       Hearing Contractions / Writing Full Forms (AK/TS)

Four sentences will be dictated. Listen and repeat. Listen and write. Listen and check. Write entire words even though you *hear* contractions.

1. _____ (6 words)

2. _____ (5)

3. _____ (9)

4. _____ (7)

(Lab: Stop the tape and ask students to read their answers. Start the tape and have students check their work.)

Practice the sentences using natural rhythm and contractions.

(Lab: Stop the tape for individual practice and self-monitoring.)

Part 5—Test Sentences for Self-Monitoring and Self-Testing

Practice the following sentences using natural rhythm, stress, and contractions. Record. Listen and monitor your pronunciation.

1. Does 'e want a cup o' coffee?
2. Is 'e fr'm Mexico 'r Canada?
3. I want s'm' cake 'n' s'm' ice cream.
4. 't 's time f'r lunch.

Resource Material

Part 1

The following sentences use words from the word list on page 46 (lesson 9) and contractions from lessons 11 and 12. As a class activity, ask students to rewrite each sentence using the full forms for each contraction. As an individualized activity, ask one student to read the sentence using full forms; ask another student to read the sentence with contracted forms. Remind students that these forms are used in speaking but not in writing. This mark (|) indicates a short pause.

1. I_want_s'm'_cake | 'n'_s'm'_ice_cream.

   _____

2. Does_'e_want_'n_apple | 'r_'n_orange?

   _____

3. Did_'e_ask_'er_to_wait?

   _____

4. What's_'s_name | 'nd_where's_'e_from?

   _____

5. I'_she_drinking_a_cup_o'_tea | 'r_a_cup_o'_coffee?

   _____

Part 2

As an individualized activity, ask students to fill in the blanks below with the correct words from the list at the right of each sentence. Practice the sentences.

1. I _____ waited _____ almost _____ hour.

   an
   for
   have

2. _____ _____ want _____ red car?

   does
   he
   the

3. No, _____ wants _____ blue one.

   he
   the

4. _____ _____ order _____ hamburger _____

   _____ hotdog?

   a   he
   a   or
   did

5. He _____ waiting _____ _____ friend.

   for
   his
   was

63

Part 3

As a class activity, ask students to pronounce these pairs of rhyming words.

Is 'e	dizzy	D' you	few
I' she	fishy	Does 'e	fuzzy
's it	bit	Was 'e	fuzzy

Part 4

Ask students to practice the following limericks, with special attention to contractions and reductions, rhythm and stress. Discuss the hidden meaning and humor of each limerick.

1. There once was a fellow named Brian,
   Who smiled as he rode on a lion
     They returned from the ride,
     With Brian inside,
   And the smile on the face of the lion!

2. There once was a man from the city,
   Who met what he thought was a kitty.
     He gave it a pat,
     And said, "Nice little cat."
   They buried his clothes, out of pity!

   (The "kitty" referred to is a *skunk*, which is called a "black and white striped kitty.")

Lesson 13

Contractions and Sound Changes

I'm (gonna) study at the lab.

Part 1—Review

In section D we studied the *rhythm* of English sentences including *sentence stresses, reduced words,* and *linking*. Repeat.

I ate a <u>chick</u>en-salad <u>sand</u>wich.   (sentence stresses)

~~The~~ students ~~are going to~~ Chicago.   (reduced words)

He was waiting at the bus : stop.   (linking words and lengthening sounds)

In lessons 11 and 12 we practiced two kinds of *contractions*. In contractions, sounds are omitted. Repeat.

He isn't coming.   (two-word contractions)

The boys 'n' girls were late.   (one-word contractions and linking)

Part 2—Contractions and Sound Changes

In this lesson we will work with contractions and sound changes. At the juncture point, where one word ends and the next word begins, two sounds touch. Sometimes one of the two sounds forces the other sound to change. For example, *meet + you* becomes *meet + chou*; then *ou* is reduced to /ə/, and we have *meetcha*, a contraction with sound changes.

As with one-word contractions, these forms are natural in informal conversational English. However, they are spoken forms which are never written. The spellings used here would be incorrect in any other context.[10] Notice that the *a* is pronounced as schwa, /ə/, at the ends of these words. Repeat.

---

10. Written forms of these words with sound changes will be found in certain kinds of fiction writing, in comic strips, and in cartoons.

1. $t + y = tch$
   can't you
   canʼtcha

2. $d + y = dj$
   did you
   didja

3. $nt + t = nn$
   want to
   wanna

4. $ng + t = nn$
   going to
   gonna

5. $v + t = ft$
   have to
   hafta

Part 3—Pronunciation Practice

Both full forms and a range of contracted forms with sound changes will be heard in natural spoken English.[11] As an ESL student, it probably is best for you to use full forms. However, train yourself to hear and to understand these contracted forms when they are heard in the natural conversational fast speech of English. Listen carefully and practice the following sentences in order to experience the feeling of this special kind of contraction. Repeat, first the full form, then the contracted form with sound changes.

Full Form	*Contracted Form with Sound Changes*
1. I have to work on Saturday.	I hafta work on Saturday.
2. I will meet you after class.	I'll meetcha after class.
3. We are going to study at the lab.	We're gonna study at the lab.[12]
4. He has to finish his homework.	He hasta finish his homework.

Repeat the sentences again using natural rhythm, stress, and contracted forms with sound changes.

(Lab: Stop the tape for individual practice and self-monitoring.)

---

11. The spoken use of these forms varies from speaker to speaker and according to the conditions in which the speaker is speaking.
12. The form *gonna* is used only before a verb. Examples:
    going to work = gonna work
    going to study = gonna study
    This verb form is sometimes called the *going to* future form. The form *gonna* is *never* used in a adverb of place phrase such as *going to Chicago* or *going to class*.

Part 4—Matching Self-Test (AK/TS)

Test yourself. Match the phrases in column 2 to the contracted forms with sound changes in column 1. The words in column 1 will be read. Repeat. Find the matching phrase in column 2 and write the letter on the line.

Column 1   *Column 2*

Group 1

    1. gonna ____   a. want to

    2. don'no ____   b. going to

    3. wanna ____   c. don't know

Group 2

    1. hafta ____   a. give me

    2. gimme ____   b. has to

    3. hasta ____   c. have to

Group 3

    1. can'tcha ____   a. won't you

    2. don'tcha ____   b. can't you

    3. won'tcha ____   c. what (are) you

                                what (do) you

    4. whatcha ____   d. don't you

Group 4

    1. didja ____   a. should you

    2. hadja ____   b. would you

    3. couldja ____   c. had you

    4. wouldja ____   d. did you

    5. shouldja ____   e. could you

Group 5

    1. whydja ____   a. where did you

    2. wheredja ____   b. who did you

    3. whendja ____   c. why did you

    4. whodja ____   d. how did you

    5. howdja ____   e. when did you

(Lab: Stop the tape and have students give their answers. Start the tape. Have students check their work as the answers are given.)

Part 5—Test Sentences for Self-Monitoring and Self-Testing

Practice the following sentences using natural rhythm, stress, contractions, and sound changes. Record. Listen and monitor your pronunciation.

1. When didja see him?
2. I hafta study tonight.
3. Where wouldja like to go?
4. Can'tcha come, or don'tcha wanna?

Resource Material

Part 1

The items below in group 1 contain examples of "fast speech" forms with sound changes. They are all real examples from real conversations. ESL students should be alerted to listen for these forms, even though they probably should not be encouraged to use them in their own spoken English.

As a group activity, match the contracted forms in group 1 to the full forms in group 2; ask students to write the matching numbers on the lines in group 1; practice both groups. As an individualized activity, ask one student to read a line from group 2, and ask another student to reply with the matching line from group 1.

Group 1

_____ 1. Let'sko eat.

_____ 2. 'djeat lunch yet?

_____ 3. C'elp you?

_____ 4. 'djave time t'_wait?

_____ 5. 's_cool today.

_____ 6. 'jever visit London?

_____ 7. 't's time for class.

_____ 8. 's_it to go?

Group 2

1. It is cool today. (It's cool today.)

2. Let us go eat. (Let's go eat.)

3. Did you ever visit London?

4. Can I help you? (*Situation*: heard in an airport; spoken by a Skycap [porter]. *Meaning*: "May I help you by carrying your suitcases for you?" A fee is charged for each suitcase.)

5. Do you have time to wait?

6. Did you eat lunch yet?

7. Is it to go? (*Situation*: heard in a fast food restaurant. *Meaning*: "Are you going to eat it in the restaurant or take it out with you?"

8. It is time for class. (It's time for class.)

Part 2

Most ESL students have learned dialogues—short conversations—in their grammar classes. These two-line dialogues are rhymalogues. The last two words in each line rhyme. Rhymalogues have a special rhythm and stress pattern.

Ask students to practice the rhymalogues, imitating the rhythm and stress pattern exactly. Encourage students to monitor their contractions and sound changes, rhythm, and stress.

1. *Jane*: Didja come on the <u>bus</u>, | <u>Gus</u>?

   Gus: No, I came on the <u>train</u>, | <u>Jane</u>.
   (*Didja* is a contracted form of *did + you*.)

2. *Kate*: Whendja get <u>back</u>, | <u>Jack</u>?

   Jack: I got back about <u>eight</u>, | <u>Kate</u>
   (*Whendja* is a contracted form of *when + did + you*.)

3. *Ted:* Howdja break ~~your~~ <u>leg</u>, | <u>Greg</u>?

   Greg: I fell out ~~of~~ <u>bed</u>, | <u>Ted</u>.

   (*Howdja* is a contracted form of *how + did + you.*)

4. *Joe:* Howdja like ~~the~~ <u>play</u>, | <u>Kay</u>?

   Kay: I didn't get ~~to~~ <u>go</u>, | <u>Joe.</u>

   (*Howdja* is a contracted form of *how + did + you.*)

5. *Dirk:* Whydja quit ~~your~~ <u>job</u>, | <u>Bob</u>?

   Bob: I didn't like ~~the~~ <u>work</u>, | <u>Dirk</u>.

   (*Whydja* is a contracted form of *why + did + you.*)

Section F—Intonation

Section Notes

Section F has three lessons. There is resource material for additional practice at the end of each lesson.

Intonation is the most complex of all the aspects of English stress, rhythm, and intonation patterns. It is difficult to analyze; it is difficult to interpret to students; it is difficult to provide meaningful and useful practice.

Three patterns are presented in section F. Lesson 14 presents intensive listening/speaking practice with rising/falling intonation (final). Lesson 15 presents similar material for rising intonation (final). Lesson 16 presents work with one use of nonfinal intonation.

The major goals of these lessons are: (1) to make students aware of the importance of intonation in listening to and in speaking English and (2) to build a sensitivity to English intonation patterns. A special adaptation of echo practice is used to help students build sensitivity.

These lessons study the ways the speaker uses intonation patterns to help the listener understand the meanings of sentences. Rhythm, stress, reductions, linking, contractions, and assimilations all work together within the intonation patterns of the rising and falling tones of the voice.

Some of the meaning of spoken English is transmitted through the intonation patterns. Intonation adds meaning in two ways: (1) it shows the relationship of words within and between sentences, (2) it tells something about the feelings of the speaker. In listening to the meaning of intonation, we listen to *how* speakers talk, as well as *what* they say. The how and the what together give us the meaning of spoken English.

Teachers may wish to discuss chart 10 with students for an overview, or as a review, of this section.

Chart 10
INTONATION

$_2$I'm hungry.

Rising/Falling Intonation (Final)
Intonation is the voice pattern of rising and falling tones. If the tone rises from tone 2 to tone 3, then falls to tone 1, the listener knows the speaker has completed a statement (or short answer), a request, or a *Wh* question.

$_2$Am I late?

Rising Intonation (Final)
If the tone rises from tone 2 to tone 3 and ends there, the listener knows that the speaker has completed a question which asks for an answer of yes or no.

$_2$I bought hotdogs, $_2$French fries,

$_2$apples, $_2$and candy.

Nonfinal Intonation
If the tone rises from tone 2 to tone 3 and then returns to tone 2, the listener knows that the speaker has not finished, that more is to follow. There are many variations of nonfinal intonation. One use is when the speaker is telling several things in a series.

71

Lesson 14

Rising/Falling Intonation (Final)

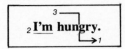

Part 1—Intonation

In lessons 8, 9, and 10, we worked with rhythm and the way the speaker uses stress and linking to help the listener get the sense (or meaning) of the sentence. In lessons 14, 15, and 16, we will study intonation and the use the speaker makes of it.

Intonation is the voice pattern of rising 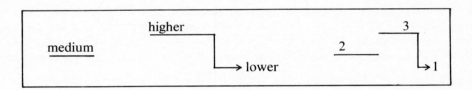 and falling voice tones. The speaker uses voice tones to help the listener understand the meaning of the sentence.

If the speaker raises the tone of voice from tone 2 to tone 3, then ends with a final fall to tone 1, the listener knows that the speaker has completed a statement (or short answer), a request, or a *Wh* question. Look at the box.[1]

Notice that the intonation rises from tone 2 to tone 3, then falls to tone 1. Look at the next box. Lines have been drawn to show the two parts of the tone group. Notice the *change point* in the tone group, that is, the place where the second part of the tone group begins.[2]

The first syllable in the second part of the tone group is the *change syllable*. It receives the tone accent. Repeat. Imitate the rising/falling tones.

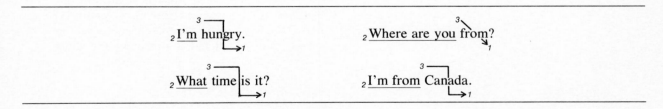

(See footnotes 2 and 3 on page 10 for notes on *step-down* and *glide-down*.)

---

1. The three tones used here are: a relative *medium* tone (2), a *higher* tone (3), and a *lower* tone (1). They are not intended to represent any particular linguistic intonational reference.
2. The graphic notations used here do not include indications of down-stepping or up-stepping, only the broad lines of the pattern in a "neutral reading" of the line. Pattern variations will be taken up later in the program. Teachers should model the sentences within their own personal intonation pattern. At any point where your pattern differs from the markings, you are urged to make whatever changes necessary in the text and to point them out to your students.

Part 2—Pronunciation Practice: Rising/Falling Intonation

As you work with these conversations notice that some of the meaning is carried by the intonation which is added to each group of words. Intonation adds meaning in two ways:

1. it shows the relationship of words within and between sentences;
2. it tells something about the feelings of the speaker.

In listening to the meaning of intonation, we listen to *how* speakers talk as well as *what* they say. The how and the what together give us the meaning of spoken English.

Look at the conversations which follow. The left-hand column has *information-asking* questions which begin with *Wh* words, (*who, what, when, where, why*), and *how*. The right-hand column has *statements* and *short answers*. The rising/falling intonation is used for both of these. Whether the questions or answers are long or short, they must be fitted into the *two* parts of the tone group. Use natural speed; notice now that rhythm, stress, linking, contractions, and reductions all work together within the tone pattern of spoken English. Listen and repeat. Use your pencil to punctuate the tone group change points.

Information-Asking Questions

1a. ₂What would you like?

2a. ₂What'll you have?

3a. ₂Where're you going?

4a. ₂What time is it?

5a. ₂Where's your lab book?

6a. ₂Where do you think you left it?

Statements and Short Answers

1b. ₂I'd like a chicken-salad sandwich.

2b. ₂I'll have a hotdog and a Coke.

3b. ₂To the lab.

4b. ₂It's a quarter past four.

5b. ₂I lost it.

6b. ₂I don't remember.

Part 3—Pronunciation Practice: Echoing

Listen and repeat the following conversations by echoing.[3] To echo means to trace the words of the speaker—with your voice—with a delay of one part of the tone group, as marked. You must begin speaking the *first* part of the tone group as soon as the speaker begins speaking the *second* part and continue to *echo* the words in this way to the end of the sentence.[4]

---

3. Echoing is an adaptation of tracking, a technique developed by Kenneth Pike, Department of Linguistics at the University of Michigan. For detailed information on the ESL use of tracking, see William Crawford, "Tracking: An Alternate Approach to the Teaching of Intonation" (Paper delivered at TESOL, 1975).
4. Practice with echoing is excellent for building student awareness of English intonation. It is useful in helping students to hear and to imitate English tone, rhythm, and stress. If teachers prefer to use this portion of the lesson for regular choral practice, however, the same purpose of student awareness will be served.

Listen to the following examples of echoing. Repeat.

Examples:

First Voice: $_2$Where's your lab|book? ^{3} → $_1$

Second Voice: $_2$Where's your lab|book? ^{3} → $_1$

First Voice: $_2$I lost|it. ^{3} → $_1$

Second Voice: $_2$I lost|it. ^{3} → $_1$

(Lab: Give students a signal when they should begin speaking in chorus with the second speaker. You may want to rewind this section of the tape and to replay it to help students master the skill of echoing. If teachers prefer, they may use the echoing portion of the intonation lessons for additional choral practice instead of echoing.)

Practice the following questions and answers using echoing. Follow the signal given by the teacher when you are to begin. As the second speaker, you should begin speaking the first part of the tone group when the first speaker begins speaking the second part.[5]

(Lab: Have students practice echoing by taking the part of the second speaker and speaking in chorus with the voice. Give students a signal when they are to begin speaking.)

1a. What would you like?

      What would you like?

1b. I'd like a chicken-salad sandwich.

      I'd like a chicken-salad sandwich.

2a. What'll you have?

      What'll you have?

2b. I'll have a hotdog and a Coke.

      I'll have a hotdog and a Coke.

3a. Where're you going?

      Where're you going?

3b. To the lab.

      To the lab.

4a. What time is it?

      What time is it?

4b. It's a quarter past four.

      It's a quarter past four.

---

5. You may want to bring in another teacher to serve as the model (i.e., first speaker) so that you can echo along with the students. As a follow-up practice, make up sentences for students to echo, so that they may experience spontaneous echoing (i.e., without knowing what the sentence is going to be). This is an excellent technique for helping students develop a sensitivity to English intonation contours.

5a. Where's your lab book?   5b. I lost it.

            Where's your lab book?   I lost it.

6a. Where do you think you left it?   6b. I don't remember.

            Where do you think you left it?   I don't remember.

(Lab: Rewind the tape. Have students close their books as they listen to the tape a second time. Give students a signal when they are to begin speaking.)

Part 4—Drawing Intonation Lines (AK/TS)

Listen carefully. Draw the intonation lines. Then listen and check. Listen and repeat.

(Lab: Stop the tape and allow students time to draw the intonation lines for each item after they hear it.)

Example: ₂I'm hungry.

1a. What would you like?   1b. I'd like a sandwich and a glass of milk.

2a. Where are you living?   2b. I have an apartment.

3a. Where are you from?   3b. I'm from Canada.

4a. How long have you been here? 4b. I've been here a month.

5a. What are you studying?   5b. I'm in law school.

Check the answers with your teacher. Practice the conversations again using natural rhythm, stress, and intonation.

(Lab: Then stop the tape for a few minutes of individual practice and self-monitoring.)

Part 5—Test Conversations for Self-Monitoring and Self-Testing

Practice the following conversations. Record. Listen and monitor your pronunciation.

1a. ₂Where're you from?   1b. ₂I'm from Mexico.

2a. ₂What time is it?   2b. ₂It's a quarter past nine.

75

3a. $_2$<u>What would you</u> l^{3}ike?$_{\searrow 1}$ 3b. $_2$<u>I'd like a</u> ho^{3}tdog.$_{\rightarrow 1}$

4a. $_2$<u>When's the</u> te^{3}st?$_{\searrow 1}$ 4b. $_2$<u>It's on</u> Fr^{3}iday.$_{\rightarrow 1}$

Resource Material

This resource material contains a few of the many questions which are a part of everyday conversation. The questions listed here are information-asking questions often used when two people are introduced and begin to get acquainted with each other. In particular, they are some of the questions ESL learners may be asked when they meet English-speaking persons, either in an English-speaking country or a non-English speaking country.

Part 1

These three dialogues are variations of the exchange used following introduction. You may want to add variations in levels of formality to fit your particular situation. Notice that the second speaker, *B*, can repeat a question which the first speaker, *A*, has asked, and change the meaning simply by shifting the change point for the tone group to the word *you*.

Practice the dialogues. Follow the intonation lines as marked.

1. *A:* ₂How do you do? ₂I'm pleased to meet you.

   B: Thank you. ₂ I'm pleased to meet you.

2. *A:* ₂How do you do?

   B: ₂How do you do? ₂I'm pleased to meet you.

   A: Thank you. ₂I'm pleased to meet you.

3. *A:* ₂How do you do?

   B: ₂How do you do?

   A: ₂I'm happy to meet you.

   B: Thank you. ₂I'm happy to meet you.

Part 2

As a class activity, ask students to practice the intonation patterns in the questions below. As an individualized activity, ask students to write their own answers to the questions. Then ask one student to read a question; ask another student to reply with a personalized answer. Encourage students to monitor their intonation.

1. ₂Where're you from? (Where do you come from?)

_____

2. ₂How long have you been here?

_____

3. ₂Where're you living? (Where are you staying?)

_____

4. ₂What're you studying?

_____

5. ₂How long will you be here? (How long are you staying?)

_____

6. ₂How do you like it here?

_____

7. ₂How's it going? (How're you doing?)

_____

(If a stranger asks one of the questions in number 7, it may be answered with a general statement: "Very well, thank you." "Pretty well, thank you." "Just fine, thank you." If a friend asks these questions, a more specific answer may be given.)

As a homework assignment, ask students to bring in additional questions which they have encountered in daily conversations.

Lesson 15
Rising Intonation (Final)

Part 1—Rising Intonation

In lesson 14 we studied the final rising/falling intonation pattern. The rising/falling intonation pattern is used in English for statements (and short answers), requests, and *Wh* and *how* questions.

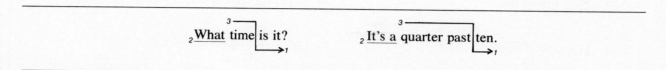

A second final intonation pattern is *rising intonation*. If the speaker raises the tone of voice from tone 2 to tone 3 and ends there, the listener knows that the speaker has completed a special kind of English question which asks for an immediate answer of yes or no. ESL students study this intonation pattern when they study *Yes/No* questions in their grammar class.[6] Look at the box.

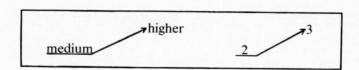

Notice that the intonation rises from tone 2 to tone 3 and does not fall.[7] Look at the sentences. Repeat. Imitate the rising tone of the voice.

---

6. Refer students to their grammar books for information on forms of *Be, Do, Have,* and the modals which begin this kind of question. You may want to point out the manner in which a statement can be shifted to a *Yes/No* question solely by a change to this rising intonation pattern.
7. As in lesson 14, the graphic notations used here indicate only the broad outline of the pattern.

Part 2—Pronunciation Practice: Rising Intonation

Look at the conversations. Notice the left-hand column has *Yes/No* questions. The right-hand column has answers. The rising intonation is used for the questions. The rising/falling intonation is used for the answers. Notice that some of the answers contain direct *Yes/No* answers, while others imply yes or no in the statement or short answer which follows.[8]

Yes/No Questions
(Rising Intonation)

Answers
(Rising/Falling Intonation)

1a. ₂Are you coming later?

1b. ₂If I can.

2a. ₂May I help you?

2b. ₂Yes, I'll have a chicken-salad sandwich.

3a. ₂Is it cold outside?

3b. ₂It's very cold.

4a. ₂Shall I wait for you?

4b. ₂No, you go ahead.

5a. ₂Did he bring his money?

5b. ₂No, he forgot it.

6a. ₂Would you like any dessert?

6b. ₂Yes, I'll have some ice cream.

Part 3—Pronunciation Practice: Echoing

Listen and repeat the following conversations by echoing. To echo means to trace the words of the speaker—with your voice—with a delay of one part of the tone group as marked. You must begin speaking the *first* part of the tone group as soon as the speaker begins speaking the *second* part and continue to echo the words in this way to the end of the sentence.

Listen to the following examples of echoing. Repeat.

Examples:

First Voice: ₂Does he want an answer now?

Second Voice: ₂Does he want an answer now?

First Voice: ₂Shall I wait for you?

Second Voice: ₂Shall I wait for you?

_____

8. At any point where your pattern differs from the markings, you are urged to make whatever changes necessary in the text and to point them out to your students. The yes or no which is followed by a statement is subject to considerable variation for nuances of meaning. Here, these sentences are marked with tone 2 (medium) for the *Yes/No* without a pause before the remainder of the sentence. An alternative falling pattern from tone 3 to tone 2 on the *yes* or *no* is often used.

Practice the following questions and answers using echoing. Follow the signal given by the teacher when you are to begin. As the second speaker, you should begin speaking the first part of the tone group when the first speaker begins speaking the second part.

(Lab: Have students practice echoing by taking the part of the second speaker and speaking in chorus with the voice. Give students a signal when they are to begin speaking.)

1a. Are you coming later?   1b. If I can.

         Are you coming later?   If I can.

2a. May I help you?   2b. Yes, I'll have a chicken-salad sandwich.

         May I help you?   Yes, I'll have a chicken-salad
                                                       sandwich.

3a. Is it cold outside?   3b. It's very cold.

         Is it cold outside?   It's very cold.

4a. Shall I wait for you?   4b. No, you go ahead.

         Shall I wait for you?   No, you go ahead.

5a. Did he bring his money?   5b. No, he forgot it.

         Did he bring his money?   No, he forgot it.

6a. Would you like any dessert?   6b. Yes, I'll have some ice cream.

         Would you like any dessert?   Yes, I'll have some ice cream.

Part 4—Drawing Intonation Lines (AK/TS)

Listen carefully. Draw the intonation lines. Then listen and check. Listen and repeat.

(Lab: Stop the tape and allow students time to draw the intonation lines for each item after they hear it.)

Example: ₂Am I late?

1a. Are you going to the picnic?   1b. I can't. I have an appointment.

2a. Have all the students gone?   2b. All but John.

3a. Isn't John going?   3b. He's waiting for a friend.

4a. Can they catch a bus later?   4b. Sure, they run every half hour.

Check the answers with your teacher. Practice the conversations again using natural rhythm, stress, intonation, and reductions.

(Lab: Stop the tape for a few minutes of individual practice and self-monitoring.)

Part 5—Test Conversations for Self-Monitoring and Self-Testing

Practice the following conversations. Record. Listen and monitor your pronunciation.

1a. ₂Can you come to the party?   1b. ₂Yes, I can.

2a. ₂Did she lose it?   2b. ₂No. She just forgot it.

3a. ₂Have you been waiting long?   3b. ₂About an hour.

4a. ₂Are you hungry?   4b. ₂No, I ate on the plane.

Resource Material

The following are questions which ESL students may expect to hear frequently in English-speaking countries. They request either a direct or indirect answer of yes or no.

Practice the examples. Both questions and answers are given in the examples. Follow the intonation lines as marked.

Examples:

A: ₂May I help you?

B: No, thank you. ₂I'm just looking.

A: ₂May I help you?

B: Yes, thank you. ₂I'm looking for a notebook.

These two examples are variations of one of the conversational exchanges used in shopping. You may want to add variations which fit your particular situation. You may wish to vary the levels of formality.

As a class activity ask students to practice the intonation patterns in the questions below. As a group activity write several possible direct or indirect answers to the questions. Then ask one student to read a question and ask another student to give an answer. Encourage self-monitoring.

1. ₂Are you ready to order?   (*Situation*: in a restaurant)

_____

2. ₂Do you take cream?   (*Situation*: in a restaurant or in a private home or at a formal tea table)

_____

3. ₂Shall we go?   (*Situation*: any situation where people are getting ready to leave)

_____

4. ₂Are you ready to go?   (*Situation*: any situation where people are getting ready to leave)

5. ₂Are you being helped? (*Situation*: in a store or at a reception desk or counter)

6. ₂Is someone waiting on you? (*Situation*: in a store or at a reception desk or counter)

7. ₂Did you lose something? (*Situation*: asked when it appears that a person is looking for something)

8. ₂Is this yours? (*Situation*: asked when a person nearby finds something)

9. ₂Are you feeling all right? (*Situation*: asked when it appears that a person is tired or ill)

10. ₂Are you all right? (*Situation*: asked when it appears that a person is unhappy or upset or recovering from a mishap)

Part 2

Ask students to practice the following rhymalogues. Encourage self-monitoring. Encourage students to work for control of rhythm, stress, and intonation. This mark (|) indicates a pause.

1. *Gus:* ₂Did you come on the train, | Jane?   3. *Ann:* ₂Are you going to the show, | Joe?

     Jane: ₂No, I came on the bus, | Gus.   *Joe:* ₂I don't think I can, | Ann.

2. *Dan:* ₂Can you loan me a penny, | Jenny?   4. *Ray:* ₂Did your team win, | Lynn?

     Jenny: ₂I certainly can, | Dan.   *Lynn:* ₂They didn't play today, | Ray.

Review the rhymalogues in the resource material of lessons 8, 13, and 15 (this lesson). As a homework assignment, ask each student to make up one or two rhymalogues. Check the rhymalogues in class; make any necessary corrections; ask a student to lead the class in practicing a rhymalogue.

Lesson 16

Nonfinal Intonation

Part 1—Nonfinal Intonation[9]

In lesson 14 we studied the final rising/falling intonation pattern. With this intonation pattern the speaker tells the listener that a statement (or short answer), a request, or a *Wh* or *how* question has been completed. Repeat.

₂I'm hungry.

In lesson 15 we studied the final rising intonation pattern. With this intonation pattern the speaker tells the listener that a *Yes/No* question has been completed.

₂Am I late?

In this last lesson we will work with nonfinal intonation. If a speaker uses a rising tone, from tone 2 to tone 3, then returns to tone 2, it tells the listener that more is to follow, that the speaker is not finished. This is nonfinal intonation or "to-be-continued" intonation. There are many variations of nonfinal intonation and many uses.

One use of this pattern is when a speaker is telling several things, either several connected short statements or a list of items in a series. Look at the box.

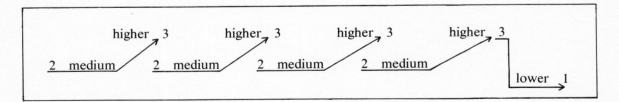

Look at the sentences. Notice that each item in the series begins with tone 2 followed by a rise to tone 3, until the end of the list. Then the speaker signals that the series is finished by using the rising/falling pattern from tone 3 to tone 1 on the last item. Repeat. Imitate the rising and falling tones.

---

9. As in lessons 14 and 15, at any point where your pattern differs from the markings, you are urged to make whatever changes necessary in the text and to point them out to your students.

₂She's worked in Boston, ₂in Detroit, ₂in New York, ₂and in Miami.

₂He likes baseball, ₂football, ₂basketball, ₂and hockey.

₂I need some soap, ₂some toothpaste, ₂and some Kleenex.

Part 2—Pronunciation Practice

Look at the conversations below. Notice the left-hand column has *Wh* questions. The right-hand column has answers. Each answer has a series of things listed. The rising/falling intonation is used for each question. The answers use nonfinal intonation until the end of the series where the final rising/falling intonation pattern is used.

Listen and repeat the following. Follow the intonation lines.

Questions	*Answers*
1a. ₂Where did you go?	1b. ₂We went to London, ₂Paris, ₂Athens, ₂and Cairo.
2a. ₂What did you buy?	2b. ₂I bought a magazine, ₂some cigarettes, ₂a candy bar, ₂and some gum.
3a. ₂How shall we go?	3b. ₂We can go by air, ₂or by train, ₂or by bus, ₂or by car.
4a. ₂What are your students studying?	4b. ₂Our students are in law, ₂medicine, ₂chemistry, ₂and physics.
5a. ₂What took you so long?	5b. ₂I had to do the dishes, ₂water the plants, ₂feed the cat, ₂and pack my suitcase.
6a. ₂Why is she leaving?	6b. ₂She doesn't like her job, ₂she doesn't like her boss, ₂she doesn't like her apartment, ₂and she doesn't like the town.

Part 3—Pronunciation Practice: Echoing

Listen and repeat the following conversations by echoing. To echo means to trace the words of the speaker—with your voice—with a delay of one part of the tone group, as marked. You must begin speaking the *first* part of the tone group as soon as the speaker begins speaking the *second* part and continue to echo the words in this way to the end of the sentence.

Listen to the following examples of echoing. Repeat.

Examples:

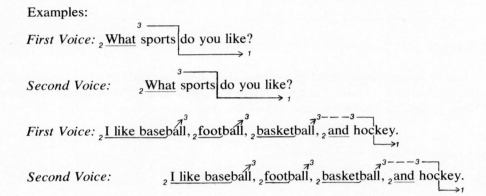

Practice the following questions and answers using echoing. Follow the signal given by the teacher when you are to begin. As the second speaker, you should begin speaking the *first* part of the tone group when the first speaker begins speaking the *second* part.

(Lab: Have students practice echoing by taking the part of the second *speaker and speaking in chorus with the voice. Give students a signal when they are to begin speaking.)*

1a. What did you buy?

      What did you buy?

1b. I bought a magazine, some cigarettes, a candy bar, and some gum.

      I bought a magazine, some cigarettes, a candy bar, and some gum.

2a. How shall we go?

      How shall we go?

2b. We can go by air, or by train, or by bus, or by car.

      We can go by air, or by train, or by bus, or by car.

3a. What are your students studying?

What are your students studying?

3b. Our students are in law, medicine, chemistry, and physics.

Our students are in law, medicine, chemistry, and physics.

4a. What took you so long?

What took you so long?

4b. I had to do the dishes, water the plants, feed the cat, and pack my suitcase.

I had to do the dishes, water the plants, feed the cat, and pack my

suitcase.

Part 4—Drawing Intonation Lines (AK/TS)

Listen carefully. Draw the intonation lines. Then listen and check. Listen and repeat.

(Lab: Stop the tape and allow students time to draw the intonation lines for each item after *they hear it.)*

1a. What sports do you like?   1b. I like baseball, football, basketball, and hockey.

2a. Have all the students gone?   2b. No, I saw John, and Bill, and Jack, and Mary.

3a. What did you have?   3b. I had some soup and crackers, a salad, a hotdog, and a Coke.

4a. Where have you lived?   4b. I've lived in Boston, in Detroit, in New York, and in Miami.

Check the answers with your teacher.

Practice the conversations again using natural rhythm, stress, intonation, and reductions.

(Lab: Then stop the tape for a few minutes of individual practice and self-monitoring.)

Part 5—Test Conversations for Self-Monitoring and Self-Testing

1a. ₂What did you get for your birthday?

1b. ₂ I got a billfold, ₂ a camera, ₂ a radio, ₂ and a chess set.

2a. ₂What cities did you visit?

2b. ₂We visited London, ₂ Paris, ₂ Rome, ₂ Athens, ₂ and Cairo.

Resource Material

Part 1

As a class activity have students practice the following sequences of sentences. In each set the list of items is increased gradually. Encourage students to monitor their intonation, rhythm, stress, and reductions.

Group 1

1. ₂We have classes on Monday,₂Tuesday,₂Thursday,₂and Friday.

2. ₂We have classes on Monday,₂Tuesday,₂Wednesday,₂Thursday,₂and Friday.

3. ₂We have classes on Monday,₂Tuesday,₂Wednesday,₂Thursday,₂Friday,₂and Saturday.

Group 2

1. ₂They visited New York,₂Miami,₂and Denver.

2. ₂They visited New York,₂Miami,₂Denver,₂and Boston.

3. ₂They visited New York,₂Miami,₂Denver,₂Boston,₂and Dallas.

Group 3

1. ₂Many of our students are in law,₂medicine,₂chemistry,₂business administration,₂and physics.

2. ₂Many of our students are in law,₂medicine,₂chemistry,₂business administration,₂physics,₂and education.

3. ₂Many of our students are in law,₂medicine,₂chemistry,₂business administration,₂physics,₂education,₂and science.

Part 2

This dialogue has been scripted from a real telephone conversation. Ask students to practice the conversation, and to monitor intonation, rhythm, stress, and reductions.

A: Greyhound.

B: Is this the Greyhound bus terminal?

A: Yes, Ma'am.

B: I'd like some information, please. What is the bus schedule to Chicago?

A: Next one'll be leaving here at eleven-thirty, then one-ten, one-forty, three-twenty-five,

three-fifty, five-fifteen, six-twenty-five, eight-fifteen, and ten-ten tonight.

B: What about—uh—earlier in the morning?

A: Six-thirty, eight-fifteen, and ten-five.

B: Thank you.

A: M-hm.

As a homework assignment, give each student the telephone number of a local business and a list of two or three items of information desired. Ask students to write out the questions and to practice them. Then ask students to make the telephone calls and report the information.

Section G—Rapid Review and Testing

Section Notes

Section G has four lessons. Lessons 17, 18, and 19 are a series of rapid review lessons which highlight significant features of English stress, rhythm, and intonation. Lesson 20 is a self-evaluative test lesson.

Lesson 17 presents fourteen selected features of English stress, rhythm, and intonation in chart form. Students are asked to practice each key sentence on the chart and to discuss it briefly with the teacher in preparation for the next two review lessons and the final test.[1]

Lessons 18 and 19 present a rapid review of each of the fourteen features selected for study. The review lessons present two or three explanatory sentences for each feature, followed by a brief section of practice items.

Lesson 20 is a ten-part self-evaluation test.

Intermediate and advanced students, even those who have not used the instructive material in this unit, have found these four lessons to provide helpful review and self-evaluation before beginning advanced work in English stress, rhythm, and intonation.

---

1. Teachers have found it helpful to ask students to summarize the importance of each feature of stress, rhythm, and intonation as studied in this unit.

Lesson 17

Rapid Review of the Key Sentences

Directions: Look at chart 11 below. Each sentence is a key sentence for an important feature of English stress, rhythm, and intonation. Read and discuss with your teacher. Practice.

Chart 11
KEY SENTENCES FOR STRESS, RHYTHM, AND INTONATION

Accented/Unaccented Syllables

---

1. I forgót my péncil.
   1 2   1 2

Two-Syllable Words

---

2. Tomórrow is Sáturday.
   1 2 3   1 2 3

Three-Syllable Words

---

3. Call me toníght aróund séven.
        x   x   x

Reduced Syllables and Schwa

Syllables and Suffixes

---

4. I closed the door and wáited for the bus.
   1   1 2

Past Tense

---

5. I bought four books for my two clásses.
   1   1   2

Plural

Sentence Sense: Rhythm and Stress

---

6. I ate a chicken-salad sandwich.

Rhythm and Sentence Stresses

---

7. The students are going to Chicago.

Rhythm and Reduced Words

---

8. He was waiting at the bus : stop.

Rhythm and Linking

Elisions and Assimilations

---

9. He isn't coming.

Two-Word Contractions

---

10. The boys (n) girls were late.

One-Word Contractions and Linking

---

11. I'm (gonna) study at the lab.

Contractions and Sound Changes

Intonation

12. $_2$ I'm hungry.   *Rising/Falling Intonation (Final)*

13. $_2$ Am I late?   *Rising Intonation (Final)*

14. $_2$ I bought hotdogs, $_2$ French fries, $_2$ apples, $_2$ and candy.   *Nonfinal Intonation*

Lesson 18

Rapid Review of Words and Syllables and Sentence Sense

Words and Syllables

Part 1—Accented Syllables, Unaccented Syllables, and Reduced Syllables

Many English words have only one syllable. Repeat.

me	yes	book	tree	class
1	1	1	1	1

In words with two or more syllables, one of the syllables is accented. Repeat the following. Give more strength to the accented syllables.

táble	Énglish	forgót	vacátion	Chicágo	ádvertise
1 2	1 2	1 2	1 2 3	1 2 3	1 2 3

Listen to the following sentences. The accented syllables have been marked. Repeat.

I belíeve the class begíns at ten.   She's a wónderful musícian.

In the natural rhythm of spoken English, many unaccented syllables are reduced. Schwa, the sound /ə/, is pronounced instead of a strong vowel. It replaces the *a, e, i, o,* or *u.* Repeat the following. Reduce the syllable with this mark (x) under the vowel.

toníght	todáy	aróund	télephone
x	x	x	x

Look at the following sentences. The reduced syllables have been marked. Repeat.

I'll see you toníght.   My télephone was ringing.
　　　　　　x　　　　　　　x

Part 2—Past Tense

The regular past tense in English is formed by adding *-ed* to the verb. If the verb ends in *t* or *d* it must be pronounced as an extra syllable. Repeat the following pairs of words.

wait	wáited	need	néeded	start	stárted	decíde	decíded
1	1 2	1	1 2	1	1 2	1 2	1 2 3

If the verb ends in any other sound, it is not pronounced as an extra syllable. It is pronounced only as the added sound of /t/ or /d/. The e in -ed is a silent letter. Repeat the following pairs of words. (The ȼ means a silent e.)

rain	rainȼd	closȼ	closȼd	wish	wishȼd	arrívȼ	arrívȼd
1	1	1	1	1	1	1 2	1 2

Look at the following sentences. Repeat.

He seemed unhappy.   I wáited for the bus.
         1   1 2

Part 3—Plurals

The regular plural in English is formed by adding -s or -es to the noun. If the noun ends in a sibilant or affricate sound spelled x, s (or se or ce), z (or ze), ge (or dge), ch, or sh, the plural must be pronounced as an extra syllable. Repeat the following pairs of words.

box	bóxes	church	chúrches	class	clásses	prómisȼ	prómises
1	1 2	1	1 2	1	1 2	1 2	1 2 3

If the noun ends in any other sound, it is not pronounced as an extra syllable. It is pronounced only as the added sound of /s/ or /z/. The e in -es is a silent letter. Repeat the following pairs of words. (The ȼ means a silent e.)

book	books	rope	ropȼs	wavȼ	wavȼs	mistákȼ	mistákȼs
1	1	1	1	1	1	1 2	1 2

Look at the following sentences. Repeat.

The boys ate sixteen sándwiches.   The books cost five dóllars.
      1   1   2   3   1   1   2

Sentence Sense: Rhythm and Stress

Part 1—Rhythm and Sentence Stresses

Every English sentence has one or more sentence stresses. Sentence stresses may be thought of as the strong beats in the rhythm of a sentence similar to the strong beats in the rhythm of music. The speaker gives more strength to the especially important words to help the listener get the sense (or meaning) of the sentence. Look at the following sentences. Each sentence stress has a line under it. Repeat. Give more strength to the sentence stresses.

The kitten was hungry and thirsty.

The classes started on Monday.

The students are going to Chicago.

Part 2—Rhythm and Reduced Words

Sentence stresses are the strong rhythmic beats of English sentences, as seen above. Reduced words are the opposite—the weak beats of English sentences. The speaker gives less strength to reductions. Reductions are the shortened pronunciations of words as they are pronounced in natural speech. Look at the following sentences. Notice each reduced word has a line through it. Repeat. Weaken each reduced word.

The children danced and sang.

Get ready for the test.

They can catch the bus at ten.

Part 3—Rhythm and Linking

In natural speech, words are linked together in groups. The speaker links words together in groups to help the listener get the sense (or meaning) of the sentence. In short sentences, all words are linked together with no pauses. The end of one word blends into the beginning of the next word. Repeat the following sentences.

I'm waiting for the bus.   I'll be late for class.

In places where the same sound is at the end of one word and at the beginning of the next word, the sound is pronounced only once. If it is a continuant sound, it is lengthened slightly. Repeat.

I wish : she would come.   Meet me at the bus : stop.

If it is a plosive sound, it is held briefly before it is released.

What : time is it?   He's a bad : dog.

Lesson 19

Rapid Review of Elisions and Assimilations and Intonation

Elisions and Assimilations

Part 1—Two-Word Contractions

Most ESL students study contractions as they study English grammar. In two-word contractions, two words are combined into one word and one or two sounds are omitted. Repeat the following. An apostrophe shows where one or more sounds have been omitted in the formation of the contraction.

I'm late.	I can't come.	How've you been?
He's early.	I didn't go.	I should've waited.

Part 2—One-Word Contractions and Linking

In contrast to two-word contractions, you will not find the following contractions in grammar books because they are spoken but never written. One-word contractions are like the reductions of lesson 9, but in addition to reduction of a vowel to schwa, /ə/, they can be marked by omissions of consonants or vowels or both, and the remaining sounds must be linked to the words on one or both sides. Look at the following sentences. Apostrophes show where sounds have been omitted. These written forms would be incorrect in any other context. Repeat.

When's ‿er birthday.	't ‿'s‿time f'r‿lunch.
Is ‿'e coming?	I saw ‿er yesterday.
I like ‿'im very much.	Was ‿'e late?

Part 3—Sound Changes and Contractions

In fast speech, when words are spoken rapidly, in addition to contractions, changes in sounds take place. These special contractions are heard most often in informal speech. Repeat the sentence in column 1. Then repeat the sentence in column 2. Underline the words with sound changes.

Column 1	*Column 2*
1. I don't want to study.	I don't wanna study.
2. I'm going to play tennis.	I'm gonna play tennis.
3. I have to work.	I hafta work.
4. I'll meet you after class.	I'll meetcha after class.

Intonation

Part 1—Rising/Falling Intonation (Final)

Intonation is the voice pattern of rising 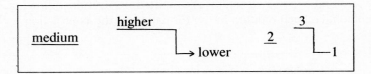 and falling voice tones. The speaker uses voice tones to help the listener get the sense (or meaning) of the sentence. If the speaker raises the tone of voice from tone 2 to tone 3, then ends with a final fall to tone 1, the listener knows that the speaker has completed a sentence (or short answer), a request, or a *Wh* question. Look at the box. Notice that the intonation pattern rises from tone 2 to tone 3, then falls to tone 1.

```
                    higher                      3
medium                                    2      ┌─┐
                        └─→ lower                └─1
```

Repeat the following. Imitate the rising/falling intonation pattern.

₂I'm hungry.   ₂Where are you from?

₂What time is it?   ₂I'm from Canada.

Part 2—Rising Intonation (Final)

If the speaker raises the tone of voice from tone 2 to tone 3 and ends there, the listener knows it is a special English question form which asks for an immediate answer of yes or no. Look at the box.

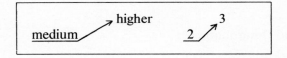

Notice that this intonation pattern rises from tone 2 to tone 3 and does not fall. Repeat the following. Imitate the rising intonation pattern.

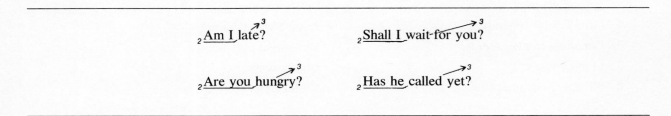

₂Am I late?   ₂Shall I wait for you?

₂Are you hungry?   ₂Has he called yet?

Part 3—Nonfinal Intonation

If the speaker uses a rising tone, from tone 2 to tone 3, then returns to tone 2, it has a special meaning in English. The meaning is this: the speaker tells the listener that more is to follow, that the speaker is not finished. This is a nonfinal or "to-be-continued" intonation pattern. One use of this nonfinal intonation pattern is when a speaker is telling several things, or giving a list in a series. Look at the box.

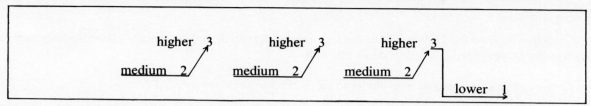

Notice that each item in the list has the same pattern—tone 2 followed by a rise to tone 3—until the end of the list. Then the last item on the list falls to tone 1. Repeat the following sentences. Imitate the intonation—several nonfinal patterns, followed by a final drop to tone 1 on the last item in the list.

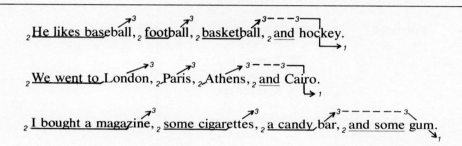

Lesson 20

Test of Stress, Rhythm, and Intonation

Lesson 20 is a review test. Listen carefully as the words or sentences are given. Follow the directions, exactly.

When you have finished the written part of the test, record the words and sentences. Listen and monitor your pronunciation as you have learned to do in this unit.

(Lab: Listen carefully as the voice on the tape gives the words or sentences.)

Part 1—Accented Syllables

Directions: Listen for the accented syllable as each word is given. Put an accent mark (´) over the vowel of the accented syllable. Listen again and check your answer.

Examples: nótebook contínue
1 2   1 2 3

1. understand
   1   2   3

2. teacher
   1   2

3. president
   1 2 3

4. telephone
   1 2   3

5. musician
   1 2 3

6. perhaps
   1   2

7. myself
   1   2

8. discover
   1   2   3

9. afternoon
   1   2   3

10. September
    1   2   3

11. tomorrow
    1   2   3

12. yesterday
    1   2   3

Part 2—Syllables and Suffixes

Directions: Listen as each word is given. Listen to the suffix. Decide how many syllables are pronounced in the word. Write the number in the blank. Listen again and check your answer.

Examples: roses _2_   waves _1_
           1 2   1

           waited _2_   worked _1_
           1 2   1

1. churches ____
2. dimes ____
3. kisses ____
4. judges ____
5. hills ____
6. wanted ____

7. missed ____
8. lived ____
9. landed ____
10. laughed ____
11. sounded ____
12. gloves ____

102

Part 3—Sentence Stresses

Directions: Listen as each sentence is given. Decide which words or parts of words received a strong sentence stress. Draw a line under each one. Listen again and check your answers. The number of stresses is given following each sentence.

Example: I ate a <u>chick</u>en-salad <u>sand</u>wich. (2 sentence stresses)

1. I'd like a sandwich. (1 sentence stress)
2. I'd like a sandwich and a cup of coffee. (2)
3. I'd like a sandwich, a cup of coffee, and some ice cream. (3)
4. The children danced and sang. (3)
5. Get ready for the test. (2)
6. I'm going to Chicago on Monday. (3)

Part 4—Reduced Words

Directions: Listen as each sentence is given. In each blank write the word which was pronounced in reduced form. Listen again and check your answers.

Example: I ___*can*___ come ___*at*___ four.

1. I _____ go _____ class.
2. He _____ come _____ ten.
3. _____ students _____ going _____ Chicago.
4. Get ready _____ _____ test.
5. I _____ hungry _____ thirsty.
6. They _____ come _____ four _____ five.

Part 5—Lengthening/Holding Sounds

Directions: Listen as each sentence is given. Draw lengthening/holding marks. Listen again and check your answer.

Examples: 1. I wi<u>sh</u> : <u>sh</u>e would come.　2. I li<u>ke</u> : <u>c</u>andy.

1. I won some money.
2. I bought a silver ring.
3. He's my favorite teacher.
4. Meet me at the bus stop.
5. We can help Paul.
6. He's a bad dog.

Part 6—Contractions

Directions: Listen as each sentence is given. In each blank write the contraction you hear. Listen again and check your answer.

Example: _How've_ you been?

1. He _____ work here.

2. _____ he crying?

3. She _____ invited.

4. _____ your mother?

5. We _____ leave until ten.

6. _____ he coming?

Part 7—Contractions and Sound Changes

Directions: Listen as each sentence is given. In the blanks write the words for the full form. Listen again and check your answer.

Example: _Did you_ go?

1. I _____ _____ study.

2. I'll _____ _____ after class.

3. We're _____ _____ study.

4. _____ _____ _____ doing?

5. I don't _____ _____ go.

6. Please _____ _____ a cup of coffee.

Part 8—Rising/Falling Intonation (Final)

Directions: Listen as each sentence is given. Draw the intonation lines. Listen again and check your answer.

Example: ₂ I'm hungry.

1. What would you like?

2. I'd like a sandwich and a glass of milk.

3. Where are you from?

4. I'm from Canada.

104

5. What are you studying?

6. I'm in law school.

Part 9—Rising Intonation (Final)

Directions: Listen as each sentence is given. Draw the intonation lines. Listen again and check your answer.

Example: ₂Am I late?

1. Have all the students gone?

2. Isn't John going?

3. Are you coming later?

Part 10—Nonfinal Intonation

Directions: Listen as each sentence is given. Draw the intonation lines. Listen again and check your answer.

Examples: ₂I bought apples, ₂candy, ₂and popcorn.

1. I bought some soap, some toothpaste, and some Kleenex.

2. I've lived in Boston, in Detroit, in New York, and in Miami.

3. I had some soup and crackers, a salad, a hotdog, and a Coke.

Unit 2
Vowels

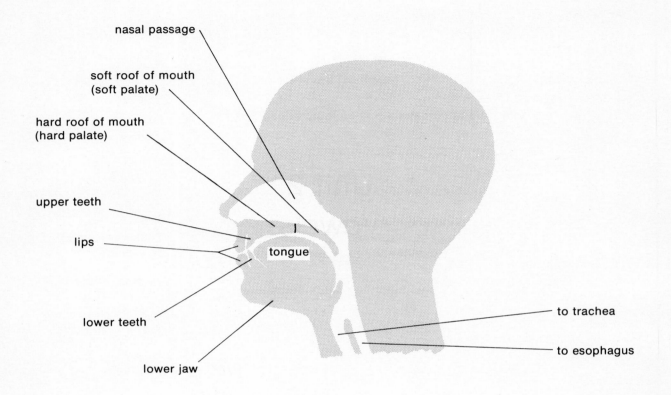

nasal passage

soft roof of mouth
(soft palate)

hard roof of mouth
(hard palate)

upper teeth

lips

tongue

lower teeth

lower jaw

to trachea

to esophagus

The side-view facial diagrams are based on this drawing. Teachers may wish to discuss the parts of the drawing with students as they study vowel articulation.

Section A—Introduction

Section Notes

Section A presents two lessons. Lesson 1 includes the following divisions.

Vowel Letters / Vowel Sounds

a. draws student attention to the basic conceptual separation of letters and sounds in English
b. notes the important role of spelling—of relating written letters to spoken sounds
c. notes the additional goal of vocabulary expansion

Vowel Articulation

a. presents a brief introduction to the flexible and self-controllable articulatory movements of the lips, the lower jaw, and the tongue
b. draws student attention to the importance of self-monitoring and self-correction—the real goals of improving spoken English

Vowel Systems

a. reviews the five basic vowel sounds shared by most languages of the world and relates them to their English pronunciations
b. relates these five vowels, which are familiar to most ESL students, to the expanded English vowel system
c. presents the Vowel Chart and provides brief practice with each key word

Resource material presents some generalized information on possible sources of problems. This material may or may not be interpreted for students, depending upon their level of language proficiency.

Lesson Two has two divisions.

Pronunciation Areas of the Vowel Chart

a. presents diagrams of the front-to-back and the high-to-low pronunciation areas of the Vowel Chart

Practice with the Vowel Chart

a. provides brief but intensive introductory practice with each of the fifteen vowel sounds of General American English
b. encourages memorization of the key words
c. discusses phonetic symbols briefly
d. again emphasizes the importance of self-monitoring

Each section of these lessons should be studied briefly but carefully as the directions to the student and the notes to the teacher indicate.

The introductory overview of the vowel system found in lessons 1 and 2 is designed to emphasize systematicity and to focus attention upon the importance of *each individual sound* as an integral part of a total pattern. Subsequent lessons will isolate each vowel sound from the system and give it brief but intensive perceptual, productive, and sound/spelling attention.

The Vowel Chart is presented as a graphic representation of the system and is a valuable classroom tool. It serves as a reference source for teachers, and a student aid for self and peer monitoring during classroom communicative activities.

Lesson 1

Introduction to the English Vowel System[1]

Vowel Letters / Vowel Sounds

Directions: Read and discuss with your teacher. Practice.

Part 1—Letters: The Alphabet of Writing

ESL students learn that English has a written alphabet of 26 letters. These 26 letters are used in *writing* English. Five of these letters are the *vowel* letters.

---

a   *e*   *i*   *o*   *u*

Sometimes the letters *w* and *y* also work as vowels. All other letters are *consonant* letters.

Every English word has at least one vowel sound.[2] Repeat.

I   it   my   strength

As studied in Unit 1, in words of two or more syllables one of the syllables is accented. That is, one of the syllables is pronounced with more strength. Repeat the following. Notice the accent mark is over the first vowel letter in the accented syllable.

ápple   páper   forgét   vocábulary
1 2   1 2   1 2   1 2 3 4 5

Part 2—Sounds: The "Alphabet" of Speaking

In contrast to the 26 letters of writing, English has a spoken "alphabet" of 39 *sounds*. These 39 sounds are used in *speaking* English. Fifteen of these 39 sounds are *vowel* sounds.

With five written vowel *letters* (*a, e, i, o, u*), but fifteen spoken vowel *sounds* in English, each written vowel letter must be pronounced in several different ways. For example, the letter *a* can be pronounced in at least four different ways. Thus, the letter *a* really has four sounds.

Sometimes the letter *a* is pronounced as the sound in *say*. Repeat.

áble   made   lake   cake   Vowel 3

---

1. The vowel system presented in this text is that of General American English. See the Preface, page viii, for comments.
2. This is oversimplification; syllabic consonants will be studied later in the program.

Sometimes the letter *a* is pronounced as the sound in *cat*. Repeat.

áfter	back	sat	fat		Vowel 5

Sometimes the letter *a* is pronounced as the sound in *father*. Repeat.

watch	fáther	part	art		Vowel 7

Sometimes the letter *a* is pronounced as the sound in *law*. Repeat.

saw	talk	call	fall		Vowel 11

To help ESL students to learn the fifteen vowel sounds of English, we will use a vowel chart (page 121). We will study a *key word* for each vowel sound. Practice these words with your teacher concentrating on the exact pronunciation of each of these key words.

Part 3—Spelling

As we study each of the fifteen vowel sounds, we will study spelling patterns for each sound. We will relate *written* letters to *spoken* sounds.

Part 4—Vocabulary

The lesson for each vowel will include a vocabulary list of thirty to forty words. These words were chosen from vocabulary lists of words which occur with relatively high frequency in spoken English.

Vowel Articulation

Directions: Read and discuss with your teacher. Practice.

(Lab: Students should have their own pronunciation mirrors.)

Part 1—Pronunciation Movements: Lips

Most languages of the world have three basic vowel sounds. They are not exactly the same in all languages but they are similar. The three sounds are the sounds in the words:

see	father	two

The symbols /i/, /a/, and /u/ from the International Phonetic Alphabet are used, as well as the English spelling letters, to represent these three vowel sounds. Phonetic symbols will be enclosed in the following marks, / /.[3]

---

3. No attempt is made to introduce students to phonemic/phonetic concepts. The slash marks, / /, represent sounds of pronunciation as distinct from letters of spelling.

Look at diagram 1. The teeth almost touch and the lips are thin and straight for /i/, s<u>ee</u>.

Look at diagram 2. The teeth are apart and the lips are rounded a little for /a/, f<u>a</u>ther.

Look at diagram 3. The lips are tightly rounded for /u/, tw<u>o</u>.

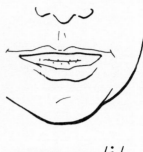

Diagram 1 /i/

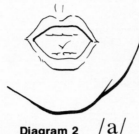

Diagram 2 /a/

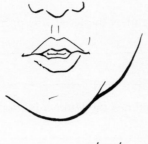

Diagram 3 /u/

Repeat these three sounds slowly. Lengthen the sounds. *Watch* the teacher. *Listen* to the sounds.

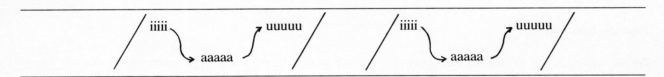

Practice again. *Feel* the movements.

Part 2—Pronunciation Movements: Lower Jaw

Look at diagram 4. The lower jaw is raised for /i/, s<u>ee</u>.

Look at diagram 5. The lower jaw is lowered for /a/, f<u>a</u>ther.

Look at diagram 6. The lower jaw is raised for /u/, tw<u>o</u>.

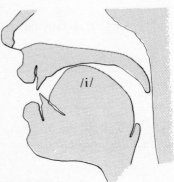

Diagram 4

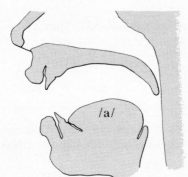

Diagram 5

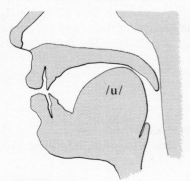

Diagram 6

Repeat. *Listen*; *watch* and *feel* the jaw movement.

Part 3—Pronunciation Movements: Tongue

Look at diagram 7.

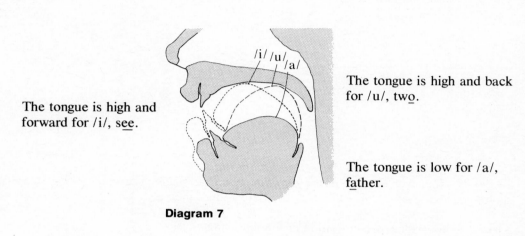

The tongue is high and forward for /i/, s<u>ee</u>.

The tongue is high and back for /u/, tw<u>o</u>.

The tongue is low for /a/, f<u>a</u>ther.

Diagram 7

Repeat the sounds. *Watch*; *feel* the tongue move to pronounce each sound. Use a pronunciation mirror.

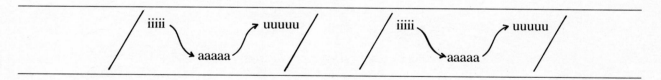

Part 4—Self-Monitoring

As discussed in Unit 1, pronunciation practice is the time for you to talk to yourself and to listen to yourself. Talking to yourself and listening to yourself are ways to self-monitor.

The three most important things in the self-monitoring of vowel pronunciations are:

  1. *watching* the movements of the lips, the lower jaw, and the tongue;

  2. *feeling* the movements of the lips, the lower jaw, and the tongue;

  3. *listening to* the differences in vowel sounds which you can make simply by changing the position and the movements of the lips, the lower jaw, and the tongue.

Vowel Systems

Directions: Read and discuss with your teacher.

Part 1—Five Basic Vowels: /i/, /e/, /a/, /o/, /u/

As we have just studied in the vowel articulation division of this lesson, most languages of the world have three basic vowel sounds. They are not exactly the same in all languages, but they are similar. In many languages these three sounds are pronounced as single *pure* sounds. Look at diagram 8.

The three basic sounds are:

/i/   /u/
    /a/

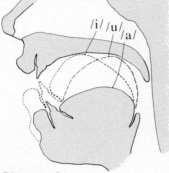

Diagram 8

In English, however, /i/ and /u/ are not pronounced as single pure sounds; they are lengthened and slightly diphthongized. That is, in addition to the pure sound, they also have a second shorter sound: /iʸ/, /uʷ/.[4]

Listen to the English pronunciation of the following words.

/iʸ/	/a/	/uʷ/
see	ma	two
need	father	food
beat	stop	truth

Most languages of the world also have two additional basic vowel sounds. They are not exactly the same in all languages, but they are similar. In many languages these two sounds are pronounced as single pure sounds. Look at diagram 9.

The two basic sounds are:

/e/   /o/

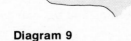

Diagram 9

---

4. Length and diphthongization vary according to the phonetic environment and the patterns of stress, rhythm, and intonation. There is also variation from speaker to speaker.

In English, however, these sounds are not pronounced as single pure sounds; they are lengthened and slightly diphthongized. That is, in addition to the pure sound, they also have a second shorter sound: /eⁱ/, /oᵘ/.

Listen to the English pronunciation of the following words.

/eⁱ/	/oᵘ/
s<u>ay</u>	n<u>o</u>
m<u>a</u>de	r<u>o</u>de
t<u>a</u>ke	h<u>o</u>pe

Look at diagram 10. Repeat: /iʸ/, /a/, /uʷ/. Notice that these three vowels are connected and form a triangle on the Vowel Chart (Vowels 1, 7, and 8).

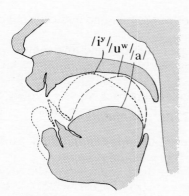

Diagram 10
THE THREE VOWELS

Look at diagram 11. Repeat: /iʸ/, /eⁱ/, /a/, /oᵘ/, /uʷ/. Notice that these five vowels are circled on the Vowel Chart. They are connected by a dotted line (Vowels 1, 3, 7, 10, and 8).

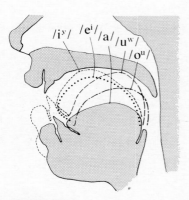

Diagram 11
THE FIVE VOWELS

115

Part 2—Key Words for the Fifteen Vowel Sounds

Directions: Read and discuss with your teacher. Practice.

Look at the Vowel Chart. Look at the front vowels. Notice there are two high front vowels: Vowels 1 and 2, /iʸ/ as in **see**, /ɪ/ as in **it**. Repeat: **see   it   see it.**

Notice there are two mid front vowels: Vowels 3 and 4, /eⁱ/ as in **say**, /ɛ/ as in **yes**. Repeat: **say   yes say yes.**

Notice there is one low front vowel: Vowel 5, /æ/ as in **fat**. Repeat: **fat   fat**. Repeat the front vowels: /iʸ/   /ɪ/   /eⁱ/   /ɛ/   /æ/   **see it   say yes   fat.**

Look at the central vowels. Notice there is one high central vowel: Vowel 12, /ɝ/ as in **bird**. Repeat: **bird   bird**.

Notice there is one mid central vowel: Vowel 6, /ʌ/ as in **bus**. Repeat: **bus   bus**.

Notice there is one low central vowel: Vowel 7, /a/ as in **stop**. Repeat: **stop   stop**. Repeat the central vowels: /ɝ/   /ʌ/   /a/   **bird   bus stop.**

Look at the back vowels. Notice there are two high back vowels: Vowels 8 and 9, /uʷ/ as in **two**, /ʊ/ as in **books**. Repeat: **two   books   two books**.

Notice there is one mid back vowel: Vowel 10, /oᵘ/ as in **no**. Repeat: **no   no**.

Notice there is one low back vowel: Vowel 11, /ɔ/ as in **law**. Repeat: **law   law**. Repeat the back vowels: /uʷ/   /ʊ/   /oᵘ/   /ɔ/   **two books   no law.**

Look at the diphthongs. Notice there are three diphthongs. Vowel 13 is /ai/ as in **my**. Vowel 14 is /au/ as in **cow**. Vowel 15 is /ɔi/ as in **boy**. Repeat: **my cowboy   my cowboy**. Repeat the diphthongs: /ai/   /au/   /ɔi/   **my cowboy.**

Repeat the key word phrases on the vowel chart.

see it   say yes   a fat bird   a bus stop   two books   no law   my cowboy

Vowel Chart

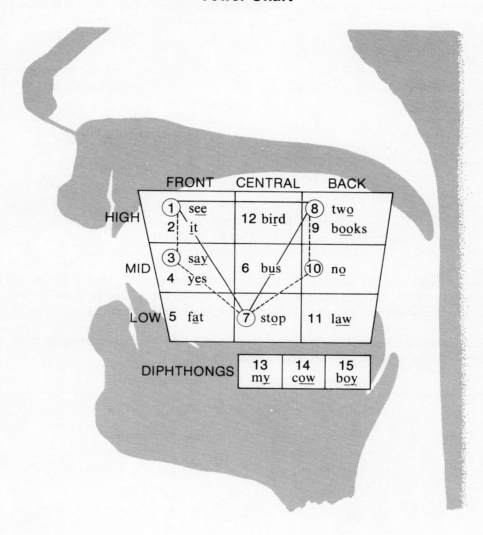

Resource Material

(This information may or may not be interpreted for students depending upon their level of language proficiency and their interests.)

Part 1—Vowels 1 to 11

In learning English as a second language some students with a system of five vowels in their first language appear to perceive and to produce these five with the following distribution pattern in relation to Vowels 1 to 11.

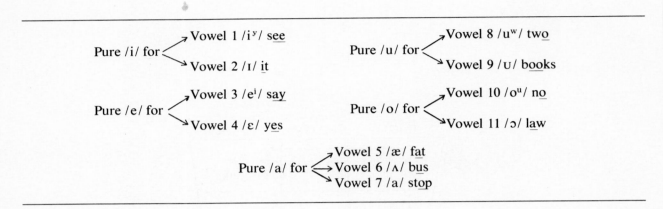

The learning task, therefore, is to examine each member of this vowel system, to practice each in appropriate vocabulary items in context, and, if necessary, to contrast it with other English vowel sounds if sufficient perceptual and production difficulties appear to be present. (See Supplement C.)

In addition, sound/spelling correspondences compound the problem. Many students have learned to read on the basis of the following sound/letter correspondences.

Letter		Sound	
i	=	/i/	(as in s<u>ee</u>)
e	=	/e/	(as in s<u>ay</u>)
a	=	/a/	(as in f<u>a</u>ther)
o	=	/o/	(as in n<u>o</u>)
u	=	/u/	(as in tw<u>o</u>)

Here are examples of possible resulting pronunciations of English words.

sit	/sɪt/	⟶	/sit/
yes	/yɛs/	⟶	/yes/
fat	/fæt/	⟶	/fat/
bus	/bʌs/	⟶	/bus/
stop	/stap/	⟶	/stop/
law	/lɔ/	⟶	/lo/

Part 2—Vowel-*r* (Vowel 12)

ESL students whose languages have a *consonant-r* but no *vowel-r* may use a trilled or tapped *consonant-r* for *vowel-r* or may omit the *vowel-r.*

Part 3—Diphthongs (Vowels 13, 14, and 15)

ESL students whose languages do not have diphthongs (i.e., complex vocalic nuclei) may fail to diphthongize in pronouncing /ai/, /au/, and /ɔi/ using the first half of the diphthong in place of the two parts of the diphthong.

Lesson 2

The Vowel Chart and the Key Words

The Pronunciation Areas of the Vowel Chart

Directions: Study these diagrams and discuss them with your teacher.

Diagram 12

This diagram shows the pronunciation areas—front, central, back.

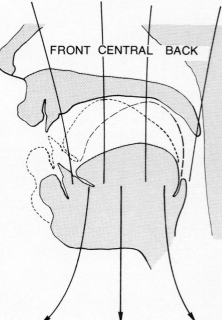

Diagram 13

This diagram shows the pronunciation areas—high, mid, low.

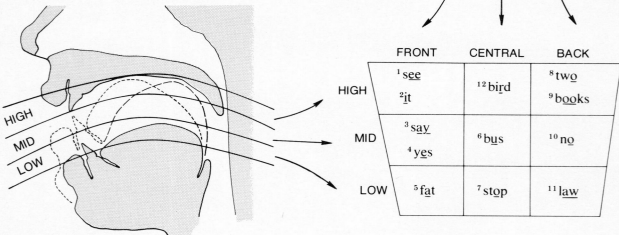

	FRONT	CENTRAL	BACK
HIGH	[1] s<u>ee</u> [2] <u>i</u>t	[12] b<u>ir</u>d	[8] tw<u>o</u> [9] b<u>oo</u>ks
MID	[3] s<u>ay</u> [4] y<u>e</u>s	[6] b<u>u</u>s	[10] n<u>o</u>
LOW	[5] f<u>a</u>t	[7] st<u>o</u>p	[11] l<u>aw</u>

Vowel Chart

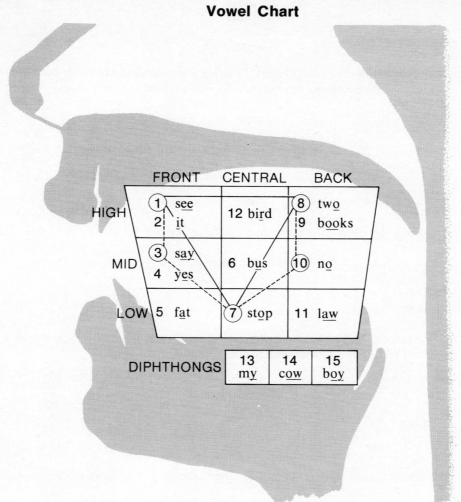

Practice with the Vowel Chart

Part 1—The Front Vowels

Look at the front vowels on the Vowel Chart. Practice the following words for each sound. Concentrate on *listening* carefully, *watching* the teacher, and *feeling* the movements for each sound. Some of the pronunciation movements may seem strange to you because some of the English sounds are different from those in your own language. Exaggerate the sounds slightly.[5]

Vowel 1:	me	read	seem	éasy	see	/i^y/	**see**
Vowel 2:	win	did	him	ríver	it	/ɪ/	**it**
Vowel 3:	day	may	rain	áble	say	/e^y/	**say**
Vowel 4:	red	head	ten	réady	yes	/ɛ/	**yes**
Vowel 5:	add	bad	man	ánswer	fat	/æ/	**fat**

Pronounce each front vowel by itself. Use a mirror. Watch the way the teeth almost touch for /i^y/ but are apart for /æ/. Feel the lower jaw drop from the high sound to the low sound.

$$/i^y \rightarrow \iota \rightarrow e^i \rightarrow \varepsilon \rightarrow æ/ \qquad /i^y \rightarrow \iota \rightarrow e^i \rightarrow \varepsilon \rightarrow æ/$$

---

5. In Vowel 2 and Vowel 5 words the letters *i* and *a* are not pronounced as they are in many languages of the world.

121

Part 2—The Central Vowels

Look at the three central vowels on the Vowel Chart. Practice the following words for each sound. Concentrate on listening, watching, and feeling the movements for each sound.

Vowel 12:[6]	he<u>r</u>	wo<u>r</u>d	tu<u>r</u>n	sé<u>r</u>vice	bi<u>r</u>d	/ɝ/	**bi<u>r</u>d**

(This is the vowel-*r* sound of English. The vowel before the *r* is not pronounced; it is *silent*.)

Vowel 6:[7]	f<u>u</u>n	r<u>u</u>n	s<u>u</u>n	stú<u>d</u>y	b<u>u</u>s	/ʌ/	**b<u>u</u>s**
Vowel 7:[8]	j<u>o</u>b	M<u>o</u>m	J<u>o</u>hn	cóllege	st<u>o</u>p	/a/	**st<u>o</u>p**

Pronounce each central vowel by itself. Use a mirror. Feel the lower jaw drop from the high sound to the low sound.

$$/ ɝ \rightarrow ʌ \rightarrow a/ \quad / ɝ \rightarrow ʌ \rightarrow a/$$

Part 3—The Back Vowels

Look at the four back vowels on the Vowel Chart. Practice the following words for each sound. Concentrate on listening, watching, and feeling the movements for each sound.

Vowel 8:	t<u>oo</u>	r<u>oo</u>m	J<u>u</u>ne	rú<u>l</u>er	tw<u>o</u>	/uʷ/	**tw<u>o</u>**
Vowel 9:	g<u>oo</u>d	w<u>oo</u>d	st<u>oo</u>d	cóokie	b<u>oo</u>ks	/ʊ/	**b<u>oo</u>ks**
Vowel 10:	g<u>o</u>	sh<u>ow</u>	dr<u>o</u>ve	ópen	n<u>o</u>	/oᵘ/	**n<u>o</u>**
Vowel 11:	s<u>aw</u>	s<u>o</u>ng	d<u>o</u>g	Aúgust	l<u>aw</u>	/ɔ/	**l<u>aw</u>**

Pronounce each back vowel by itself. Use a mirror. Feel the lower jaw drop from the high sound to the low sound.

$$/uʷ \rightarrow ʊ \rightarrow oᵘ \rightarrow ɔ/ \quad /uʷ \rightarrow ʊ \rightarrow oᵘ \rightarrow ɔ/$$

Part 4—Diphthongs

Look at the three diphthongs on the Vowel Chart. These sounds are called *diphthongs* because they are made up of two parts. There is a distinct change in sound quality between the two parts of each diphthong. Practice the following words for each sound. Concentrate on listening, watching, and feeling the movements for each sound.

Vowel 13:[9]	t<u>ie</u>	w<u>i</u>de	n<u>i</u>ne	decíde	m<u>y</u>	/ai/	**m<u>y</u>**
Vowel 14:[10]	n<u>ow</u>	h<u>ow</u>	d<u>ow</u>n	aróund	c<u>ow</u>	/au/	**c<u>ow</u>**
Vowel 15:[11]	t<u>oy</u>	n<u>oi</u>se	j<u>oi</u>n	enjóy	b<u>oy</u>	/ɔi/	**b<u>oy</u>**

---

6. Notice that the numbering of Vowel 12 is not in sequence. The 11 standard vowels have been numbered 1 through 11 with vowel-*r* numbered as 12 and the three diphthongs as 13, 14, and 15. Vowel-*r* has a corresponding consonant-*r* sound.
7. In these words the letter *u* is not pronounced as it is in many languages.
8. In these words the letter *o* is not pronounced as it is in many languages.
9. If this diphthong ends a word, the second part sounds more like Vowel 1. If it comes in the middle of a word, it sounds more like Vowel 2.
10. If this diphthong ends a word, the second part sounds more like Vowel 8. If it comes in the middle of a word, it sounds more like Vowel 9.
11. If this diphthong ends a word, the second part sounds more like Vowel 1. If it comes in the middle of a word, it sounds more like Vowel 2.

Pronounce each diphthong by itself. Use a mirror. Watch the lower jaw movement for each.

$$/ai \rightarrow au \rightarrow \mathit{oi}/ \qquad /ai \rightarrow au \rightarrow \mathit{oi}/$$

Part 5—Memorizing the Fifteen *Key* Words

Practice the key words in the vowel box. Do strong, rapid, group practice, first with individual words. Concentrate on the way each word *sounds* and the way it *feels*. Repeat each word two times.

¹s<u>ee</u> ²<u>i</u>t	¹²b<u>ir</u>d	⁸tw<u>o</u> ⁹b<u>oo</u>ks
³s<u>ay</u> ⁴y<u>e</u>s	⁶b<u>u</u>s	¹⁰n<u>o</u>
⁵f<u>a</u>t	⁷st<u>o</u>p	¹¹l<u>aw</u>

¹³m<u>y</u>	¹⁴c<u>ow</u>	¹⁵b<u>oy</u>

Practice each word once *silently*. *Watch* the teacher; *feel* the movements.

Now repeat the phrase groups. *Do not pause* between words in the phrase groups. Run the words together in each phrase.

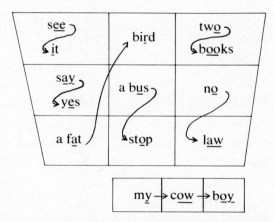

As you work with the lessons in this unit, concentrate on the pronunciation of each of these key words. Practice them again and again. These key words will provide you with a key tool which will help you in improving your spoken English.

Part 6—Vowel Sounds and Phonetic Symbols

English spelling is confusing to ESL students. For example, the letter *a* can be pronounced in at least four different ways so that the letter *a* really has four sounds.

l<u>a</u>ke	(Vowel 3	s<u>ay</u>)
c<u>a</u>t	(Vowel 5	f<u>a</u>t)
f<u>a</u>ther	(Vowel 7	st<u>o</u>p)
c<u>a</u>ll	(Vowel 11	l<u>aw</u>)

Phonetic symbols will be used to help with this spelling/pronunciation problem. A special phonetic symbol for each of the fifteen sounds is listed below. Phonetic symbols are useful because there is a one-to-one relationship between the symbol and the corresponding sound when spoken by a native speaker.[12]

Do not try to memorize the phonetic symbols now.[13] You will learn them as you study the vowel lessons in this unit.

Vowel	Sound	Key word
Vowel 1	/iʸ/	s<u>ee</u>
Vowel 2	/ɪ/	<u>i</u>t
Vowel 3	/eⁱ/	s<u>ay</u>
Vowel 4	/ɛ/	y<u>e</u>s
Vowel 5	/æ/	f<u>a</u>t
Vowel 6	/ʌ/	b<u>u</u>s
Vowel 7	/a/	st<u>o</u>p
Vowel 8	/uʷ/	tw<u>o</u>
Vowel 9	/ʊ/	b<u>oo</u>ks
Vowel 10	/oᵘ/	n<u>o</u>
Vowel 11	/ɔ/	l<u>aw</u>
Vowel 12	/ɝ/	b<u>ir</u>d
Vowel 13	/ai/	m<u>y</u>
Vowel 14	/au/	c<u>ow</u>
Vowel 15	/ɔi/	b<u>oy</u>

12. There is a danger in the idea of international phonetic alphabet. The *symbols* are international, but their *spoken interpretation* can be only for a particular language as spoken by a native speaker. For example, the symbol /i/ has one quality of sound in General American English speech, but the symbol /i/, when pronounced as a part of the Spanish or French vowel system, has a somewhat different sound quality. See the Preface, page ix, for comments on phonetic symbols.
13. No attempt is made to introduce students to phonemic/phonetic concepts.

Part 7—You, as Your Own Pronunciation Teacher: Self-Monitoring/Self Correction

(Some teachers may wish to delay use of this section until later in the course.)

As you use the vowel lessons in this unit, you will increase in your ability to "match" the vowel sounds in new words to those in the key words by the sound and by the feel of the movements. It will become easier for you to pronounce the appropriate vowels in new words the first time by yourself. Eventually you will not need to have the teacher pronounce them for you. The teacher will help you by telling you which key word a new word matches and by guiding you to change sounds which are not quite correct. Bit by bit it will become easier for you to monitor yourself and to control your own pronunciation for more intelligible spoken English.

Examples:

Student: What vowels are pronounced in these words?

pron<u>ou</u>nce pro<u>nu</u>nci<u>a</u>tion lea<u>r</u>n

Teacher: (writing the vowel numbers and referring to the key words on the Vowel Chart) These vowels.

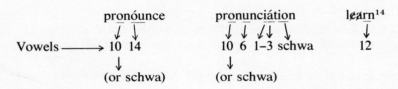

```
        pronóunce        pronunciátion      leárn¹⁴
          ↓ ↓              ↓  ↓ ↓↓  ↓          ↓
Vowels → 10 14           10  6 1–3 schwa      12
          ↓                ↓
        (or schwa)       (or schwa)
```

Teacher: You used sounds more like Vowel 1 in place of Vowel 2 in this sentence. Practice again and try for Vowel 2.

```
         This is my sister
           ↓  ↓   ↓  ↓ ↓
Vowels →   2 2   13  2 12
```

---

14. A slash mark through a letter (¢) indicates a silent letter.

Using the Intensive Vowel Lessons
in Sections B, C, D, and E

Each vowel lesson includes brief, but intensive, perception, pronunciation, and sound/spelling work. Activities in each lesson are varied, involve active student participation, provide for feedback and self-evaluation, and encourage speech awareness and self-monitoring.

Each part of each lesson has a specific function. The parts of each lesson are:

Articulation
  a. presents two or three explanatory sentences which highlight significant articulatory features of the sound and its placement within the Vowel Chart.
  b. encourages students to *observe* articulatory movements, to *listen* to sounds, and to *feel* articulatory movements

Pronunciation Practice
  a. presents four or five sentences for rapid, vigorous oral practice; uses the graphic notations for linking and reductions studied in Unit 1
  b. asks students to do a second cycle of self-monitored oral practice; vigorous practice is suggested in order to help students to develop a tactile and kinesthetic "feel" for English vowels

Reading/Listening Practice
  a. presents four sentences for silent reading and underlining of words whose spelling indicates probable pronunciation with the given sound (i.e., spelling/sound correspondences)
  b. gives students a brief time to complete the underlining; asks students to give answers and to check their own work immediately
  c. asks students to do a cycle of self-monitored oral practice exaggerating the vowel sounds slightly, but using natural rhythm, stress, and reductions

Dictation
  a. presents four dictated sentences; asks students to listen and repeat, listen and write, listen and check; suggests that teachers write a sentence on the chalkboard as the students finish writing it in their books
  b. asks students to underline all words with the sound; asks students to give answers and to check their own work immediately
  c. asks students to do a cycle of self-monitored oral practice exaggerating the vowel sounds slightly, but using natural rhythm, stress, and reductions

Spelling
  a. presents short sets of dictated words which represent selected spelling patterns; calls attention to spelling book designations and dictionary symbols
  b. suggests that teachers write the words on the chalkboard as students write them in their books, followed by discussion of the spelling pattern for each set of words

Test Sentences for Self-Monitoring and Self-Testing
  a. presents four sentences for practice, self-monitored recording, and self-analysis
  b. encourages students to record themselves and to monitor their pronunciation

Dictionary Homework
  a. presents selected words and asks students to consult their dictionaries for pronunciations
  b. encourages students to use their dictionaries for pronunciation guidance as well as for word meanings

Summary of Pronunciation
  a. provides a short reference summary of articulatory information; includes one or two self-monitoring cues for students; these focus on articulatory differences between sounds and often suggest working from known to unknown sounds and movements

Following each lesson is resource material for each vowel; it provides an additional short resource of spelling, vocabulary, and pronunciation information.

Section B—Front Vowels

Section Notes

Section B has six lessons. Lessons 3 and 4 present intensive listening/speaking practice with the two tense front vowels: /iʸ/ and /eⁱ/. Lessons 5, 6, and 7 present similar practice with the three lax front vowels: /ɪ/, /ɛ/, and /æ/. Lesson 8 presents a four-part self-evaluative test of front vowels.

The tense/lax distinction has been selected for front vowel presentation as an aid in building student awareness of spelling, acoustic, and physiological similarities and dissimilarities. It also provides a useful framework for later work with spelling and word stress. Notes on the tense vowels (page 128) and the lax vowels (page 140) are provided for more advanced classes. Teachers may wish only to paraphrase these notes briefly for some classes.

Teachers may wish to use the following diagrams, vowel boxes, and notes with students for a front vowel overview.

Many languages have only two front vowels, /i/ and /e/. As just reviewed in lesson 1 of this unit, the /i/ and /e/ are two of the five basic vowels found in most languages of the world: /i/, /e/, /a/, /o/, and /u/. English has /iʸ/ and /eⁱ/ (tense vowels) and three additional front vowels, /ɪ/, /ɛ/, and /æ/ (all lax vowels), for a total of five front vowels.

Vowel 1 is a very high front vowel (tense).
   /iʸ/—s<u>ee</u>

Vowel 2 is a lower high front vowel (lax).
   /ɪ/—<u>i</u>t

Vowel 3 is a mid front vowel (tense).
   /eⁱ/—s<u>ay</u>

Vowel 4 is a lower mid front vowel (lax).
   /ɛ/—y<u>e</u>s

Vowel 5 is a low front vowel (lax).
   /æ/—f<u>a</u>t

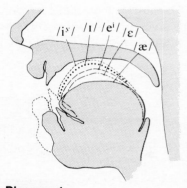

Diagram 1

¹s<u>ee</u> /iʸ/	i		
²<u>i</u>t /ɪ/			
³s<u>ay</u> /eⁱ/	e		
⁴y<u>e</u>s /ɛ/			
⁵f<u>a</u>t /æ/			

Diagram 2

Look at diagram 2.

The large symbols represent the two basic front vowels: /i/ and /e/.

The small symbols represent the five English front vowels: /iʸ/, /ɪ/, /eⁱ/, /ɛ/, and /æ/.

When students have completed the lessons in section B, practice material from Supplement B (Practice in Context for Unit 2) and/or Supplement C (Vowel Contrasts for Unit 2) may be used to provide continued attention to the front vowels. Students should be encouraged to monitor their front vowel pronunciation during classroom speaking activities.

Notes on the Two Tense Front Vowels

(Some teachers may wish only to paraphrase these notes briefly at this time and return to them later in the course for detailed discussion.)

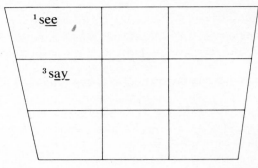

Two of the English front vowels are tense.[1]

/iʸ/—see is the high tense vowel

/eⁱ/—say is the mid tense vowel

In English these sounds are not pronounced as single pure sounds but are lengthened and slightly diphthongized. That is, in addition to the pure sound, they also have a second shorter sound. The length and the quality of this second shorter sound vary considerably according to the phonetic environment and the rhythm and stress pattern of the sentence. It is most noticeable in stressed syllables. Diagrams 3 and 4 show the tongue movements necessary to form the two parts of /iʸ/ and /eⁱ/.

Some ESL students have difficulty with the lengthening and diphthongizing of /iʸ/ and /eⁱ/. Special attention should be given to this so that students learn to modify the pure /i/ and /e/ in order to achieve the special English pronunciation of /iʸ/ and /eⁱ/.

/iʸ/—see

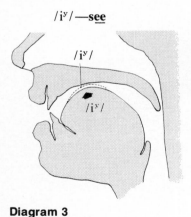

The movement is a small one for /iʸ/. The tongue is pulled up a little closer to the roof of the mouth from /i/ to /iʸ/.

/eⁱ/—say

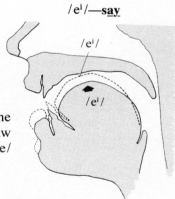

The movement is a larger one for /eⁱ/. In fact, the lower jaw is raised from half-open for /e/ to nearly closed for /eⁱ/.

Diagram 3   **Diagram 4**

Tense vowels /iʸ/ and /eⁱ/ are *open* vowels. That is, they are found not only in an initial or medial position in a word, but also can come at the end of a word and leave the word *open* or without a final *closing* consonant.[2]

---

1. Tense vowels can be distinguished from lax vowels in the following ways:
    a. the tongue moves farther from the rest position in their pronunciation
    b. there is more muscle tension
    c. they are slightly longer in duration
    d. they occur in both open and closed stressed syllables
    e. they are easier to distinguish auditorily
2. This is in contrast to lax front Vowels 2 (as in *it*), 4 (as in *yes*), and 5 (as in *fat*), which are closed vowels and must have a final or closing consonant following the vowel sound.

Examples: s<u>ee</u>   sa<u>y</u>

              m<u>e</u>   wa<u>y</u>

              sh<u>e</u>   awa<u>y</u>

              t<u>ea</u>   sta<u>y</u>

              s<u>ea</u>   pla<u>y</u>

(Notice the letter *y* is pronounced as part of the vowel, not as a consonant.)

Lesson 3

Intensive Practice with Vowel 1—see /iʸ/

Part 1—Articulation[3]

Vowel 1 is the highest front vowel. It is not a pure /i/ as in some languages.[4] It has an /i/ followed by a /y/ glide.[5] Practice these words: see   me   read.

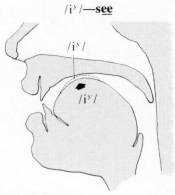

/iʸ/—see

Diagram 5

Part 2—Pronunciation Practice[6]

Listen, watch, and practice. (Follow the linking lines (‿); shorten the unstressed weak words such as ~~the~~, ~~was~~, ~~some~~.)

1. these
   éasy

   These‿books‿are‿easy!

2. he
   léaving

   He's‿leaving‿at‿noon.

3. she
   sléeping

   ~~Was~~‿she‿sleeping?

4. téacher
   needs

   ~~The~~‿teacher‿needs‿~~some~~‿chalk.

5. please
   see
   me

   Please‿see‿me‿after‿class.

Practice each sentence again using natural rhythm, stress, and reductions.[7] Exaggerate the /iʸ/ sounds slightly.

(Lab: Stop the tape for a few minutes of individual practice and self-monitoring.)

---

3. Encourage students to use pronunciation mirrors. Encourage them to listen to the sound and to feel the movements of the lips, the lower jaw, and the tongue as they practice.
4. Contrast the sounds in Spanish *sí* and French *oui* with the sounds in English *see* and *we*.
5. When /iʸ/ is in the middle of a word followed by a voiceless consonant, the glide (or diphthongization) is shorter and harder to hear. In unstressed syllables it may disappear altogether.
6. *Lab:* As the students practice, move about the room and monitor their pronunciation. Give additional suggestions wherever students are having difficulty.
7. This brief segment of practice which encourages natural rhythm, stress, and reductions is important. *Lab:* Have students remove headphones for individual and choral practice.

Part 3—Reading/Listening Practice (AK/TS)

Read each sentence silently. Find the words which you would guess are pronounced with Vowel 1. Draw a line under these words.

1. We must leave at three. (Find 3 words with /iʸ/.)
2. These books seem easy to read. (4)
3. Does he need these keys? (4)
4. Please meet me at the beach. (4)

(Lab: Stop the tape and ask students to give their answers. Then start the tape and have students check their work as the words for each line are given.)

Practice the sentences using natural rhythm, stress, and reductions. Exaggerate the /iʸ/ sounds slightly.

(Lab: Stop the tape for a few minutes of individual practice and self-monitoring.)

Part 4—Dictation[8] (AK/TS)

Four sentences will be dictated. Listen and repeat. Listen and write. Listen and check. Underline each occurrence of Vowel 1. Check your spelling.

1. _____ (6 words)
2. _____ (6)
3. _____ (5)
4. _____ (5)

(Lab: Stop the tape and ask students to read their /iʸ/ words. Then start the tape and have students check their work as the words for each line are given.)

Practice the sentences again using natural rhythm, stress, and reductions.[9] Exaggerate the /iʸ/ sounds slightly.

(Lab: Stop the tape for a few minutes of individual practice and self-monitoring.)

Part 5—Spelling[10] (AK/TS)

The /iʸ/ is the high tense front vowel. As a tense vowel it can come at the end of a word and leave the word open—without a closing consonant. In spelling books /iʸ/ sometimes is called the "long *e*" sound. Many dictionaries use this symbol (ē) as the pronunciation guide for this sound. Listen and write. Repeat the words to yourself as you write. (A capital letter *C* stands for any consonant; a slash mark [ȼ] through a letter indicates a silent letter; a capital letter *V* stands for any vowel or vocalic *y*.)

---

8. Write each sentence on the chalkboard as the students write it in their books. Ask students to identify the words with /iʸ/; underline each word and write *1* under it.
9. This brief segment of practice which encourages natural rhythm, stress, and reductions is important; students should note that some of the /iʸ/ sounds are longer and some are shorter depending upon the stress and rhythm of the sentence.
10. Write the words in each group on the chalkboard as the students write them in their books. Stop after each group and discuss briefly. Several of the high frequency spelling patterns for /iʸ/ are given here and in the resource material. (Consult the Hanna et al. reference given on page viii for detailed frequency information.) The notational detail on environments has been kept to a bare minimum with examples given to illustrate the patterns. Expanded information will be studied later in the program. (Consult the R. L. Venezky and Cronnell references for detailed spelling rule information.)

Group 1	e (including eC¢)			
be	_____	_____	_____	_____
Group 2	ee (including eeC¢)			
see	_____	_____	_____	_____
Group 3	ea (including eaC¢)			
tea	_____	_____	_____	_____
Group 4	ieC(C) (including ieC¢)			
field	_____	_____		

Part 6—Test Sentences for Self-Monitoring and Self-Testing

Practice the following sentences using natural rhythm, stress, and reductions. Exaggerate the /iʸ/ sounds slightly. Record. Listen and monitor your pronunciation.

1. We need these keys.
2. Meet me at three.
3. We'll meet you at the beach.
4. These books are easy.

Part 7—Dictionary Homework

Look up the following words in your dictionary. Copy the pronunciation exactly. Include the syllable accent marks. Notice the symbol your dictionary uses as a pronunciation guide for this sound.

1. people _____   3. relief _____   5. neither _____

2. police _____   4. magazine _____   6. completion _____

Summary—Pronunciation of /iʸ/

The /iʸ/ sound is pronounced with the tongue high, front, and tense. In fact, the tongue is arched upward and forward in the highest front articulatory position for English vowels. It is not a pure /i/ as in some languages. It has an /i/ followed by a /y/ glide: /iʸ/   /iʸ/.

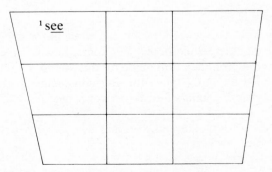

For more detailed articulatory information see the contrasts in Supplement C.

Resource Material

Part 1—Notes

The sound /i^y/ is fifth in general usage among the fifteen vowel sounds.

The following are major spelling patterns for /i^y/, with percentages for frequency of occurrence.[11]

e	as in *we*	72%	(including eC¢, 2%)
ee	as in *see*	10%	(including eeC¢)
ea	as in *tea*	11%	(including eaC¢)
ieC(C)	as in *field*	2%	(including ieC¢)

ESL interference / learning problems may include the following:

a. Sound: a shorter pure sound /i/ may be used for /i^y/

b. Spelling: in some languages the letter *e* is pronounced with the sound /e/ (as in s<u>ay</u>); this may lead to spelling/pronunciation confusion

Part 2—Major Spelling Patterns

Ask students to study and practice the following words, which represent major spelling patterns for /i^y/.[12] Add to the lists.[13]

Group 1   e, eCV

be	me	éven
he	we	équal
she		Péter

Group 2   eC¢

| these | Pete |
| scene | compléte |

Group 3   ee[14]

see	need	betwéen	feel
free	week	sleep	heel
seem	indéed	green	

Group 4   eeC¢

| breeze | freeze |
| sneeze | cheese |

---

11. A (*C*) means an additional consonant is optional.
12. Students find it useful to extend practice with these words into sentences and/or conversational dialogues.
13. For carryover, alert students to look for these words in daily classwork and encourage students to monitor themselves and others as these words occur in classroom conversations.
14. The /i^y/ before final /l/ may have a schwa, /ə/, glide following the vowel, as in *feel* and *heel*. This varies in length according to the sentence rhythm and stress pattern. There also is considerable variation from speaker to speaker.

Group 5   ea

eat	tea	beach
each	sea	repéat
east	mean	speak

Group 6   eaC¢

please	leave
peace	

Group 7   ieC(C), ieC¢

field	belíef	niece
thief	belíeve	piece

Part 3—Other Spelling Patterns

Group 1   iC¢

políce	machíne

Group 2   ey

key

Group 3   eiC, eiC¢

recéive	éither	néither

Group 4   oe

péople

Part 4—Practice with /iʸ/ before Voiced / Voiceless Consonants

Ask students to practice these pairs of words with attention to lengthening the vowel before the voiced consonant—the first word in each pair. The lengthening mark (:) has been added to emphasize the lengthening before the voiced consonant. Add to the list. See page 29 for voiced / voiceless sound charts.

1. nee:d	neat
2. pea:s ($s = $ /z/)	piece ($c = $ /s/)
3. knee:s ($s = $ /z/)	niece ($c = $ /s/)
4. lea:ve	leaf
5. see:d	seat

Lesson 4

Intensive Practice with Vowel 3—s<u>ay</u> /eⁱ/

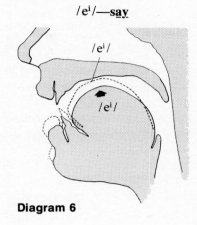

/eⁱ/—s<u>ay</u>

Diagram 6

Part 1—Articulation

Vowel 3 is the mid front vowel. It is not a pure /e/ as in some languages.[15] It has an /e/ followed by a glide to /i/.[16] The tongue is mid front, then moves up toward high front /i/ for /eⁱ/. Practice these words: w<u>ay</u> d<u>ay</u> c<u>a</u>me.

Part 2—Pronunciation Practice[17]

Listen, watch, and practice. (Follow the linking lines (-); shorten the unstressed weak words such as ~~the~~, ~~was~~, ~~some~~.)

1. tr<u>ai</u>n   <u>The</u> tr<u>ai</u>n ~~was~~ l<u>a</u>te.
   l<u>a</u>te

2. p<u>á</u>per   Put ~~your~~ papers <u>on</u> ~~the~~ table.
   t<u>á</u>ble

3. tod<u>áy</u>   Tod<u>a</u>y <u>is</u> ~~the~~ <u>ei</u>ghth <u>of</u> M<u>ay</u>.
   <u>ei</u>ghth
   M<u>ay</u>

4. p<u>á</u>inting   He's p<u>ai</u>nting my place <u>at</u> ~~the~~ l<u>a</u>ke.
   place
   l<u>a</u>ke

Practice each sentence again using natural rhythm, stress, and reductions.[18] Exaggerate the /eⁱ/ sounds slightly.

(Lab: Stop the tape for a few minutes of individual practice and self-monitoring.)

---

15. Contrast the sounds in Spanish *de* and French *les* with the sounds in English *day* and *lay*.
16. When /eⁱ/ is in the middle of a word followed by a voiceless consonant, the glide (or diphthongization) is shorter and harder to hear. In unstressed syllables it may disappear altogether.
17. *Lab*: As the students practice, move about the room and monitor their pronunciation. Give additional suggestions wherever students are having difficulty.
18. This brief segment of practice which encourages natural rhythm, stress, and reductions is important. *Lab*: Have students remove headphones for individual and choral practice.

Unit 2—Section B
Lesson 4

Part 3—Reading / Listening Practice (AK/TS)

Read each sentence silently. Find the words which you would guess are pronounced with Vowel 3. Draw a line under these words.

1. We were waiting for the train in the rain. (Find 3 words with /eⁱ/.)
2. He ate eighty-eight cakes! (4)
3. Jane Taylor is a famous lady. (4)
4. The rain in Spain is mainly on the plain. (4)

(Lab: Stop the tape and ask students to give their answers. Then start the tape and have students check their work as the words for each line are given.)

Practice the sentences using natural rhythm, stress, and reductions. Exaggerate the /eⁱ/ sounds slightly.

(Lab: Stop the tape for a few minutes of individual practice and self-monitoring.)

Part 4—Dictation[19] (AK/TS)

Four sentences will be dictated. Listen and repeat. Listen and write. Listen and check. Underline each occurrence of Vowel 3. Check your spelling.

1. _____ (6 words)

2. _____ (6)

3. _____ (7)

4. _____ (5)

(Lab: Stop the tape and ask students to read their /eⁱ/ words. Then start the tape and have students check their work as the words for each line are given.)

Practice the sentences again using natural rhythm, stress, and reductions.[20] Exaggerate the /eⁱ/ sounds slightly.

(Lab: Stop the tape for a few minutes of individual practice and self-monitoring.)

Part 5—Spelling[21] (AK/TS)

The /eⁱ/ is the mid tense front vowel. As a tense vowel, like /iʸ/, it can come at the end of a word and leave the word *open*—without a closing consonant. In spelling books /eⁱ/ sometimes is called the "long *a*" sound. Many dictionaries use this symbol (ā) as the pronunciation guide for this sound. Listen and write. Repeat the words to yourself as you write.

Group 1   a (including aCȼ)

   fámous   _____ _____   late   _____ _____ _____

---

19. Write each sentence on the chalkboard as the students write it in their books. Ask students to identify the words with /eⁱ/; underline each word and write *3* under it. Ask them to identify any examples of Vowel 1, /iʸ/, studied in lesson 3.
20. This brief segment of practice which encourages natural rhythm, stress, and reductions is important; students should note that some of the /eⁱ/ sounds are longer and some are shorter depending upon the stress and rhythm of the sentence.
21. Write the words in each group on the chalkboard as the students write them in their books. Stop after each group and discuss briefly.

136

Group 2   aiC   (including aiC¢)

train   _____   _____   praise   _____

Group 3   ay

day   _____   _____   _____

Group 4   eigh

weight   _____   _____

Group 5   eaC
            (not a usual spelling for /eⁱ/; memorize these words)

great   _____   _____

Part 6—Test Sentences for Self-Monitoring and Self-Testing

Practice the following sentences using natural rhythm, stress, and reductions. Exaggerate the /eⁱ/ sounds slightly. Record. Listen and monitor your pronunciation.

1. The train was late!
2. Jane was waiting by the gate.
3. He ate eighty-eight cakes!
4. They came on the eighth of May.

Part 7—Dictionary Homework

Look up the following words in your dictionary. Copy the pronunciation exactly. Include the syllable accent marks. Notice the symbol your dictionary uses as a pronunciation guide for this sound.

1. vacation _____   3. explain _____   5. mistake _____

2. neighbor _____   4. radio _____   6. April _____

Summary—Pronunciation of /eⁱ/

The /eⁱ/ sound is pronounced with the tongue mid, front, and tense. It is not a pure /e/ as in some languages. It has an /e/ followed by a glide to /i/. The lower jaw is raised from half-open for /e/ to nearly closed for /eⁱ/: /eⁱ/   /eⁱ/.[22]

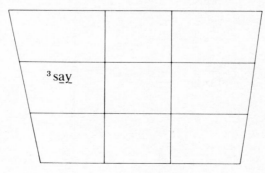

For more detailed articulatory information see the contrasts in Supplement C.

---

22. See footnote 16 on page 135.

Resource Material

The sound /eⁱ/ is eighth in general usage among the fifteen vowel sounds.

The following are major spelling patterns for /eⁱ/ with percentages for frequency of occurrence:

a	as in *famous*	80%	(including aC¢, 35%)
aiC	as in *rain*	10%	(including aiC¢)
ay	as in *say*	6%	
eigh	as in *eight*	1%	

ESL interference / learning problems may include the following:

a. Sound: a shorter pure sound /e/ may be used for /eⁱ/

b. Spelling: in some languages the letter *a* is pronounced with the sound /a/, (as in *fáther*); this may lead to spelling/pronunciation confusion

Part 2— Major Spelling Patterns

Ask students to study and practice the following words, which represent major spelling patterns for /eⁱ/.[23] Add to the lists.[24]

Group 1   aCV, aCrV

lády	lábel	nátion
Ápril	páper	vacátion
báby		státion

Group 2   aC¢, aCl¢[25]

came	escápe	ate
place	éducate	make
sale	óperate	táble

Group 3   aiC, aiC¢

rain	ráisin	praise
train	remáin	raise
mail	straight	

Group 4   ay

say	deláy	Fríday
may	todáy	stay

---

23. See footnote 12 on page 133.
24. See footnote 13 on page 133.
25. The /eⁱ/ before final /l/ may have a schwa, /ə/, glide following the vowel, as in *sale* in group 2 and *mail* in group 3. This varies in length according to the sentence rhythm and stress pattern. There also is considerable variation from speaker to speaker.

Group 5   eigh

   weight   éighty   néighbor
   eight   eightéen

Part 3—Other Spelling Patterns

Group 1   eaC
   break   great   steak
Group 2   ey
   they

Part 4—Practice with /eⁱ/ before Voiced / Voiceless Consonants

Ask students to practice these pairs of words with attention to lengthening the vowel before the voiced consonant—the first word in each pair. The lengthening mark (:) has been added to emphasize the lengthening before the voiced consonant. Add to the list.

1. ma:de   mate
2. stay:ed   state
3. rai:se ($s = /z/$)   race ($c = /s/$)
4. play:s ($s = /z/$)   place ($c = /s/$)
5. sa:ve   safe

Notes on the Three Lax Front Vowels

(Some teachers may wish only to paraphrase these notes briefly at this time and return to them later in the course for detailed discussion.)

Three of the English front vowels are lax.[26]

/ɪ/—it is the high lax vowel

/ɛ/—yes is the mid lax vowel

/æ/—fat is the low lax vowel

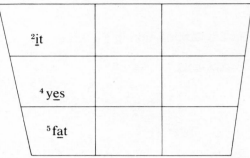

As the phonetic symbols above show, each of these sounds has only one part. However, each of these sounds, when pronounced by itself, may have a small glide[27] toward the center position so we hear /ɪə/, /ɛə/, and /æə/. Awareness of this centering glide tendency may be helpful for some students in distinguishing the following sounds.

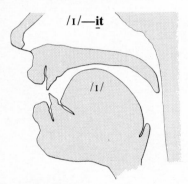 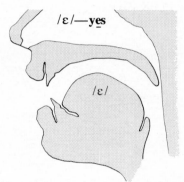 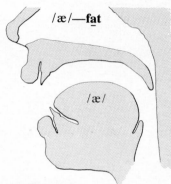

Diagram 7

ESL students may experience difficulty in distinguishing /ɪ/ from /iʸ/.

Diagram 8

ESL students may experience difficulty in distinguishing /ɛ/ from /eⁱ/.

Diagram 9

ESL students may experience difficulty in distinguishing /æ/ from /ɛ/ and from /a/, Vowel 7.

These three sounds are *closed* vowels. That is, they cannot come at the end of a word (when stressed) and leave the word *open*. They must be followed by one or more consonants which close the word.[28]

Examples:

it	then	fat
did	men	can
kiss	help	glad
thing	tell	pass
with	test	last

---

26. Lax vowels can be distinguished from tense vowels in the following ways:
    a. the tongue does not move as far from the rest position in their pronunciation
    b. the muscles of articulation are more relaxed; you can feel the difference in muscle tension between tense /iʸ/ and lax /ɪ/ and tense /eⁱ/ and lax /ɛ/
    c. they are slightly shorter in duration
    d. they occur *only* in closed syllables, when stressed; the unstressed *y* in words like *happy* is somewhat between /ɪ/ and /i/ for many speakers
    e. they are a little harder to distinguish auditorily
27. This tendency varies according to phonetic environment and the patterns of stress, rhythm, and intonation. There also is considerable variation from speaker to speaker.
28. This is in contrast to tense front Vowels 1 and 3 which can come at the end of a word without a closing consonant.

Lesson 5

Intensive Practice with Vowel 2—it /ɪ/

Part 1—Articulation

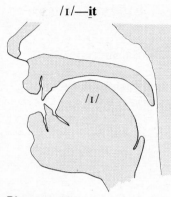

/ɪ/—it

Vowel 2 is not as high as Vowel 1 and it does not have a /y/ glide.[29] The jaw and tongue are lowered slightly from /iʸ/ to /ɪ/. Do not confuse Vowel 1 with Vowel 2. Listen to the difference: /iʸ/ /ɪ/   see it. Practice these words: this   did   bit.

Diagram 10

Part 2—Pronunciation Practice

Listen, watch, and practice. (Follow the linking lines (‿); shorten the unstressed weak words such as ~~the, was, some~~.)

1. six	He‿caught‿six‿big‿fish!	3. sítting	I‿was‿sitting‿by‿the‿river.
big		ríver	
fish			
2. this	This‿is‿my‿little‿sister.	4. lísten	Listen! ~~The~~ children‿are‿singing.
is		chíldren	
líttle		sing	
síster			

Practice each sentence again using natural rhythm, stress, and reductions. Exaggerate the /ɪ/ sounds slightly.

(Lab: Stop the tape for a few minutes of individual practice and self-monitoring.)

Part 3—Reading / Listening Practice (AK/TS)

Read each sentence silently. Find the words which you would guess are pronounced with Vowel 2. Draw a line under these words.[30]

1. Let's have dinner ~~at~~ six. (Find 2 words with /ɪ/.)
2. I put four big fish in ~~the~~ dish. (4)
3. Snow is ~~the~~ kiss ~~of~~ winter; rain is ~~the~~ kiss ~~of~~ spring! (6)
4. Which picture is in ~~the~~ window? (5)

---

29. See page 140 for a comment on a small glide toward the central position.
30. The words *is* and *in* are often pronounced with a short reduced form of Vowel 2. This weak form of Vowel 2 has the phonetic symbol of /ɪ/ with a line through it, /ɪ̵/.

(Lab: Stop the tape and ask students to give their answers. Then start the tape and have students check their work as the words for each line are given.)

Practice the sentences using natural rhythm, stress, and reductions. Exaggerate the /ɪ/ sounds slightly.

(Lab: Stop the tape for a few minutes of individual practice and self-monitoring.)

Part 4—Dictation (AK/TS)

Four sentences will be dictated. Listen and repeat. Listen and write. Listen and check. Underline each occurrence of Vowel 2. Check your spelling.

1. _____ (5 words)

2. _____ (7)

3. _____ (7)

4. _____ (9)

(Lab: Stop the tape and ask students to read their /ɪ/ words. Then start the tape and have students check their work as the words for each line are given.)

Practice the sentences again using natural rhythm, stress, and reductions. Exaggerate the /ɪ/ sounds slightly.

(Lab: Stop the tape for a few minutes of individual practice and self-monitoring.)

Part 5—Spelling (AK/TS)

The /ɪ/ sound is the high lax front vowel. As a lax vowel it cannot come at the end of a word, when stressed, and leave the word open; it *must* be followed by one or more consonants which *close* the word. In spelling books /ɪ/ sometimes is called the "short *i*" sound. Many dictionaries use this symbol (ĭ) as the pronunciation guide for this sound. Listen and write. Repeat the words to yourself as you write.

Group 1	iC(C)				
big	_____	_____	_____	_____	
Group 2	iCC				
	(Notice the letter *i* is the lax sound /ɪ/ before the doubled consonant.)				
giggle	_____	_____	_____	_____	_____
Group 3	yC(C)				
bicycle	_____	_____			
Group 4	uC, uiC				
	(not a usual spelling for /ɪ/; memorize these words)				
business	_____	build	_____	_____	_____

Part 6—Test Sentences for Self-Monitoring and Self-Testing

Practice the following sentences using natural rhythm, stress, and reductions. Exaggerate the /ɪ/ sounds slightly. Record. Listen and monitor your pronunciation.

1. Let's have dinner at six.
2. Jim caught a big fish.
3. I was sitting by the river.
4. This is a picture of my sister.

Part 7—Dictionary Homework

Look up the following words in your dictionary. Copy the pronunciation exactly. Include the syllable accent marks. Notice the symbol your dictionary uses as a pronunciation guide for this sound.

1. guitar _____   3. symbol _____   5. syllable _____

2. nickel _____   4. deliver _____   6. sixteen _____

Summary—Pronunciation of /ɪ/

The /ɪ/ sound is pronounced with the tongue quite high but lax. It does not have the /y/ glide of /iʸ/. Feel the difference: /iʸ/ → /ɪ/   /iʸ/ → /ɪ/   see it.

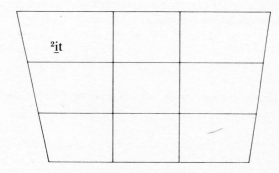

For more detailed articulatory information see the contrasts in Supplement C.

Resource Material

Part 1—Notes

The sound /ɪ/ is first in general usage among the fifteen vowel sounds.

The following are major spelling patterns for /ɪ/ with percentages for frequency of occurence:

iC(C)	as in *it, míddle*	68%
yC(C)	as in *rhýthm*	
y	as in *báby*	24%
ey	as in *móney*	

(This 24% includes the unstressed *y* at the ends of words such as *báby*, *lády*, and *cíty*, and the unstressed *ey* at the end of words such as *móney* and *válley*. Some dictionaries give a short unaccented /i/ instead of /ɪ/.)

ESL interference/learning problems may include the following:

    a. Sound: a pure tense vowel /i/ may be used for the lax /ɪ/

    b. Spelling: in many languages the letter *i* is pronounced with the sound /i/ (as in *see*); this may lead to spelling/pronunciation confusion

Part 2—Major Spelling Patterns

Ask students to study and practice the following words, which represent major spelling patterns for /ɪ/. Add to the lists.

Group 1[31]   iC(C)

this	bring	lísten
with	síster	whísper
big	dídn't	wíndow
líttle	wrítten	fill

Group 2   yC(C)

rhýthm	sýllable	sýmpathy
sýmbol	sýmptom	

Group 3   y (final) and ey (final), unstressed

(Many speakers use a short unaccented /i/ in these words instead of /ɪ/.)

báby	fúnny	mónkey
lády	fríendly	móney
cíty	válley	hóney

---

31. The /ɪ/ before final /l/ may have a schwa, /ə/, glide following the vowel, as in *fill*. This varies in length according to the sentence rhythm and stress pattern. There also is considerable variation from speaker to speaker.

Part 3—Other Spelling Patterns

Group 1   ivV, ixV
   give   live   míxer
                                                  ríver

Group 2   uC and uiC
   búsy   búsiness
   quit   quick   guitár
   build   búilding   built

Group 3   Exceptions
   prétty   been   wómen

Part 4—Practice with /ɪ/ before Voiced/Voiceless Consonants

Ask students to practice these pairs of words with attention to lengthening the vowel before the voiced consonant—the first word in each pair. The lengthening mark (:) has been added to emphasize the lengthening before the voiced consonant. Add to the list.

1. pi:g   pick
2. ri:b   rip
3. ki:d   kit
4. bi:d   bit
5. ri:dge   rich
6. hi:d   hit
7. wi:g   wick

Lesson 6

Intensive Practice with Vowel 4—y<u>e</u>s /ɛ/

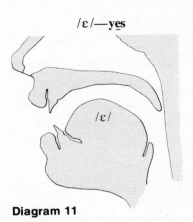

/ɛ/—y<u>e</u>s

Diagram 11

Part 1—Articulation

Vowel 4 is not as high as Vowel 3 and it does not have an /i/ glide. The jaw and tongue are lowered slightly from /eⁱ/ to /ɛ/. Do not confuse Vowel 3 with Vowel 4. Listen to the difference: /eⁱ/ /ɛ/ s<u>a</u>y y<u>e</u>s. Practice these words: l<u>e</u>ss get m<u>e</u>n.

Part 2—Pronunciation Practice

Listen, watch, and practice. (Follow the linking lines (‿); shorten the unstressed weak words such as ~~the,~~ ~~was,~~ ~~some.~~)

1. b<u>e</u>st He's‿my‿best‿friend.
   fri<u>e</u>nd
2. wh<u>e</u>n When's‿the‿next‿test?
   n<u>e</u>xt
   t<u>e</u>st
3. r<u>é</u>ady I'll‿be‿ready‿at‿ten-twenty.
   t<u>e</u>n
   tw<u>é</u>nty
4. r<u>e</u>d I‿found‿a‿red‿pen.
   p<u>e</u>n

Practice each sentence again using natural rhythm, stress, and reductions. Exaggerate the /ɛ/ sounds slightly.

(Lab: Stop the tape for a few minutes of individual practice and self-monitoring.)

Part 3—Reading / Listening Practice (AK/TS)

Read each sentence silently. Find the words which you would guess are pronounced with Vowel 4. Draw a line under these words.

1. It's twenty past ten. (Find 2 words with /ɛ/.)
2. I met my best friend ~~at the~~ restaurant. (4)
3. Every lesson will end with ~~a~~ test. (4)
4. I left my pencil on ~~the~~ desk. (3)

(Lab: Stop the tape and ask students to give their answers. Start the tape and have students check their work as the words for each line are given.)

Practice the sentences using natural rhythm, stress, and reductions. Exaggerate the /ɛ/ sounds slightly.

(Lab: Stop the tape for a few minutes of individual practice and self-monitoring.)

Part 4—Dictation (AK/TS)

Four sentences will be dictated. Listen and repeat. Listen and write. Listen and check. Underline each occurrence of Vowel 4. Check your spelling.

1. _____ (8 words)

2. _____ (5)

3. _____ (5)

4. _____ (5)

Practice the sentences again using natural rhythm, stress, and reductions. Exaggerate the /ɛ/ sounds slightly.

(Lab: Stop the tape for a few minutes of individual practice and self-monitoring.)

Part 5—Spelling (AK/TS)

The /ɛ/ sound is the mid lax front vowel. As a lax vowel, like /ɪ/, it cannot come at the end of a word, when stressed, and leave the word open; it *must* be followed by one or more consonants which *close* the word. In spelling books /ɛ/ sometimes is called the "short *e*" sound. Many dictionaries use this symbol (ĕ) as the pronunciation guide for this sound. Listen and write. Repeat the words to yourself as you write.

Group 1	eC(C)					
red	_____	_____	_____	_____	_____	
Group 2	eCC					
	(Notice the letter *e* is the lax sound /ɛ/ before the doubled consonant.)					
better	_____	_____	_____	_____	_____	
Group 3	eaC					
	(not a usual spelling for /ɛ/; memorize these words)					
ready	_____	_____	_____	_____	_____	
Group 4	ieC					
	(not a usual spelling for /ɛ/; memorize these words)					
friend	_____					
Group 5	ueC					
	(not a usual spelling for /ɛ/; memorize these words)					
guest	_____	_____				

Part 6—Test Sentences for Self-Monitoring and Self-Testing

Practice the following sentences using natural rhythm, stress, and reductions. Exaggerate the /ɛ/ sounds slightly. Record. Listen and monitor your pronunciation.

1. He's my best friend.
2. She bought ten red pens.
3. Spring weather is pleasant.
4. The next test is on Wednesday.

147

Part 7—Dictionary Homework

Look up the following words in your dictionary. Copy the pronunciation exactly. Include the syllable accent marks. Notice the symbol your dictionary uses as a pronunciation guide for this sound.

1. Wednesday _____ 3. February _____ 5. rescue _____

2. already _____ 4. bread _____ 6. expense _____

Summary—Pronunciation of /ɛ/

The /ɛ/ sound is pronounced with the tongue in a mid, lax, front position. The jaw is lowered from /eⁱ/ to /ɛ/. It does not have the /i/ glide of /eⁱ/. Feel the difference: /eⁱ/ → /ɛ/   /eⁱ/ → /ɛ/   say → y̲e̲s.

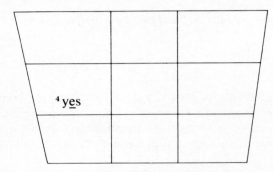

For more detailed articulatory information see the contrasts in Supplement C.

Resource Material

Part 1—Notes

The sound /ɛ/ is sixth in general usage among the fifteen vowel sounds.

The following is the major spelling pattern for /ɛ/:

    eC(C)   as in *yes*   91%

ESL interference / learning problems may include the following:

    a. Sound: a pure tense vowel /e/ may be used for the lax /ɛ/
    b. Spelling: in many languages the letter *e* is pronounced with the sound /e/ (as in *say*); this may lead to spelling/pronunciation confusion

Part 2—Major Spelling Pattern eC(C)

Ask students to study and practice the following words. Add to the lists.[32]

red	édge	mysélf	fell
get	bétter	hersélf	well
next	péncil	himsélf	tell

---

32. The /ɛ/ before final /l/ may have a schwa, /ə/, glide following the vowel, as in *fell*, *well*, *tell*. This varies in length according to the sentence rhythm and stress pattern. There also is considerable variation from speaker to speaker.

Part 3—Other Spelling Patterns

Group 1   evV, exV

séven	éxit
néver	Téxas

Group 2   eaC

head	wéather
meant	bréakfast
pléasant	réady

Group 3   aiC

said	agáin	agáinst

Group 4   aC, ieC, ueC

ány	friend	guess
mány	fríendly	guest
		quéstion

Part 4—Practice with /ɛ/ before Voiced/Voiceless Consonants

Ask students to practice these pairs of words with attention to lengthening the vowel before the voiced consonant—the first word in each pair. The lengthening mark (:) has been added to emphasize the lengthening before the voiced consonant. Add to the list.

1. le:d	let
2. dea:d	debt
3. be:d	bet
4. sai:d	set
5. e:dge	etch

Part 5—Practice with /iʸ/ — /ɛ/ Pairs of Words

Ask students to practice these pairs of words with attention to the alternation of Vowel 1, /iʸ/, and Vowel 4, /ɛ/. Add to the list. The principles of vowel alternation will be studied later in the program.

Vowel 1	*Vowel 4*
1. please	pleasant
2. feel	felt
3. sleep	slept
4. receive	reception

Lesson 7

Intensive Practice with Vowel 5—f<u>a</u>t /æ/

Part 1—Articulation

Vowel 5 is the lowest front vowel. The jaw and the tongue are lowered slightly from /ɛ/ to /æ/. As the diagram shows, the tongue is rounded and arched forward a little. Do not let the tongue pull down and back for Vowel 7, /a/. Listen, watch, and compare: /ɛ/ /æ/ /a/. Practice these words: <u>a</u>dd b<u>a</u>d f<u>a</u>t.

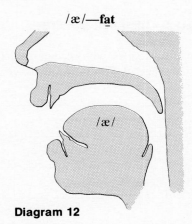

/æ/—f<u>a</u>t

/æ/

Diagram 12

Part 2—Pronunciation Practice

Listen, watch, and practice. (Follow the linking lines (‿); shorten the unstressed weak words such as ~~the~~, ~~was~~, ~~some~~.)

1. h<u>á</u>ndsome   He's‿a‿handsome‿man.
   m<u>a</u>n

2. d<u>a</u>nced   ~~The~~‿children‿danced‿and‿sang.
   s<u>a</u>ng

3. <u>á</u>fter   Meet‿me‿after‿class.
   cl<u>a</u>ss

4. <u>á</u>nswer   Please‿answer‿the‿last‿question.
   l<u>a</u>st

5. b<u>a</u>ck   I'm‿going‿back‿to‿the‿lab.
   l<u>a</u>b

Practice each sentence again using natural rhythm, stress, and reductions. Exaggerate the /æ/ sounds slightly.

(Lab: Stop the tape for a few minutes of individual practice and self-monitoring.)

Part 3—Reading / Listening Practice (AK/TS)

Read each sentence silently. Find the words which you would guess are pronounced with Vowel 5. Draw a line under these words.

1. Please pass ~~the~~ apples. (Find 2 words with /æ/.)
2. ~~The~~ fat cat sat on ~~the~~ hat. (4)
3. Sam took ~~the~~ last sandwich. (3)
4. The classes will travel ~~by~~ taxi. (3)

(Lab: Stop the tape and ask students to give their answers. Then start the tape and have students check their work as the words for each line are given.)

Practice the sentences using natural rhythm, stress, and reductions. Exaggerate the /æ/ sounds slightly.

(Lab: Stop the tape for a few minutes of individual practice and self-monitoring.)

Part 4—Dictation (AK/TS)

Four sentences will be dictated. Listen and repeat. Listen and write. Listen and check. Underline each occurrence of Vowel 5. Check your spelling.

1. _____ (7 words)

2. _____ (4)

3. _____ (6)

4. _____ (5)

(Lab: Stop the tape and ask students to read their /æ/ words. Then start the tape and have students check their work as the words for each line are given.)

Practice the sentences again using natural rhythm, stress, and reductions. Exaggerate the /æ/ sounds slightly.

(Lab: Stop the tape for a few minutes of individual practice and self-monitoring.)

Part 5—Spelling (AK/TS)

The /æ/ sound is the low lax front vowel. As a lax vowel, like /ɪ/ and /ɛ/, /æ/ is a closed vowel. It cannot come at the end of a word, when stressed, and leave the word open; it must be followed by one or more consonants which close the word. In spelling books /æ/ sometimes is called the "short *a*" sound. Many dictionaries use this symbol (ă) as the pronunciation guide for this sound. Listen and write. Repeat the words to yourself as you write.

Group 1	aC(C)				
bad	_____	_____	_____	_____	_____
Group 2	aCC				
	(Notice the letter *a* is the lax sound /æ/ before any doubled consonant except *l*.)[33]				
class	_____	_____	_____	_____	_____
Group 3	aC				
	(Notice these are *strong* forms of these words. See Unit 1, lesson 9, for discussion of weak/strong forms.)				
at	_____	_____	_____	_____	_____
Group 4	aC				
	(Write the following words and mark the accented syllable.)				
áfter	_____	_____	_____	_____	_____
Group 5	auC				
laugh	_____	_____			

---

33. With the exception of the word *shall*, which is pronounced with Vowel 5, /æ/.

Part 6—Test Sentences for Self-Monitoring and Self-Testing

Practice the following sentences using natural rhythm, stress, and reductions. Exaggerate the /æ/ sounds slightly. Record. Listen and monitor your pronunciation.

1. He's a handsome man.
2. Please pass the apples.
3. The fat cat sat on the hat.
4. Let's go back to the lab.

Part 7—Dictionary Homework

Look up the following words in your dictionary. Copy the pronunciation exactly. Include the syllable accent marks. Notice the symbol your dictionary uses as a pronunciation guide for this sound.

1. adverb _____   3. antonym _____   5. relax _____

2. hamburger _____   4. accent _____   6. contrast _____

Summary—Pronunciation of /æ/

The /æ/ sound is pronounced with the jaw lowered. The tongue is in the lowest front articulatory position for English vowels. The tongue and the jaw are lower for /æ/ than for /ɛ/, Vowel 4; the tongue is rounded and arched forward more for /æ/ than for /a/, Vowel 7. Use a mirror. Watch the movements for these three sounds: /ɛ/ /æ/ /a/.

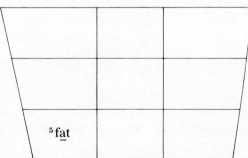

For more detailed articulatory information see the contrasts in Supplement C.

Resource Material

Part 1—Notes

The sound /æ/ is fourth in general usage among the fifteen vowel sounds.

The following is the major spelling pattern for /æ/:

    aC(C)   as in *fat*   97%

ESL interference / learning problems may include the following:

    a. Sound: a low central vowel /a/, as in *father*, may be used for the low front vowel /æ/; this may be a particular problem for students whose languages have the /a/ sound as the only low vowel sound

    b. Spelling: in many languages the letter *a* is pronounced with the sound /a/, as in *father*; this may lead to spelling/pronunciation confusion

Part 2—Major Spelling Pattern aC(C)

add	áfter	práctice	exámple
class	ánswer	lánguage	perháps
pass	básket	hándsome	understánd

Part 3—Other Spelling Patterns

Group 1   avV, axV
    trável   táxi
Group 2   auC[34]
    laugh   láughter   aunt

Part 4—Practice with /æ/ before Voiced / Voiceless Consonants

Ask students to practice these pairs of words with attention to lengthening the vowel before the voiced consonant—the first word in each pair. The lengthening mark (:) has been added to emphasize the lengthening before the voiced consonant. Add to the list.

1. c:ab   cap
2. la:b   lap
3. a:dd   at
4. ba:d   bat
5. sa:d   sat
6. ba:g   back
7. ra:g   rack
8. ha:ve   half

---

34. Many speakers of English use a sound between /æ/ and /a/ for these words.

Part 5—Practice with /eⁱ/—/æ/ Pairs of Words

Ask students to practice these pairs of words with attention to the alternation of Vowel 3, /eⁱ/, and Vowel 5, /æ/. Add to the list.

Vowel 3	Vowel 5
1. nation	national
2. nature	natural
3. Spain	Spanish
4. explain	explanatory

Lesson 8

Front Vowel Tests

Part 1—Discrimination[35] (AK/TS)

Directions: Listen to the following sentences. Draw a circle around the word (and vowel number) you think you hear.

Examples: Who bought the (paper——pepper)?   *Answer*: paper
                               3   4   3

          Who bought the (paper——pepper)?   *Answer*: pepper
                               3   4   4

These sentences will be given once, only.

1. I bought another (sheep—ship).
                          1   2

2. Do you have a (pain—pen)?
                       3   4

3. Who borrowed my (pan—pen)?
                          5   4

4. She has a new (pen—pin).
                       4   2

5. She's (sleeping—slipping).
                1   2

6. He (tasted—tested) it.
             3   4

7. I can smell the (leather—lather).
                          4   5

8. The waiter gave me the (bill—bell).
                                   2   4

9. Do you have a (pin—pain—pen—pan)?
                        2   3   4   5

10. Spell the word (seat—sit—set—sat).
                           1   2   4   5

Part 2—Spelling.[36] (AK/TS)

Directions: Put the following words in the correct column according to the vowel in their pronunciation. The teacher will *not* read the words.

(Lab: Stop the tape and complete part 2; allow 5 to 10 minutes.)

cat	easy	black	last	fish
these	rain	red	get	letter
little	test	may	gate	sang
table	big	green	she	six

Vowel 1	*Vowel 2*	*Vowel 3*	*Vowel 4*	*Vowel 5*
s<u>ee</u>	<u>i</u>t	s<u>ay</u>	y<u>e</u>s	f<u>a</u>t
___	___	___	___	___
___	___	___	___	___
___	___	___	___	___
___			___	___

35. *Lab:* At the end of part 1 stop the tape and ask students to give their answers. Write them on the chalkboard. Ask students to check their work. Replay this segment of the test for review.

36. *Lab:* At the end of part 2 stop the tape and ask students to give their answers. Write them on the chalkboard. Ask students to check their work. Pronounce them and discuss the spelling patterns.

Part 3—Test Sentences for Writing Vowel Numbers[37] (AK/TS)

Directions: Listen as the following words are pronounced. Write the number of the vowel below the line.

Vowel 1	/iʸ/	as in	see
Vowel 2	/ɪ/	as in	it
Vowel 3	/eⁱ/	as in	say
Vowel 4	/ɛ/	as in	yes
Vowel 5	/æ/	as in	fat

Repeat and write the vowel numbers.

1. He's sitting in my seat!

2. The lady set the pepper on the paper.

3. Which letter did Ted leave on the desk?

4. Betty would rather have a leather hat.

5. He put his ten sheep on the red ship.

6. Jim went to get six sandwiches and ten apples.

Part 4—Test Sentences for Self-Monitoring and Self-Testing

Directions: Practice the sentences in part 3 using natural rhythm, stress, and reductions. Exaggerate the sounds slightly. Record. Listen and monitor your pronunciation.

---

37. *Lab*: At the end of part 3 stop the tape and ask students to give the vowel numbers they have written. Replay this segment of the test and have students check their work.

Section C—Back Vowels

Section Notes

Section C has five lessons. Lessons 9, 10, and 11 present intensive listening/speaking practice with the three tense back vowels: /uʷ/, /oᵘ/, and /ɔ/. Lesson 12 presents similar practice with the one lax back vowel: /ʊ/. Lesson 13 presents a four-part self-evaluative test of back vowels. With this section the number of tense vowels is extended to five and the number of lax vowels is extended to four.

TENSE		
¹s<u>ee</u>		⁸tw<u>o</u>
³s<u>ay</u>		¹⁰n<u>o</u>
		¹¹l<u>aw</u>

LAX		
²<u>i</u>t		⁹b<u>oo</u>ks
⁴y<u>e</u>s		
⁵f<u>a</u>t		

As in section B, the tense/lax distinction has been selected for back vowel presentation. It is used as an aid in building student awareness of spelling, acoustic, and physiological similarities and dissimilarities. It also provides a useful framework for later work with spelling and word stress. Notes on the tense vowels (page 128) and the lax back vowel (page 140) are provided for more advanced classes. Teachers may wish only to paraphrase these notes briefly for some classes.

Teachers may wish to use the following diagrams and notes with students for a back vowel overview.

Many languages have only two back vowels, /u/ and /o/. English has /uʷ/ and /oᵘ/ (tense vowels) and two additional back vowels, /ɔ/ (tense) and /ʊ/ (lax) for a total of four back vowels.

Vowel 8 is a very high back vowel (tense).

    /uʷ/—tw<u>o</u>

Vowel 9 is a lower high back vowel (lax).

    /ʊ/—b<u>oo</u>ks

Vowel 10 is a mid back vowel (tense).

    /oᵘ/—n<u>o</u>

Vowel 11 is a low back vowel (tense).

    /ɔ/—l<u>aw</u>

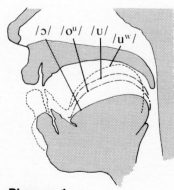

Diagram 1

Look at diagram 2.

The large symbols represent the two basic back vowels: /u/ and /o/.

The small symbols represent the four English back vowels: /u^w/, /o^u/, /ʊ/, and /ɔ/.

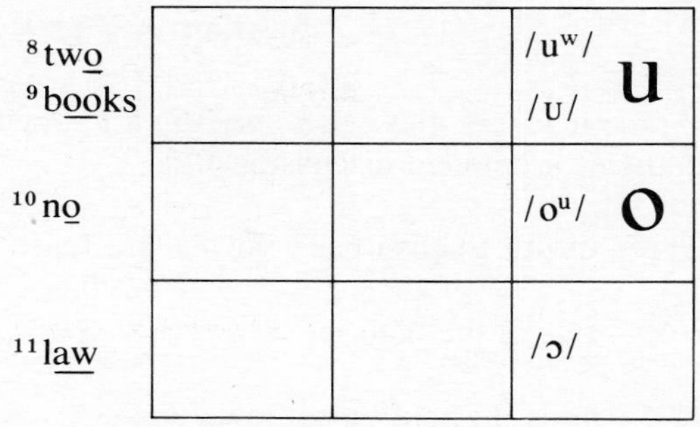

[8] tw<u>o</u> [9] b<u>oo</u>ks		/u^w/ **u** /ʊ/
[10] n<u>o</u>		/o^u/ **O**
[11] l<u>aw</u>		/ɔ/

Diagram 2

When students have completed the lessons in section C, practice material from Supplements B and C may be used to provide continued attention to the back vowels. Students should be encouraged to monitor their back vowel pronunciation during classroom speaking activities.

Notes on the Three Tense Back Vowels

(Some teachers may wish only to paraphrase these notes briefly at this time and return to them later in the course for detailed discussion.)

Three of the English back vowels are tense.[1]

/uʷ/—twọ is the high tense vowel

/oᵘ/—nọ is the mid tense vowel

/ɔ/—la̲w̲ is the low tense vowel

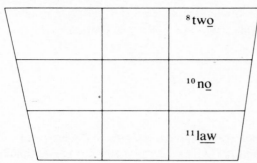

This extends the number of tense vowels to five: /iʸ/, /eⁱ/, /uʷ/, /oᵘ/, and /ɔ/.

In English the tense back vowels /uʷ/ and /oᵘ/ are not pronounced as single pure sounds, but are lengthened and slightly diphthongized. That is, in addition to the pure sound, they also have a second shorter sound. The length and the quality of this second shorter sound vary considerably according to the phonetic environment and the rhythm and stress pattern of the sentence. It is most noticeable in stressed syllables. In addition, /ɔ/, when pronounced by itself, may have a small glide toward the center position so we hear /ɔᵊ/. Awareness of this centering glide tendency for /ɔ/ may be helpful for some students who have difficulty in producing this sound. Diagrams 3, 4, and 5 show the tongue movements necessary to form the /uʷ/, /oᵘ/, and /ɔ/.

Some ESL students have difficulty with the lengthening and diphthongizing of /uʷ/ and /oᵘ/. Special attention should be given to this so that students learn to modify the pure /u/ and /o/ in order to achieve the special English pronunciation of /uʷ/ and /oᵘ/.

/uʷ/—**two**	/oᵘ/—**no**	/ɔ/—**law**
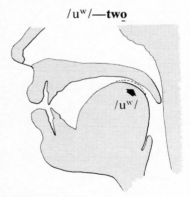	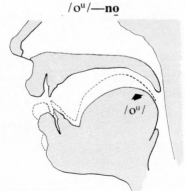	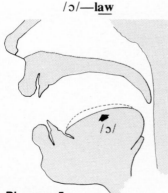

Diagram 3

The movement is a small one for /uʷ/. The tongue is pulled up a little closer to the roof of the mouth for /uʷ/.

Diagram 4

The movement is a larger one for /oᵘ/. In fact, the lower jaw is raised from half-open for /o/ to nearly closed for /u/.

Diagram 5

The tongue moves very slightly toward a centering position and the lips unround a little for /ɔ/.

These three sounds are *open* vowels. That is, they are found not only in an initial or medial position in a word, but also can come at the end of a word and leave the word open or without a final closing consonant.[2]

---

1. See footnote 1 on page 128 in section B for notes on tense vowels.
2. This is in contrast to lax back Vowel 9 (as in *books*) which is a closed vowel and must have a final or closing consonant following the vowel sound.

160

Examples: two   no   saw

          due   go   raw

          blue   slow   law

          new   grow

(Notice the letter *w* is pronounced as part of the vowel, not as a consonant.)

Lesson 9

Intensive Practice with Vowel 8—two /uʷ/

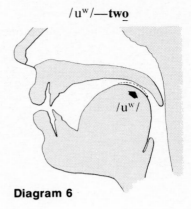

/uʷ/—two

Diagram 6

Part 1—Articulation

Vowel 8 is the highest back vowel. It is not a pure /u/ as in some languages. It has an /u/ followed by a /w/ glide: /uʷ/.[3] Practice these words: do noon two.

Part 2—Pronunciation Practice

Listen, watch, and practice. (Follow the linking lines (‿); shorten the unstressed weak words such as the, was, some.)

1. pool   The water in the pool is too cool!
   too
   cool

2. school   He'll be home from school at noon.
   noon

3. two   There are two new students.
   new
   stúdents

4. June   Please come in June or July.
   Julý

Practice each sentence again using natural rhythm, stress, and reductions. Exaggerate the /uʷ/ sounds slightly.

(Lab: Then stop the tape for a few minutes of individual practice and self-monitoring.)

Part 3—Reading / Listening Practice (AK/TS)

Read each sentence silently. Find the words which you would guess are pronounced with Vowel 8. Draw a line under these words.

1. I need a new blue suit. (Find 3 words with /uʷ/.)
2. Lou likes his new room. (3)
3. We met a group of students at the zoo. (3)
4. Sue wants some soup and some fruit. (3)

(Lab: Stop the tape and ask students to give their answers. Then start the tape and have students check their work as the words for each line are given.)

---

3. When /uʷ/ is in the middle of a word followed by a voiceless consonant, the glide (or diphthongization) is shorter and harder to hear. In unstressed syllables it may disappear altogether.

Practice the sentences using natural rhythm, stress, and reductions. Exaggerate the /uʷ/ sounds slightly.

(Lab: Stop the tape for a few minutes of individual practice and self-monitoring.)

Part 4—Dictation⁴ (AK/TS)

Four sentences will be dictated. Listen and repeat. Listen and write. Listen and check. Underline each occurrence of Vowel 8. Check your spelling.

1. _____ (8 words)

2. _____ (9)

3. _____ (7)

4. _____ (6)

(Lab: Stop the tape and ask students to read their /uʷ/ words. Then start the tape and have students check their work as the words for each line are given.)

Practice the sentences again using natural rhythm, stress, and reductions. Exaggerate the /uʷ/ sounds slightly.

(Lab: Stop the tape for a few minutes of individual practice and self-monitoring.)

Part 5—Spelling⁵ (AK/TS)

The /uʷ/ sound is the high tense back vowel. As a tense vowel, like front tense vowels /iʸ/ and /eⁱ/, the /uʷ/ can come at the end of a word and leave the word open—without a closing consonant. In spelling books /uʷ/ sometimes is called the "long *u*" sound. Many dictionaries use this symbol (ū) as the pronunciation guide for this sound. Listen and write. Repeat the words to yourself as you write.

Group 1   oo
               (In these words, the *oo* spelling is word-final, or before nasals *m* and *n*, or before *l*, *t*, *th*, *f*, or *se*.)⁶

   zoo   _____   _____   _____   _____   _____

             _____   _____

Group 2   u (including uC¢)
               (Write the following words and mark the accented syllable.)
   rúler   _____   _____   _____   June   _____
Group 3   o
   to   _____   _____

---

4. Write each sentence on the chalkboard as the students write it in their books. Ask students to identify the words with /uʷ/; underline each word and write *8* under it. Ask them to identify, by number, any other vowels studied in lessons 3 through 8.
5. Write the words in each group on the chalkboard as the students write them in their books. Stop after each group and discuss briefly.
6. Notice, however, that the words *wool*, *foot*, and *soot* are pronounced with Vowel 9, /ʊ/. Some speakers pronounce the words *roof* and *root* with Vowel 9, /ʊ/.

Group 4   ou

    you   _____   _____

Group 5   ew

    threw   _____   _____

Group 6   ue

    ávenue   _____   _____

Part 6—Test Sentences for Self-Monitoring and Self-Testing

Practice the following sentences using natural rhythm, stress, and reductions. Exaggerate the /u^w/ sounds slightly. Record. Listen and monitor your pronunciation.

1. We met a group of students at the zoo.
2. Sue wants some soup and some fruit.
3. I need a new blue suit.
4. I'll be home from school at noon.

Part 7—Dictionary Homework

Look up the following words in your dictionary. Copy the pronunciation exactly. Include the syllable accent marks. Notice the symbol your dictionary uses as a pronunciation guide for this sound.

1. argument _____   3. refuse _____   5. flu _____

2. February _____   4. approve _____   6. influenza _____

Summary—Pronunciation of /u^w/

The /u^w/ sound is pronounced with the tongue high, back, and tense. The tongue is pulled upward and backward toward the back part of the roof of the mouth. The lips are rounded. It is not a pure /u/ as in some languages. It has an /u/ followed by a /w/ glide: /u^w/   /u^w/. Compare /u^w/ with the highest front vowel /i^y/ which is made with the lips spread: /i^y/ → /u^w/   /i^y/ → /u^w/.

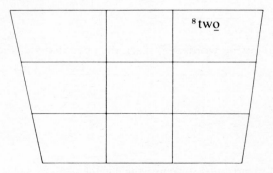

For more detailed articulatory information see the contrasts in Supplement C.

Resource Material

Part 1—Notes

The sound /uʷ/ is tenth in general usage among the fifteen vowel sounds.

The following are major spelling patterns for /uʷ/ with percentages for frequency of occurrence:

oo	as in *too*	38%
u	as in *rúler*	28.5% (including uC¢, 7.5%)
o	as in *do*	8%
ou	as in *you*	6%

ESL interference / learning problems may include the following:

a. Sound: a shorter pure sound /u/ may be used for /uʷ/

Part 2—Major Spelling Patterns

Group 1   oo[7]

room	too	pool
noon	zoo	fool
spoon	food	smooth
roof	root	tooth

Group 2   uCV

truth	stúdents
júnior	Julý
rúler	

Group 3   uC¢

June	rule	tune

Group 4   o

do	to	two
who	whom	

Group 5   ou

you	through	group

Part 3—Other Spelling Patterns

Group 1   ew

new	flew	threw
knew		

---

7. Some speakers use Vowel 9, /u/, for *roof* and *root*.

> *Group 2*   ue
>
>   blue   true   ávenue
>
> *Group 3*   oC¢
>
>   move   prove   whose
>
>   appróve   lose
>
> *Group 4*   ooC¢
>
>   loose   groove
>
> *Group 5*   uiC, uiC¢
>
>   suit   juice
>
> *Group 6*   oe
>
>   shoe

Part 4—Palatalization

In the following words the palatal sound /y/ *precedes* the /u^w/ sound for the combined pronunciation of /yu^w/.[8] Add to the list.

Word Initial	Syllable Initial after Alveolar Consonants *l*, *n*, *t*, and *d*		After Velars *c* /k/ and *g* and Labio-dentals *f* and *v*		After *h* and Labials *m*, *p*, and *b*	
use	válue	áctual	cure	fúture	huge	pure
úsual	mánual	grádual	cute	refúse	húmor	reputátion
úsually	Jánuary		árgue	view	músic	béauty
úniverse			régular	revúe	amúse	vocábulary
univérsity						

Part 5—Practice with /u^w/ before Voiced / Voiceless Consonants

Ask students to practice these pairs of words with attention to lengthening the vowel before the voiced consonant—the first word in each pair. The lengthening mark (:) has been added to emphasize the lengthening before the voiced consonant. Add to the list.

1. pro:ve   proof
2. ru:de   route
3. u:se (verb)   use (noun)
4. lo:se (verb; *s* = /z/)   loose (adjective; *s* = /s/)

---

8. Some speakers also palatalize the *u* following the alveolar consonants in *word initial* position: *t*, *d*, *n*, *l*, *s*, and *z*.

Lesson 10

Intensive Practice with Vowel 10—no /oᵘ/

Part 1—Articulation

/oᵘ/—no

Vowel 10 is the mid back vowel. It is not a pure /o/ as in some languages. It has an /o/ followed by a /u/ glide: /oᵘ/.[9] Practice these words: no own note.

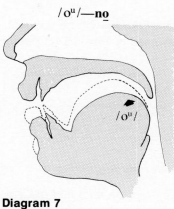

Diagram 7

Part 2—Pronunciation Practice

Listen, watch, and practice. (Follow the linking lines (‿); shorten the unstressed weak words such as the, was, some.)

1. wrote   I wrote him a note.   4. slow   This is a slow boat.
   note   boat

2. won't   I won't go!   5. old   I found an old yellow coat.
   go   yéllow

3. close   Please close the window.   coat
   window

Practice each sentence again using natural rhythm, stress, and reductions. Exaggerate the /oᵘ/ sound slightly.

(Lab: Stop the tape for a few minutes of individual practice and self-monitoring.)

Part 3—Reading / Listening Practice (AK/TS)

Read each sentence silently. Find the words which you would guess are pronounced with Vowel 10. Draw a line under these words.

1. Let's go to the show. (Find 2 words with /oᵘ/.)
2. Who owns that old yellow boat? (4)
3. I know those fellows stole the gold! (5)
4. Don't go swimming alone. (3)

(Lab: Stop the tape and ask students to give their answers. Then start the tape and have students check their work as the words for each line are given.)

---

9. When /oᵘ/ is in the middle of a word followed by a voiceless consonant, the glide (or diphthongization) is shorter and harder to hear. In unstressed syllables it may disappear altogether.

167

Practice the sentences using natural rhythm, stress, and reductions. Exaggerate the /oᵘ/ sound slightly.

(Lab: Stop the tape for a few minutes of individual practice and self-monitoring.)

Part 4—Dictation (AK/TS)

Four sentences will be dictated. Listen and repeat. Listen and write. Listen and check. Underline each occurrence of Vowel 10. Check your spelling.

1. _____ (7 words)

2. _____ (5)

3. _____ (5)

4. _____ (6)

(Lab: Stop the tape and ask students to read their /oᵘ/ words. Then start the tape and have the students check their work as the words for each line are given.)

Practice the sentences again using natural rhythm, stress, and reductions. Exaggerate the /oᵘ/ sounds slightly.

(Lab: Stop the tape for a few minutes of individual practice and self-monitoring.)

Part 5—Spelling (AK/TS)

The /oᵘ/ sound is the mid tense back vowel. As a tense vowel, like front tense vowels /iʸ/ and /eⁱ/ and back tense vowel /uʷ/, the /oᵘ/ can come at the end of a word and leave the word *open*—without a closing consonant. In spelling books /oᵘ/ sometimes is called the "long *o*" sound. Many dictionaries use this symbol (ō) as the pronunciation guide for this sound. Listen and write. Repeat the words to yourself as you write.

Group 1	o				
so	_____	_____	_____	_____	_____
Group 2	oC¢				
wrote	_____	_____	_____		
Group 3	ow				

(Write the following words and mark the accented syllable.)

slow	_____	_____	_____
Group 4	oaC		
road	_____	_____	_____

Part 6—Test Sentences for Self-Monitoring and Self-Testing

Practice the following sentences using natural rhythm, stress, and reductions. Exaggerate the /o^u/ sounds slightly. Record. Listen and monitor your pronunciation.

1. Joe broke his toe!
2. Please close the window.
3. Nobody answered the phone.
4. He sold the old boat.

Part 7—Dictionary Homework

Look up the following words in your dictionary. Copy the pronunciation exactly. Include the syllable accent marks. Notice the symbol your dictionary uses as a pronunciation guide for this sound.

1. hotel   _____   3. shoulder _____   5. although _____

2. November _____   4. radio _____   6. don't _____

Summary—Pronunciation of /o^u/

The /o^u/ sound is pronounced with the tongue mid, back, and tense. It is not a pure /o/ as in some languages. It has an /o/ followed by a glide to /u/. The lower jaw is raised from half-open for /o/ to nearly closed for /o^u/ : /o^u/   /o^u/. Compare /o^u/ with the mid front vowel /e^i/ : /e^i/ → /o^u/   /e^i/ → /o^u/.

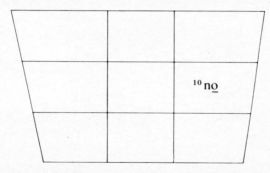

For more detailed articulatory information see the contrasts in Supplement C.

Resource Material

Part 1—Notes

The sound /o^u/ is ninth in general usage among the fifteen vowel sounds.

The following are major spelling patterns for /o^u/ with percentages for frequency of occurrence:

o	as in *no*	87% (including oC¢, 14%)
oaC	as in *road*	5%
ow	as in *show*	5%

ESL interference / learning problems may include the following:

a. Sound: a shorter pure sound /o/ may be used for /o^u/

Part 2—Major Spelling Patterns

Group 1   o, oCV, oCC (-old, -oth, -ost, -on't)

no	ópen	won't
go	most	don't
gold	sold	hold
ócean	both	

Group 2   oC¢

whole	alóne	close
broke	home	suppóse

Group 3   ow

row	féllow	show
wíndow	slow	belów

Group 4   oaC

road	load	coat
boat	soap	coal

Part 3—Other Spelling Patterns

Group 1   oul, ough

shóulder	althóugh	soul
though		

Group 2   oe

toe	Joe

Part 4—Practice with /oᵘ/ before Voiced/Voiceless Consonants

Ask students to practice these pairs of words with attention to lengthening the vowel before the voiced consonant—the first word in each pair. The lengthening mark (:) has been added to emphasize the lengthening before the voiced consonant. Add to the list.

1. ro:de   wrote
2. co:de   coat
3. clo:se (verb; $s = $ /z/)   close (adverb; $s = $ /s/)

Lesson 11

Intensive Practice with Vowel 11—law /ɔ/ [10]

Part 1—Articulation

Vowel 11 is the lowest back vowel. The jaw is lowered more than for Vowel 10. Do not confuse Vowel 10 with Vowel 11.[11] Listen to the difference: /oᵘ/ → /ɔ/   low → law. Practice these words: law   saw   caught.

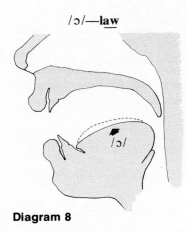

/ɔ/—law

Diagram 8

Part 2—Pronunciation Practice

Listen, watch, and practice. (Follow the linking lines (‿); shorten the unstressed weak words such as ~~the~~, ~~was~~, ~~some~~.)

1. saw   I saw him fall.
   fall
2. taught   He taught us a song.
   song
3. acróss   He lives across the hall.
   hall
4. long   We had a long talk.
   talk
5. lost   I lost my ball.
   ball

Practice each sentence again using natural rhythm, stress, and reductions. Exaggerate the /ɔ/ sounds slightly.

(Lab: Stop the tape for a few minutes of individual practice and self-monitoring.)

Part 3—Reading / Listening Practice (AK/TS)

Read each sentence silently. Find the words which you would guess are pronounced with Vowel 11. Draw a line under these words.

1. They went for a long walk. (Find 2 words with /ɔ/.)
2. The teacher taught us the wrong song. (3)

_____

10. Some speakers use Vowel 7 instead of Vowel 11 for many of the words in this lesson. If any of the pronunciations listed are different from those which you use, you are urged to make whatever changes necessary in the text and to discuss these differences with your students.
11. The tongue is pulled down and back for /ɔ/ followed by a slight centering glide toward /ə/. This distinction of a slight centering glide following /ɔ/, contrasted with an upward glide for /oᵘ/, may be a useful self-monitoring cue for some ESL students.

3. His daughter's office is across ~~the~~ hall. (4)

4. Be careful! Don't fall off ~~the~~ wall. (3)

(Lab: Stop the tape and ask students to give their answers. Then start the tape and have students check their work as the words for each line are given.)

Practice the sentences using natural rhythm, stress, and reductions. Exaggerate the /ɔ/ sounds slightly.

(Lab: Stop the tape for a few minutes of individual practice and self-monitoring.)

Part 4—Dictation (AK/TS)

Four sentences will be dictated. Listen and repeat. Listen and write. Listen and check. Underline each occurrence of Vowel 11. Check your spelling.

1. _____ (5 words)

2. _____ (4)

3. _____ (7)

4. _____ (4)

(Lab: Stop the tape and ask students to read their /ɔ/ words. Then start the tape and have students check their work as the words for each line are given.)

Practice the sentences again using natural rhythm, stress, and reductions. Exaggerate the /ɔ/ sounds slightly.

(Lab: Stop the tape for a few minutes of individual practice and self-monitoring.)

Part 5—Spelling (AK/TS)

The /ɔ/ sound is the low tense back vowel. As a tense vowel, like front tense vowels /iʸ/ and /eⁱ/ and back tense vowels /uʷ/ and /oᵘ/, the /ɔ/ can come at the end of a word and leave the word open—without a closing consonant. Many dictionaries use (ȯ) or (à) as the pronunciation guide for this sound. Listen and write. Repeat the words to yourself as you write.

(Notice the *o* spelling for /ɔ/ comes before the single voiced consonant *g*, before *ng* and *nk*, and before doubled *ss* and *ff*.)

Group 1   oC(C)

    dog   _____   _____   _____   _____

Group 2   alC (including the prefix *al* before a consonant)
                (Notice the *a* is pronounced /ɔ/ before doubled *ll*, *lk*, *lt*, or *ld*.)[12]

    call   _____   _____   _____   _____

Group 3   auC

    caught   _____   _____

---

12. Notice, however, that the *a* before *ll* in the word *shall* is pronounced with Vowel 5, /æ/.

Group 4   aw

saw   _____   _____

Group 5   ought
(not a usual spelling for /ɔ/; memorize these words)

ought   _____   _____

Part 6—Test Sentences for Self-Monitoring and Self-Testing

Practice the following sentences using natural rhythm, stress, and reductions. Exaggerate the /ɔ/ sounds slightly. Record. Listen and monitor your pronunciation.

1. The teacher taught us the wrong song.
2. They were talking in the hall.
3. I lost my dog.
4. We went for a long walk.

Part 7—Dictionary Homework

Look up the following words in your dictionary. Copy the pronunciation exactly. Include the syllable accent marks. Notice the symbol your dictionary uses as a pronunciation guide for this sound.

1. fought _____   3. August _____   5. off _____

2. almost _____   4. often _____   6. also _____

Summary—Pronunciation of /ɔ/

The /ɔ/ sound is pronounced with lowered jaw and tongue. The tongue is down and back in the lowest back articulatory position for English vowels. Compare low back /ɔ/ with low central /a/: /ɔ/ → /a/   /ɔ/ → /a/. Compare low back /ɔ/ with mid back /oᵘ/ which has an upward /u/ glide: /ɔ/ → /oᵘ/   /ɔ/ → /oᵘ/.

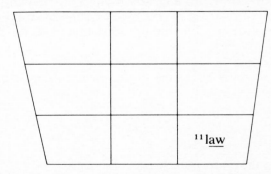

For more detailed articulatory information see the contrasts in Supplement C.

Resource Material

Part 1—Notes

The sound /ɔ/ is twelfth in general usage among the fifteen vowel sounds. Many speakers of General American English, however, use this sound in very few words. The sound /a/, Vowel 7, as in *father*, may be used for the words listed in this reference sheet. For comments on the pronunciation of /ɔ/ or /o/ before /ɝ/, see page 194 in lesson 14. The following are the major spelling patterns for /ɔ/ with percentages for frequency of occurrence:

oC(C)	as in *dog*	49%
alC	as in *call, also*	24%
auC	as in *caught*	19% (including auCȼ and augh)
aw	as in *law*	8%

ESL interference / learning problems may include the following:

a. Sound: many languages do not have a low back vowel similar to the /ɔ/ sound; the mid back vowel /o/, as in *no*, may be used for this low back sound, or the low central vowel /a/ may be used

b. Spelling: in many languages the letter *o* is pronounced with the sound /o/, as in *no*; this may lead to spelling/pronunciation confusion

c. Spelling: in many languages the letter *a* is pronounced with the sound /a/, as in *father*; this may lead to spelling/pronunciation confusion

Part 2—Major Spelling Patterns

Group 1   oC(C)

off	soft	dog	song
cross	lost	fog	wrong
loss	óften	log	honk

(The spelling *or* has not been included here. See page 193 in lesson 14.)

Group 2   alC

all	talk	álways
call	walk	álso
fall	bald	alréady

Group 3   auC, auCȼ, aught

Aúgust	aútograph	cause	taught
automátic	áutomobile	becáuse	caught
			dáughter

Group 4   aw

law	saw	láwyer
draw	dawn	

175

Part 3—Other Spelling Patterns

Group 1   ought

ought	thought	fought
bought	brought	sought

Group 2   oaC

broad

Group 3   oC¢

gone

(The spellings *or¢* and *orC¢* have not been included. See page 193 in lesson 14.)

Part 4—Practice with /ɔ/ before Voiced/Voiceless Consonants

1. saw:ed	sought
2. broa:d	brought
3. thaw:ed	thought
4. law:s (*s* = /z/)	loss (*ss* = /s/)
5. caw:ed	caught

Notes on the Lax Back Vowel

(Some teachers may wish only to paraphrase these notes briefly at this time and return to them later in the course for detailed discussion.)

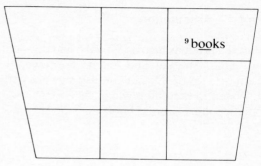

One of the English back vowels is lax.[13] The /ʊ/, as in *books*, is a high lax back vowel. This extends the number of lax vowels to four: /ɪ/, /ɛ/, /æ/, and /ʊ/.

As the phonetic symbol above shows, this sound has only one part. However, when pronounced by itself, it may have a small glide toward the center position so we hear: /ʊᵊ/. Awareness of this centering glide tendency may be helpful for some students in distinguishing between /uʷ/ and /ʊ/.[14]

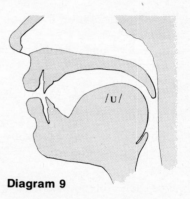

Diagram 9

The /ʊ/ is a *closed* vowel. That is, it cannot come at the end of a word (when stressed) and leave the word *open*. It must be followed by one or more consonants which close the word.[15]

Examples: pull   book   could
           push   foot   would

---

13. See footnote 26 on page 140 in section B for notes on lax vowels.

14. This tendency varies according to phonetic environment and the patterns of stress, rhythm, and intonation. There also is considerable variation from speaker to speaker.

15. This is in contrast to tense back Vowels 8 (as in *two*), 10 (as in *no*), and 11 (as in *law*) which can come at the end of a word without a closing consonant.

Lesson 12

Intensive Practice with Vowel 9—b<u>oo</u>ks /ʊ/

Part 1—Articulation

Vowel 9 is not as high as Vowel 8 and does not have a
/w/ glide. The jaw and tongue are lowered slightly
from /uʷ/ to /ʊ/. Do not confuse Vowel 8 with Vowel
9. Listen to the difference: /uʷ/ → /ʊ/ tw<u>o</u> b<u>oo</u>ks.
Practice these words: b<u>oo</u>k   st<u>oo</u>d   p<u>u</u>t.

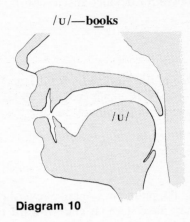

/ʊ/—b<u>oo</u>ks

Diagram 10

Part 2—Pronunciation Practice

Listen, watch, and practice. (Follow the linking lines (‿); shorten the unstressed words such as ~~the~~,
~~was, some~~.)

1. g<u>oo</u>d   My‿Mom's‿a good‿cook.
   c<u>oo</u>k

2. t<u>oo</u>k   Who‿took‿my‿book?
   b<u>oo</u>k

3. sh<u>ou</u>ld   We‿should‿buy‿~~some~~‿sugar.
   súgar

4. w<u>ou</u>ld   ~~Would‿you~~‿like‿a‿cookie?
   c<u>óo</u>kie

Practice each sentence again using natural rhythm, stress, and reductions. Exaggerate the /ʊ/ sound slightly.

(Lab: Stop the tape for a few minutes of individual practice and self-monitoring.)

Part 3—Reading / Listening Practice (AK/TS)

Read each sentence silently. Find the words which you would guess are pronounced with Vowel 9. Draw a
line under these words.

1. He shouldn't put ~~his~~ foot on ~~the~~ table. (Find 3 words with /ʊ/.)

2. Where should I put ~~the~~ wood? (3)

3. ~~The~~ boy stood on one foot. (2)

4. Put ~~the~~ books on ~~the~~ table. (2)

*(Lab: Stop the tape and ask students to give their answers. Then start the tape and have students check their
work as the words for each line are given.)*

Practice the sentences using natural rhythm, stress, and reductions. Exaggerate the /ʊ/ sounds slightly.

(Lab: Stop the tape for a few minutes of individual practice and self-monitoring.)

Part 4—Dictation (AK/TS)

Four sentences will be dictated. Listen and repeat. Listen and write. Listen and check. Underline each occurrence of Vowel 9. Check your spelling.

1. _____ (8 words)

2. _____ (6)

3. _____ (9)

4. _____ (6)

(Lab: Stop the tape and ask students to read their /ʊ/ words. Then start the tape and have students check their work as the words for each line are given.)

Practice the sentences again using natural rhythm, stress, and reductions. Exaggerate the /ʊ/ sounds slightly.

(Lab: Stop the tape for a few minutes of individual practice and self-monitoring.)

Part 5—Spelling (AK/TS)

The /ʊ/ sound is the only lax back vowel. As a lax vowel, like front lax vowels /ɪ/, /ɛ/, and /æ/, the /ʊ/ cannot come at the end of a word, when stressed, and leave the word open; it must be followed by one or more consonants which close the word. Many dictionaries use this symbol (u̇) as the pronunciation guide for this sound. Listen and write. Repeat the words to yourself as you write.

Group 1   uC(C)
           (Notice the *u* spelling is pronounced /ʊ/ before doubled *ll* in *pull* and *full* and before *sh* in these words.)[16]

   put   _____   _____   _____   _____

Group 2   ooC
           (Notice the *oo* spelling is before plosive consonants *d* and *k* in these words.)[17]

   good   _____   _____   _____

Group 3   ould
           (Notice these are the strong forms of these words. See Unit 1, lesson 9, for discussion of strong/weak forms.)

   should   _____   _____   _____   _____

Part 6—Test Sentences for Self-Monitoring and Self-Testing

Practice the following sentences using natural rhythm, stress, and reductions. Exaggerate the /ʊ/ sounds slightly. Record. Listen and monitor your pronunciation.

1. Who took my book?
2. Put the sugar on the table.

---

16. Notice, however, that the *u* before *ll* in the words *dull, cull, null,* and *mull* is pronounced with Vowel 6, /ʌ/.
17. Notice, however, that the words *food* and *brood* are pronounced with Vowel 8, /uʷ/, and the words *blood* and *flood* are pronounced with Vowel 6, /ʌ/.

3. Where should I put the wood?

4. I couldn't find the cookies.

Part 7—Dictionary Homework

Look up the following words in your dictionary. Copy the pronunciation exactly. Include the syllable accent marks. Notice the symbol your dictionary uses as a pronunciation guide for this sound.

1. woman _____

3. sugar _____

5. cushion _____

2. shouldn't _____

4. undertook _____

6. bushel _____

Summary—Pronunciation of /ʊ/

The /ʊ/ sound is pronounced with the back of the tongue quite high but lax and the lips rounded only a little. It does not have the /w/ glide of /uʷ/. Feel the difference: /uʷ/ → /ʊ/   /uʷ/ → /ʊ/.

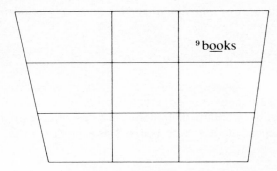

For more detailed articulatory information see the contrasts in Supplement C.

Resource Material

The sound /ʊ/ is thirteenth in general usage among the fifteen vowel sounds.

The following are major spelling patterns for /ʊ/ with percentages for frequency of occurrence:

uC(C)	as in *push*	54%
ooC	as in *book*	31%
ould	as in *could*	7%

ESL interference / learning problems may include the following:

a. Sound: a *pure* tense vowel /u/ may be used for the lax /ʊ/

b. Spelling: in many languages the letter *u* is pronounced with the sound /u/, as in *two*; this may lead to spelling/pronunciation confusion

c. Spelling: the double *oo* spelling pattern of English leads to spelling/pronunciation confusion although some general rules may be studied (see the spelling sections of lessons 9 and 12)

Part 2—Major Spelling Patterns

Group 1   uC(C)

push	pull	cúshion
bush	full	
put	súgar	

Group 2   ooC

took	cook	good
look	shook	wood
book	wool	stood
cóokie	foot	

Group 3   ould

should	could	would
shóuldn't	cóuldn't	wóuldn't

Part 3—Exception

wóman

Lesson 13

Back Vowel Tests

Part 1—Discrimination[18] (AK/TS)

Directions: Listen to the following sentences. Draw a circle around the word (and vowel number) you think you hear.

Examples: I was (cold—called).   *Answer*: cold
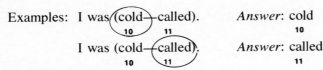
            10   11   10

           I was (cold—called).   *Answer*: called
            10   11   11

These sentences will be given once, only.

1. It was a golden (hawk—hook)!
                    11   9

2. He's in the (low—law) school.
              10   11

3. It was a long (pull—pool).
               9   8

4. Who paid for the (wool—wall)?
                  9   11

5. Mr. White is very (bold—bald)!
                 10   11

6. The (suit—soot) was black.
           8   9

7. It isn't (Fall—full) yet!
           11   9

8. Whose (bowl—ball) is this?
          10   11

9. It looks (fullish—foolish)!
         9   8

10. Spell the word (pool—pull—pole—Paul).
           8   9   10   11

11. Spell the word (cooed—could—code—cawed).
           8   9   10   11

12. Spell the word (bull—bowl—ball).
           9   10   11

Part 2—Spelling.[19] (AK/TS)

Directions: Put the following words in the correct column according to the vowel in their pronunciation. The teacher will *not* read the words.

(Lab: Stop the tape and complete part 2; allow 5 to 10 minutes.)

school	caught	push	talk	pull
ball	could	pole	you	bold
bull	boot	rule	long	taught
cold	code	rose	do	would

Vowel 8	*Vowel 9*	*Vowel 10*	*Vowel 11*
tw<u>o</u>	b<u>oo</u>ks	n<u>o</u>	l<u>aw</u>
_____	_____	_____	_____
_____	_____	_____	_____
_____	_____	_____	_____
_____	_____	_____	_____
_____	_____	_____	_____

---

18. *Lab*: At the end of part 1 stop the tape and ask students to give their answers. Write them on the chalkboard and have students check their work. Replay this segment of the test for review.

19. *Lab*: At the end of part 2 stop the tape and ask students to give their answers. Write them on the chalkboard and have students check their work. Pronounce them and discuss the spelling patterns.

Part 3—Test Sentences for Writing Vowel Numbers[20] (AK/TS)

Directions: Listen as the following words are pronounced. Write the number of the vowel below the line.

Vowel 8	/uʷ/	as in	tw<u>o</u>
Vowel 9	/ʊ/	as in	b<u>oo</u>ks
Vowel 10	/oᵘ/	as in	n<u>o</u>
Vowel 11	/ɔ/	as in	l<u>aw</u>

Repeat and write the vowel numbers.

1. Wh<u>o</u> t<u>oo</u>k my g<u>oo</u>d n<u>ew</u> c<u>oo</u>kb<u>oo</u>k?

2. The l<u>aw</u>yer's d<u>augh</u>ter is a g<u>oo</u>d c<u>oo</u>k!

3. We t<u>oo</u>k a l<u>o</u>ng w<u>a</u>lk in the w<u>oo</u>ds.

4. I th<u>ough</u>t P<u>au</u>l was g<u>o</u>ing h<u>o</u>me.

5. W<u>oo</u>dy pushed L<u>ou</u>ie into the p<u>oo</u>l!

6. D<u>o</u>n't g<u>o</u> 'til the l<u>aw</u>yer c<u>a</u>lls!

Part 4—Test Sentences for Self-Monitoring and Self-Testing

Directions: Practice the sentences in part 3 using natural rhythm, stress, and reductions. Exaggerate the sounds slightly. Record. Listen and monitor your pronunciation.

---

20. *Lab*: At the end of part 3 stop the tape and ask students to give the vowel numbers they have written. Replay this segment of the test and have students check their work.

Section D—Central Vowels

Section Notes

Section D has four lessons. Lesson 14, 15, and 16 present intensive listening/speaking practice with the central vowels: *vowel-r* /ɝ/, lax /ʌ/, and tense /a/. Lesson 17 presents a four-part self-evaluative test of central vowels.

The lax/tense distinction is used in the presentation of /ʌ/ and /a/; the vowel-r /ɝ/ is not designated as either tense or lax. With this section the number of tense vowels is extended to six and the number of lax vowels is extended to five.

	TENSE	
¹ s<u>ee</u>		⁸ tw<u>o</u>
³ s<u>ay</u>		¹⁰ n<u>o</u>
	⁷ st<u>o</u>p	¹¹ l<u>aw</u>

	LAX	
² <u>i</u>t		⁹ b<u>oo</u>ks
⁴ y<u>e</u>s		⁶ b<u>u</u>s
	⁵ f<u>a</u>t	

Notes on each of the three central vowels are provided for more advanced classes, on page 185, 194, and 200. Teachers may wish only to paraphrase these notes briefly for some classes. Teachers may wish to use the following diagrams and notes with students for a central vowel overview.

Many languages have only one central vowel, /a/. General American English has /a/ (tense) and two additional central vowels, /ʌ/ (lax) and vowel-*r*, for a total of three central vowels.

Vowel 12 is a high central vowel.

    /ɝ/—bi<u>r</u>d

Vowel 6 is a mid central vowel (lax).

    /ʌ/—b<u>u</u>s

Vowel 7 is a low central vowel (tense).

    /a/—st<u>o</u>p

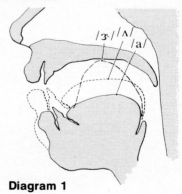

Diagram 1

Look at diagram 2.

The large symbol represents the one basic central vowel: /a/.

The small symbols represent the three English central vowels: /ɝ/, /ʌ/, and /a/.

When students have completed the lessons in section D, practice material from Supplements B and C may be used to provide continued attention to the central vowels. Students should be encouraged to monitor their central vowel pronunciation during classroom speaking activities.

¹² bi<u>r</u>d		/ɝ/	
⁶ b<u>u</u>s		/ʌ/	
⁷ st<u>o</u>p f<u>a</u>ther		/a/ **a**	

Diagram 2

Notes on the High Central Vowel-r

(Some teachers may wish only to paraphrase these notes briefly at this time and return to them later in the course for detailed discussion.)

The /ɝ/, as in *bird*, is the high *central* vowel of English. It is similar to the high *front* vowel, /iʸ/, and the high *back* vowel, /uʷ/, in three ways.

1. Each has the highest position in the three sets of vowels, the front vowels, the back vowels, the central vowels.

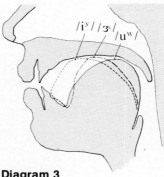

   a. For /iʸ/—s<u>ee</u>, the tongue is pulled up close to the *front* part of the roof of the mouth.

   b. For /ɝ/—b<u>i</u>rd, the tongue is pulled up close to the *center* part of the roof of the mouth.

   c. For /uʷ/—tw<u>o</u>, the tongue is pulled up close to the *back* part of the roof of the mouth.

Diagram 3

Practice silently, then aloud; feel the movement: /iʸ/ → /ɝ/ → /uʷ/.

2. Each of these three vowels has a matching consonant. These three consonants are the vocalic or semivowel consonants. Try the following gliding technique to move from the vowel to the matching vocalic consonant *without* putting in a hard articulatory contact. This gliding technique may be especially helpful for students who use a trilled or tapped *r* for /ɝ/, or a /dʒ/ before /y/, or a /g/ before /w/.

   a. Consonant *y*, as in *you*, matches vowel /iʸ/.
      Practice silently, then aloud: s<u>ee</u> : <u>y</u>ou.

   b. Consonant *r*, as in *room*, matches vowel /ɝ/.
      Practice silently, then aloud: he<u>r</u> : <u>r</u>oom.

   c. Consonant *w*, as in *weeks*, matches vowel /uʷ/.
      Practice silently, then aloud: tw<u>o</u> : <u>w</u>eeks.

FRONT	CENTRAL	BACK
/iʸ/	/ɝ/	/uʷ/
Vowel 1	**Vowel 12**	**Vowel 8**

3. All three sounds are open vowels. That is, they can come at the end of a word and leave the word open or without a final consonant sound.

Examples:	/iʸ/	/ɝ/	/uʷ/
	m<u>e</u>	he<u>r</u>	tw<u>o</u>
	s<u>ee</u>	si<u>r</u>	sh<u>oe</u>
	t<u>ea</u>	fu<u>r</u>	bl<u>ue</u>

   In the words *her*, *sir*, and *fur*, the vowel before the *r* sound is silent. They are pronounced as if they were spelled: *h'r, s'r, f'r*.

Some students have particular difficulty with /ɝ/. It often is omitted by ESL students, or a trilled or tapped *r* is used instead. See the Summary—Pronunciation of /ɝ/ on page 189 for some self-monitoring cues.

Vowel-*r* is hard for some students to pronounce when it comes just *before* the sound /l/, as in curl, girl, and Earl. Try slow careful attention to sliding the tongue forward from the *center* to the *front* of the roof of the mouth for r‿‿‿l, cur‿l, cur‿l. (The velar /k/ in *curl* helps get the tongue into position for /ɝ/.)

Vowel-*r* is hard for some students to pronounce when it comes just *after* the sound /l/, as in lurk. Try slow careful attention to sliding the tongue back from the *front* to the *center* of the roof of the mouth for l‿‿‿rk, l‿rk, l‿rk.

Lesson 14

Intensive Practice with Vowel 12—bird /ɝ/

Part 1—Articulation[1]

Vowel 12 is the high central vowel, /ɝ/, the vowel-*r* sound. The /ɝ/ is made with the tongue in the same position as for the consonant sound. The tongue is pulled up high close to the center of the hard roof of the mouth.[2] In these words the vowel before the sound is *silent*: b~~i~~rd w~~o~~rk h~~e~~r. They are pronounced as if they were spelled: *b'rd* *w'rk* *h'r.* Practice these words: bird work her.

/ɝ/—**bird**

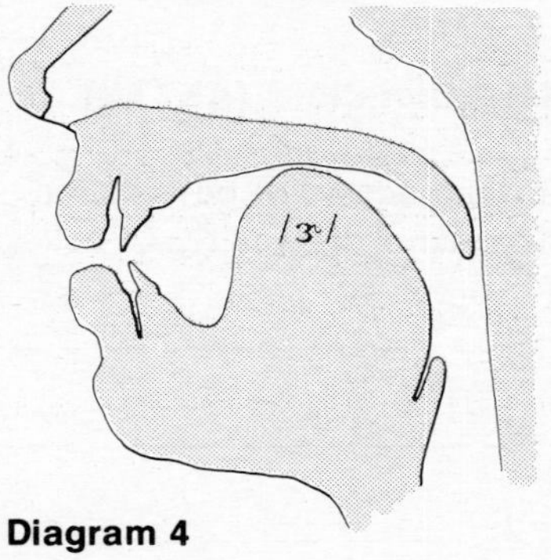

Diagram 4

Part 2—Pronunciation Practice

Listen, watch, and practice. (Follow the linking lines (‿); shorten the unstressed weak words such as ~~the~~, ~~was~~, ~~some~~.)

1. síster, téacher — My‿sister‿is‿~~a~~‿teacher.
2. nurse, her, purse — ~~The~~‿nurse‿lost‿~~her~~‿purse.
3. thírty, birds — I‿saw‿thirty‿birds.
4. works, church — He‿works‿~~at~~‿~~the~~‿church.

Practice each sentence again using natural rhythm, stress, and reductions. Exaggerate the /ɝ/ sounds slightly.

(Lab: Stop the tape for a few minutes of individual practice and self-monitoring.)

Part 3—Reading / Listening Practice (AK/TS)

Read each sentence silently. Find the words which you would guess are pronounced with Vowel 12. Draw a line under these words.

1. ~~The~~ nurse burned ~~the~~ shirt. (Find 3 words with /ɝ/.)
2. It's ~~a~~ modern church. (2)
3. Learn thirty new words. (3)
4. Thirty purple birds were sitting on ~~the~~ curb. (5)

---

1. It is especially important to encourage students to use pronunciation mirrors to help them to visualize the articulation of /ɝ/. Encourage them to listen to the sound and to feel the movement of the tongue. For students who have difficulty in forming /ɝ/, see the notes on pronunciation at the end of this lesson. For students who have difficulty with *r* and *l*, the notes on page 186 may be helpful.
2. Some speakers form the /ɝ/ in an alternative manner with the tip and front of the tongue down and only the mid portion of the tongue bunched up toward the hard roof of the mouth.

(Lab: Stop the tape and ask students to give their answers. Then start the tape and have students check their work as the words for each line are given.)

Practice the sentences using natural rhythm, stress, and reductions. Exaggerate the /ɝ/ sounds slightly.

(Lab: Stop the tape for a few minutes of individual practice and self-monitoring.)

Part 4—Dictation[3] (AK/TS)

Four sentences will be dictated. Listen and repeat. Listen and write. Listen and check. Underline each occurrence of Vowel 12. Check your spelling.

1. _____ (5 words)

2. _____ (6)

3. _____ (6)

4. _____ (5)

(Lab: Stop the tape and ask students to read their /ɝ/ words. Then start the tape and have students check their work as the words for each line are given.)

Practice the sentences again using natural rhythm, stress, and reductions. Exaggerate the /ɝ/ sounds slightly.

(Lab: Stop the tape for a few minutes of individual practice and self-monitoring.)

Part 5—Spelling (AK/TS)

The vowel /ɝ/ is the high central vowel-*r* sound. It can occur in all three word positions, initial, medial, and final. Many dictionaries use this symbol (ər) as their pronunciation guide for the sound /ɝ/. Listen and write. Repeat the words to yourself as you write.

Group 1	er(C)		
her	_____	_____	_____
Group 2	ur(C)		
fur	_____	_____	_____
Group 3	ir(C)		
sir	_____	_____	_____
Group 4	or(C)		
world	_____	_____	_____
Group 5	earC		

(Notice the C is obligatory in this pattern; the *ea* is silent and only the /ɝ/ is pronounced before the following consonant.)

heard	_____	_____	_____

---

3. Write each sentence on the chalkboard as the students write it in their books. Ask students to identify the words with /ɝ/; underline each word and write 12 under it. Ask them to identify, by number, any other vowels studied in lessons 3 through 13.

Part 6—Test Sentences for Self-Monitoring and Self-Testing

Practice the following sentences using natural reductions. Exaggerate the /ɝ/ sounds slightly. Record. Listen and monitor your pronunciation.

1. Dinner is served.
2. I heard a bird singing.
3. I never work on Thursday.
4. My sister bought a purple skirt.

Part 7—Dictionary Homework

Look up the following words in your dictionary. Copy the pronunciation exactly. Include the syllable accent marks. Notice the symbol your dictionary uses as its pronunciation guide for the sound /ɝ/.

1. earthquake _____
2. furniture _____
3. earnest _____
4. Thursday _____
5. certain _____
6. curtain _____

Summary—Pronunciation of /ɝ/

The /ɝ/, vowel-r, is made with the tongue in the same position as for the English consonant-r sound. The tongue is pulled up high and bunched close to the center of the hard roof of the mouth. The sides of the tongue touch the backs of the upper back teeth. The front and the tip of the tongue are pointed upward, and, for some speakers a little backward: /ɝ/   /ɝ/.

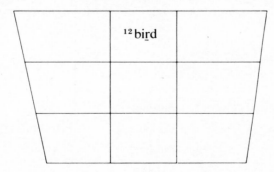

Special Notes for /ɝ/
1. Use a mirror. Try the following in order to feel the tongue position for /ɝ/: begin with the velar sound /g/, keep the tongue in nearly the same place but change the sound to /ɝ/. Repeat: g:rrrrr   g:rrrrr.

2. Use a mirror. Try the following in order to feel the way the air stream passes over the tongue to make the /ɝ/: begin with the sound of *sh*, /ʃ/, continue making the sound, slowly slide the tongue back, change the sound to /ɝ/. Repeat: sh:rrrrr   sh:rrrrr. (In making /ɝ/, a shallow grooving in the front and the tip of the tongue is formed near the roof of the mouth. This grooving is similar to that of the sibilant sound *sh*, /ʃ/.)

3. Some speakers form the /ɝ/ in an alternative manner with the tip and front down and only the mid portion of the tongue bunched up toward the hard roof of the mouth.

Resource Material

Part 1— Notes

The sound of syllabic or vowel-*r*, /ɝ/, is third highest in general usage among the fifteen vowel sounds.

The following are major spelling patterns with percentages for frequency of occurrence:

Stressed				*Unstressed*[4]	
er	as in *her*	40%	er	as in *father*	77%
ur	as in *fur*	26%	or	as in *actor*	12%
ir	as in *sir*	13%			
or	as in *work*	7%			

ESL interference / learning problems may include the following:

a. Sound: some languages have a consonant-*r* sound, which is a trilled or tapped *r*, but do not have a syllabic vowel-*r*; the consonant-*r* sound may be used for the syllabic vowel-*r* sound /ɝ/

b. Sound: some languages have no *r*-colored central vowel;[5] a mid or high *r*-less central vowel may be used for /ɝ/

c. Sound: some students have particular difficulty with words in which *r* is preceded or followed by *l*; see page 186 for special notes

d. Spelling: some students may need special help in learning to omit the vowel preceding the *r* in order to avoid pronunciations such as /ɛɝθ/ for /ɝθ/ in the word *earth*

Part 2— Major Spelling Patterns

Group 1 ̶er(C)

her	pérson	percént	páper
fern	cértain	perháps	óther
term	sérvice	módern	óver
err	preféŕ	páttern	síster

Group 2 ̶ur(C)

fur	church	púrpose	retúrn
hurt	nurse	cúrtain	occúr
turn	purse	Thúrsday	surpríse
burn	curl[6]	húrry[7]	surróund

---

4. The phonetic symbol for unstressed vowel -*r* is /ɚ/.
5. Some dialects of English, both British and American, have no *r*-colored central vowel. Students who have studied English with speakers of these dialects must decide whether or not they wish to add the /ɝ/ sound to their personal dialect.
6. The /ɝ/ before /l/ (as in *curl* in group 2 and *world* in group 5) is difficult for some students. The notes on page 186 may be helpful in giving them self-monitoring cues.
7. Some speakers pronounce *hurry* and *surround* in group 2, *worry* in group 5, and others like them with the /ʌ/ sound before the *r*. Example: /hʌrɪ/.

Group 3 ur¢

(These words have an unaccented syllable spelled *ure*; the *u* is silent and the preceding consonant is palatalized before the vowel-*r* sound.)

pléasure	cápture	méasure	pícture
tréasure	fúture	ínjure	

Group 4 ir(C)

sir	shirt	bird	skirt
firm	thírty	girl	dírty
first	círcle	third	confírm

Group 5 ør(C)

word	work	worm	worse
worth	world	wórry	cólor
áctor	dóctor	néighbor	vísitor
hónor	informátion		

Part 3—Other Spelling Patterns

Group 1 ¢arC

(In these words the *ea* is silent and only the /ɝ/ is pronounced before the following consonant. Notice the C is obligatory in this pattern.)

earn	earth	eárthquake
heard	learn	eárly

Group 2 ár(C)

áltar	dóllar	cóllar	cóward
éastward	báckward	símilar	régular

Group 3 øur

glámour

Group 4 i¢r

sóldier

Group 5 Exception

were

Resource Material

Syllabic Vowel-*r* Following Other Vowels

^{1} /iʸ/ *or* ^{2} /ɪ/	^{12} /ɝ/	^{8} /uʷ/ *or* ^{9} /ʊ/
^{3} /eⁱ/ *or* ^{4} /ɛ/		^{10} /oᵘ/ *or*
	^{7} /a/	^{11} /ɔ/

Part 1—Notes

The pronunciation of vowels in combination with the vowel-*r* sound /ɝ/ varies among speakers of English. This vowel box shows five vowel areas; one sound from each is combined with the /ɝ/. In four of the five areas speakers use *either* the higher or the lower sound or one which is somewhere between the two. Teachers may want to discuss these individual differences with their students.

The pronunciation of the three diphthongs in combination with the vowel-*r* sound is also marked by variation among speakers.

Part 2—Vowels in Combination with Vowel-*r*

Group 1   Vowel 1 /iʸ/ or Vowel 2 /ɪ/ + /ɝ/

/iʸ/ ⎫
      ⎬ + /ɝ/
/ɪ/ ⎭

ear	erɇ	eer
hear	here	beer
dear		deer
near		cheer
tear (*noun*)		
fear		
ear		

Group 2   Vowel 3 /eⁱ/ or Vowel 4 /ɛ/ + /ɝ/

/eⁱ/ ⎫
      ⎬ + /ɝ/
/ɛ/ ⎭

air	arɇ	ear	erɇ	eir	ar(r)	er(r)
hair	bare	bear	there	their	Máry	véry
pair	share	wear	where	heir	márry	mérry
fair	fare	tear (*verb*)			cárry	
chair	care					

Group 3   Vowel 7 /a/ + /ɝ/

/a/ + /ɝ/

ar		arge	arɇ
art	part	large	are
park	dark	barge	aren't
far	car		
start	star		

192

Group 4   Vowel 8 /uʷ/ or Vowel 9 /ʊ/ + /ɝ/

(The words spelled with *ure* and *ur* and pronounced /uʷ/ or /ʊ/ + /ɝ/ are preceded by /y/—palatalization of the consonant.)

/uʷ/	our	oor	ure	ur
} + /ɝ/	pour	poor	sure	fúry
/ʊ/	tour		pure	búreau
			cure	

Group 5   Vowel 10 /oᵘ/ or Vowel 11 /ɔ/ + /ɝ/

/oᵘ/	or̵e	or	ar	our
} + /ɝ/	pore	or	war	four
/ɔ/	more	for	ward	source
	tore	stóry	wart	course
	shore	form		
	store	storm		
	befóre	horse		

Part 3—Diphthongs in Combination with Vowel-*r*[8]

Group 1   Vowel 13 /ai/ + /ɝ/

/ai/ + /ɝ/	ire	er
	fire	crýer
	hire	hígher
	retíre	buýer
	tire	

Group 2   Vowel 14 /au/ + /ɝ/

/au/ + /ɝ/	our	ower
	flour	flówer
	hour	pówer
	our	tówer
		shówer

Group 3   Vowel 15 /ɔi/ + /ɝ/

/ɔi/ + /ɝ/	oyer
	Bóyer
	cóyer

---

8. Some speakers make a more definite two-syllable distinction in pronouncing the words in the second column in groups 1 and 2.

Notes on the Mid Central Vowel

(Some teachers may wish only to paraphrase these notes briefly at this time and return to them later in the course for detailed discussion.)

The /ʌ/, as in *bus*, is the mid central vowel. It is called the mid-central neutral vowel because it is not front, back, high, nor low, but in the middle of the pronunciation area. The /ʌ/ is a lax vowel. This completes the set of five lax vowels: /ɪ/, /ɛ/, /æ/, /ʊ/ and /ʌ/.[9]

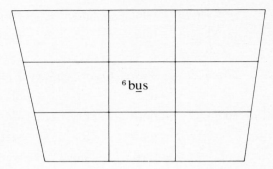

As the phonetic symbol shows, this sound has only one part.

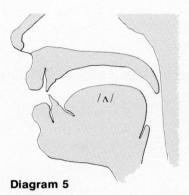

Diagram 5

The /ʌ/ is a *closed* vowel. That is, it cannot come at the end of a word (when stressed) and leave the word open. It must be followed by one or more consonants which close the word.

Examples: bus   run   jump
           sun   son   young

---

9. The vowel /ʌ/ has a weak form schwa, /ə/, which is used in unstressed reduced syllables and reduced words as studied in lessons 5 and 9 of Unit 1.

Lesson 15
Intensive Practice with Vowel 6—b<u>u</u>s /ʌ/

Part 1—Articulation

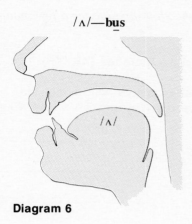

/ʌ/—b<u>u</u>s

Vowel 6 is the mid central vowel. The tongue is in a mid position and the jaw is partly raised for /ʌ/. Do not confuse /ʌ/ with high Vowel 12, /ɝ/. Feel the tongue rise from mid to high for /ɝ/. Repeat: /ʌ/ → /ɝ/   /ʌ/ → /ɝ/. Do not confuse /ʌ/ with low Vowel 7, /a/. Feel the jaw lower from /ʌ/ to /a/. Repeat: /ʌ/ → /a/   /ʌ/ → /a/. Practice these words: b<u>u</u>s   s<u>u</u>n   r<u>u</u>n.

Diagram 6

Part 2—Pronunciation Practice

Listen, watch, and practice. (Follow the linking lines (‿); shorten the unstressed weak words such as ~~the~~, ~~was~~, ~~some~~.)

1. bró ther   My‿brother‿loves‿money!
   lóves
   móney

2. wónder   I‿wonder‿who's‿coming‿to‿lunch?
   cóming
   lunch

3. run   I‿was‿running‿to‿catch‿the‿bus.
   bus

4. cóusin   My‿cousin‿lives‿in‿the‿country.
   cóuntry

Practice each sentence again using natural rhythm, stress, and reductions. Exaggerate the /ʌ/ sounds slightly.

(Lab: Stop the tape for a few minutes of individual practice and self-monitoring.)

Part 3—Reading / Listening Practice (AK/TS)

Read each sentence silently. Find the words which you would guess are pronounced with Vowel 6. Draw a line under these words.

1. ~~The~~ Number One bus comes ~~at~~ one. (5 words) (Do not count reduced words *the* and *at*.)[10]
2. His brother can't come until Monday. (4)
3. June ~~is~~ ~~a~~ lovely summer month. (3) (Do not count reduced word *a*.)
4. Her mother cooked ~~a~~ wonderful supper. (3) (Do not count reduced word *a*.)

---

10. In sentences 1, 3, and 4, the words *the*, *at*, and *a* are reduced. The vowel sound in each is the weak form of Vowel 6, schwa, /ə/. Do not count these reduced words in the totals for Vowel 6 pronunciations in these three sentences. Count only the stressed /ʌ/ sound.

(Lab: Stop the tape and ask students to give their answers. Then start the tape and have students check their work as the words for each line are given.)

Practice the sentences using natural rhythm, stress, and reductions. Exaggerate the /ʌ/ sounds slightly.

(Lab: Stop the tape for a few minutes of individual practice and self-monitoring.)

Part 4—Dictation (AK/TS)

Four sentences will be dictated. Listen and repeat. Listen and write. Listen and check. Underline each occurrence of Vowel 6. Check your spelling.

1. _____ (5 words)

2. _____ (6)

3. _____ (6)

4. _____ (6)

(Lab: Stop the tape and ask students to read their /ʌ/ words. Then start the tape and have students check their work as the words for each line are given.)

Practice the sentences again using natural rhythm, stress, and reductions. Exaggerate the /ʌ/ sounds slightly.

(Lab: Stop the tape for a few minutes of individual practice and self-monitoring.)

Part 5—Spelling (AK/TS)

The /ʌ/ sound is the lax central vowel. As a lax vowel, like the front lax vowels /ɪ/, /ɛ/, and /æ/, and the lax back vowel /ʊ/, the /ʌ/ cannot come at the end of a word, when stressed; it must be followed by one or more consonants which close the word. In spelling books /ʌ/ sometimes is called the "short *u*" sound. Many dictionaries use the schwa symbol (ə) as their pronunciation guide to this sound. Listen and write. Repeat the words to yourself as you write.

Group 1	uC(C)		
	(Notice the letter *u* is the lax sound /ʌ/ before a doubled consonant.)[11]		
sun	_____	_____	_____
Group 2	oC, oCȼ		
	(The C in this pattern is usually *n*, *m*, *v*, or voiced *th*.)		
son	_____	_____	_____
Group 3	ouC		
cousin	_____	_____	_____

---

11. Notice, however, that the *u* before *ll* in the words *pull*, *full*, and *bull* is pronounced with Vowel 9, /ʊ/.

Part 6—Test Sentences for Self-Monitoring and Self-Testing

Practice the following sentences using natural rhythm, stress, and reductions. Exaggerate the /ʌ/ sounds slightly. Record. Listen and monitor your pronunciation.

1. What color is the bus?
2. My cousin came for lunch.
3. My brother loves money.
4. I must study on Sunday.

Part 7—Dictionary Homework

Look up the following words in your dictionary. Copy the pronunciation exactly. Include the syllable accent marks. Notice the symbol your dictionary uses as a pronunciation guide for this sound.

1. country _____ 3. enough _____ 5. won _____

2. company _____ 4. color _____ 6. one _____

Summary—Pronunciation of /ʌ/.

The /ʌ/ sound is pronounced with the jaw partly raised and the tongue in a lax mid-central or neutral position, neither high, low, front, nor back. Use a mirror. Compare /ʌ/ with the lax front vowel /ɪ/ and the lax back vowel /ʊ/. Feel the tongue move front for /ɪ/, mid central for /ʌ/ and back for /ʊ/: /ɪ/ → /ʌ/ → /ʊ/ /ɪ/ → /ʌ/ → /ʊ/. Compare /ʌ/ with the low central vowel /a/ and the high central vowel /ɝ/. Feel the jaw open for /a/, half close for /ʌ/, and close for /ɝ/: /a/ → /ʌ/ → /ɝ/   /a/ → /ʌ/ → /ɝ/.

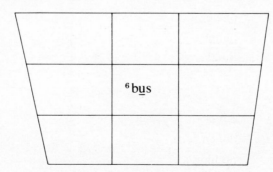

For more detailed articulatory information see the contrasts in Supplement C.

Resource Material

Part 1—Notes

The sound /ʌ/ is second in general usage among the fifteen vowel sounds.

The following are major spelling patterns for /ʌ/ with percentages for frequency of occurrence:

uC(C)	as in *bus*	86%
oC	as in *won*	10% (including oC¢, 2%)
ouC	as in *young*	2%

ESL interference / learning problems may include the following:

a. Sound: the low central vowel /a/, as in *father*, may be used for the mid central vowel /ʌ/; this may be a particular problem for students whose languages have the /a/ sound as the only central vowel sound

b. Spelling: in many languages the letter *o* is pronounced with the sound /o/, as in *no*; this may lead to spelling/pronunciation confusion

c. Spelling: in many languages the letter *u* is pronounced with the sound /u/, as in *two*; this may lead to spelling/pronunciation confusion

Part 2—Major Spelling Patterns

Group 1   uC(C)

bus	lunch	úncle
run	jump	húngry
sun	cup	Súnday
súnny	untíl	

Group 2   oC

son	móney	cóver
won	hóney	dózen
ton	month	nóthing
	cólor	Mónday

Group 3   oC¢

love	abóve
come	done
some	one

Group 4   ouC

enóugh	cóuntry
cóuple	tróuble
young	cóusin

198

Part 3—Other Spelling Patterns

Group 1   ood

  blood   flood

Group 2   Exceptions

  what   does

Part 4—Practice with /ʌ/ before Voiced / Voiceless Consonants

1. cu:b   cup
2. bu:d   but
3. bu:zz   bus

Part 5—Practice with /ʌ/—/u/ Pairs of Words

Ask students to practice these pairs of words with attention to the alternation of Vowel 6, /ʌ/, and Vowel 8, /uʷ/. Add to the list.

Vowel 6	*Vowel 8*
1. study	student
2. number	numerical
3. judge	judicial

Notes on the Low Central Vowel

(Some teachers may wish only to paraphrase these notes briefly at this time and return to them later in the course for detailed discussion.)

The /a/, as in *stop*, is the low central vowel. As the phonetic symbol shows, this sound has only one part. However, when /a/ is pronounced by itself or at the end of a word, it may have a small glide toward center so we hear /aᵊ/ in words such as *ma*, /maᵊ/ or *pa*, /paᵊ/.

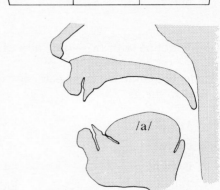

Diagram 7

The /a/ is an open vowel but there are very few monosyllabic words in English in which the /a/ comes at the end of a word.

Examples: ma   ha   bah

                  pa   schwa   ah

However, in multisyllabic words the /a/ may come at the end of the stressed *syllable*.

Examples: fáther   prócess

Some speakers use Vowel 7, /a/, in place of Vowel 11, /ɔ/.

Examples: saw   /sɔ/ becomes /sa/

                  law   /lɔ/ becomes /la/

The /a/ sound is not a difficult one for most ESL students. One problem which does occur, however, is when the sound /a/ is spelled with the letter *o* (as in *job, college, problem*). ESL students often pronounce these words with Vowel 10, /oᵘ/, in place of Vowel 7, /a/.

Many languages have only this one low vowel sound. They do not have low front /æ/ or low back /ɔ/. In addition, many languages do not have the mid central vowel /ʌ/ of English. The /a/ often is substituted for all these sounds. For example, the /a/, as in *stop*, may be used for the following four words:

cat	/kæt/—Vowel 5	
cot	/kat/—Vowel 7	
caught	/kɔt/—Vowel 11	
cut	/kʌt/—Vowel 6	

	FRONT	CENTRAL	BACK
HIGH			
MID		[6] /ʌ/—cut	
LOW	[5] /æ/—cat	[7] /a/—cot	[11] /ɔ/— caught

For ESL students who have this problem, practice with sets of words having all four sounds (as cat, cot, caught, and cut) may be helpful.

Lesson 16

Intensive Practice with Vowel 7—stop /a/

Part 1—Articulation

Vowel 7 is the lowest central vowel. It is not difficult for most ESL students. The jaw is lowered and the tongue is pulled down from the rest position. Practice these words: clock   not   stop.

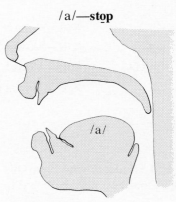

/a/—stop

Diagram 8

Part 2—Pronunciation Practice

Listen, watch, and practice. (Follow the linking lines (_); shorten the unstressed weak words such as ~~the~~, ~~was~~, ~~some~~.)

1. fáther   My father's a doctor.
   dóctor

2. drop   He dropped the clock
   clock

3. watch   My watch has stopped.
   stop

4. Mom   Mom got some hotdogs.
   got
   hótdog

Practice each sentence again using natural rhythm, stress, and reductions. Exaggerate the /a/ sounds slightly.

(Lab: Stop the tape for a few minutes of individual practice and self-monitoring.)

Part 3—Reading / Listening Practice (AK/TS)

Read each sentence silently. Find the words which you would guess are pronounced with Vowel 7. Draw a line under these words.

1. John forgot his promise. (3 words)
2. Is the doctor at the hospital? (2)
3. I got a spot on my collar. (3)
4. We stopped at the shop for a bottle of pop. (4)

(Lab: Stop the tape and ask students to give their answers. Then start the tape and have students check their work as the words for each line are given.)

Practice the sentences using natural rhythm, stress, and reductions. Exaggerate the /a/ sounds slightly.

(Lab: Stop the tape for a few minutes of individual practice and self-monitoring.)

Part 4—Dictation (AK/TS)

Four sentences will be dictated. Listen and repeat. Listen and write. Listen and check. Underline each occurrence of Vowel 7. Check your spelling.

1. _____ (4 words)

2. _____ (9)

3. _____ (6)

4. _____ (8)

(Lab: Stop the tape and ask students to read their /a/ words. Then start the tape and have students check their work as the words for each line are given.)

Practice the sentences again using natural rhythm, stress, and reductions. Exaggerate the /a/ sounds slightly.

(Lab: Stop the tape for a few minutes of individual practice and self-monitoring.)

Part 5—Spelling (AK/TS)

The /a/ sound is the low central vowel. It occurs primarily in the initial and medial word positions, although it can occur in the final position. In spelling books /a/ sometimes is called the "short *o*" sound. Many dictionaries use this symbol (ä) as the pronunciation guide for this sound. Listen and write. Repeat the words to yourself as you write.

> *Group 1*   oC(C)
> (The spelling *o* before doubled consonants is pronounced /a/ with certain exceptions.)[12]
>
> not   _____   _____   _____   _____
>
> *Group 2*   aC(C)
> father   _____   _____

---

12. The *o* before *ff* and *ss* and *gg* is pronounced with Vowel 11, /ɔ/, in such words as *off*, *cross*, and *foggy*.

Part 6—Test Sentences for Self-Monitoring and Self-Testing

Practice the following sentences using natural rhythm, stress, and reductions. Exaggerate the /a/ sounds slightly. Record. Listen and monitor your pronunciation.

1. He dropped the clock.
2. His father's a doctor.
3. Mom got some hotdogs.
4. My watch has stopped.

Part 7—Dictionary Homework

Look up the following words in your dictionary. Copy the pronunciation exactly. Include the syllable accent marks. Notice the symbol your dictionary uses as a pronunciation guide for this sound.

1. college _____
2. October _____
3. collar _____
4. promise _____
5. product _____
6. shock _____

Summary—Pronunciation of /a/

The low central /a/ sound is pronounced with the jaw lowered and the tongue pulled down from the rest position. Use a mirror. Compare /a/ with the low front vowel /æ/ and the low back vowel /ɔ/. Feel the tongue move front for /æ/, central for /a/, and back for /ɔ/: /æ/ → /a/ → /ɔ/. Compare /a/ with the mid central vowel /ʌ/ and the high central vowel /ɝ/. Feel the jaw open for /a/, half close for /ʌ/ and close for /ɝ/: /a/ → /ʌ/ → /ɝ/.

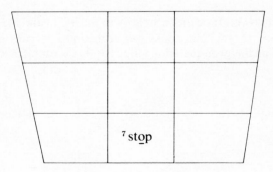

Resource Material

Part 1— Notes

The sound /a/ is seventh in general usage among the fifteen vowel sounds.

The following are major spelling patterns for /a/ with percentages for frequency of occurrence:

oC(C)	as in *stop*	69%
aC(C)	as in *father*	26%

ESL interference / learning problems may include the following:

a. Spelling: in many languages the letter *o* is pronounced with the sound /o/, as in *no*; this may
lead to spelling/pronunciation confusion

Part 2— Major Spelling Patterns[13]

Group 1   oC(C)

spot	shop	job	cóllege	sórry
hot	top	got	cóllar	doll
not	rock	prómise	cómmon	
lot	shock	módern	bóttle	

Group 2   aC(C)

father	watch
wash	want

Part 3— Other Spelling Patterns

Group 1   odge

lodge	dodge

Group 2   ow

knówledge

Part 4— Practice with /a/ before Voiced / Voiceless Consonants

1. go:d	got
2. ro:d	rot
3. no:d	not
4. co:b	cop

---

13. Some speakers use Vowel 11 instead of Vowel 7 for *sorry* in group 1 and *wash, watch,* and *want* in group 2.

Part 5—Practice with /oᵘ/—/a/ Pairs of Words

Ask students to practice these pairs of words with attention to the alternation of Vowel 10, /oᵘ/, and Vowel 7, /a/. Add to the list.

	Vowel 10	*Vowel 7*
1.	know	knowledge
2.	cone	conical
3.	pose	posture
4.	holy	holiday

Lesson 17

Central Vowel Tests

Part 1—Discrimination.[14] **(AK/TS)**

Directions: Listen to the following sentences. Draw a circle around the word (and vowel number) you think you hear.

Examples: Who owns the (duck—dock)?   *Answer*: dock
                           6   7   7

Who owns the (duck—dock)?   *Answer*: duck
                      6   7   6

These sentences will be given once, only.

1. The (bird—bud) is beautiful?
       12   6

2. Was it (hot—hurt)?
            7   12

3. My (lock—luck) was good!
         7   6

4. The (cub—curb) was black.
          6   12

5. Who (shut—shot) it?
          6   7

6. That was a good (shirt—shot)!
                         12   7

7. Which (curlers—collars—colors) did she buy?
            12   7   6

8. Where are the (ducks—docks)?
                       6   7

9. I didn't see the (cub—curb—cob).
                        6   12   7

10. Spell the word (lock—lurk—luck).
                        7   12   6

Part 2—Spelling[15] **(AK/TS)**

Directions: Put the following words in the correct column according to the vowel in their pronunciation. The teacher will *not* read the words.

(Lab: Stop the tape and complete part 2; allow 5 to 10 minutes.)

---

14. *Lab*: At the end of part 1 stop the tape and ask students to give their answers. Write them on the chalkboard and have students check their work. Replay this segment of the test for review.

15. *Lab*: At the end of part 2 stop the tape and ask students to give their answers. Write them on the chalkboard and have students check their work. Pronounce them and discuss the spelling patterns.

cot	hurt	drop	luck	not	cut	lunch
shirt	duck	fun	sun	shut	top	clock
lock	work	her	nurse	shot	church	word

Vowel 12	*Vowel 6*	*Vowel 7*
bi<u>r</u>d	b<u>u</u>s	st<u>o</u>p

_____	_____	_____
_____	_____	_____
_____	_____	_____
_____	_____	_____
_____	_____	_____
_____	_____	_____
_____	_____	_____

Part 3—Test Sentences for Writing Vowel Numbers.[16] (AK/TS)

Directions: Listen as the following words are pronounced. Write the number of the vowel below the line.

Vowel 12	/ɝ/	as in	bi<u>r</u>d
Vowel 6	/ʌ/	as in	b<u>u</u>s
Vowel 7	/a/	as in	st<u>o</u>p

Repeat and write the vowel numbers.

1. W<u>o</u>rst l<u>u</u>ck! S<u>o</u>me<u>o</u>ne b<u>u</u>rned the b<u>u</u>ns!

2. The r<u>o</u>bber dr<u>o</u>pped the r<u>u</u>bber d<u>u</u>ck!

3. B<u>o</u>b's c<u>o</u>llar is a f<u>u</u>nny c<u>o</u>lor!

4. The r<u>o</u>bber sh<u>u</u>t his shi<u>r</u>t in the l<u>o</u>cker.

5. Di<u>r</u>k's d<u>u</u>ck was on the d<u>o</u>ck.

6. The c<u>u</u>rler and the c<u>o</u>llar were the same c<u>o</u>lor!

Part 4—Test Sentences for Self-Monitoring and Self-Testing

Directions: Practice the sentences in part 3 using natural rhythm, stress, and reductions. Exaggerate the sounds slightly. Record. Listen and monitor your pronunciation.

---

16. *Lab*: At the end of part 3 stop the tape and ask students to give the vowel numbers they have written. Replay this segment of the test and have students check their work.

Section E—Diphthongs

Section Notes

Section E has four lessons. Lessons 18, 19, and 20 present intensive listening/speaking practice with the three diphthongs: /ai/, /au/, and /ɔi/. Lesson 21 presents a four-part self-evaluative test of diphthongs. Teachers may wish to use the following notes with students for a diphthong overview.

Many languages do not have diphthongs. English has three diphthongs. Diphthongs are double sounds. Each of them is made up of two distinct parts, that is, two different sounds.

Vowel 13 is the diphthong /ai/, as in *my*. It begins with the low central sound /a/ and ends with a high front /i/ or /ɪ/.[1]

Vowel 14 is the diphthong /au/, as in *cow*. It begins with the low central sound /a/ and ends with a high back /u/ or /ʊ/.[2]

Vowel 15 is the diphthong /ɔi/, as in *boy*.[3] It begins with the low back sound /ɔ/ and ends with a high front /i/ or /ɪ/.[4]

/ai/—**my**

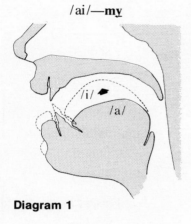

Diagram 1

/au/—**cow**

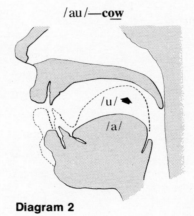

Diagram 2

/ɔi/—**boy**

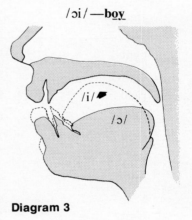

Diagram 3

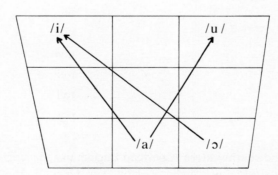

---

1. If diphthong /ai/ comes at the end of a word, the second part is more like Vowel 1. If it comes in the middle of a word, it is more like Vowel 2.
2. If diphthong /au/ comes at the end of a word, the second part is more like Vowel 8. If it comes in the middle of a word, it is more like Vowel 9.
3. If diphthong /ɔi/ comes at the end of a word, the second part is more like Vowel 1. If it comes in the middle of a word, it is more like Vowel 2.
4. For some speakers of English the first part of Vowel 15 is more like the first part of Vowel 10, /o/, for the diphthong /oi/.

The diphthongs are open vowels. That is, they are found not only in initial and medial positions in a word, but also can come at the end of a word and leave the word open or without a final closing consonant.

Examples: tie   now   toy

               lie   how   joy

               my   cow   boy

(Notice the letters *y* and *w* are pronounced as parts of the vowels, not as consonants.)

As the phonetic symbols show, each diphthong is a double sound. Some students have difficulty with the length and the glide of the diphthongs and do not pronounce the second part of the diphthong. Special attention should be given to pronouncing both parts of each diphthong so that they are not confused with the single sounds /a/ or /ɔ/.

Contrast.

Vowel 13 /ai/—my	*Vowel 7* /a/—stop	*Vowel 14* /au/—cow	*Vowel 7* /a/—stop
light	lot	shout	shot
night	not	doubt	dot
right	rot	down	Don
find	fond	noun	non-
time	Tom	pound	pond
like	lock	found	fond
ride	rod	cloud	clod
I	ah		
high	ha	*Vowel 15* /ɔi/—boy	*Vowel 11* /ɔ/—law
pie	pa		
		oil	all
		boil	ball
		coil	call
		foil	fall
		toil	tall
		poise	pause

Some dialects of southeastern and southwestern American English use the single sounds /a/ and /ɔ/, in place of the double (diphthong) sounds /ai/, /au/, and /ɔi/. However, General American English uses the three diphthongs as presented in this lesson.

Lesson 18

Intensive Practice with Vowel 13—my /ai/

Part 1—Articulation

Vowel 13 is a diphthong made up of the sounds /a/ and /i/: /ai/   /ai/.[5]

Practice these words: my   right   nice.

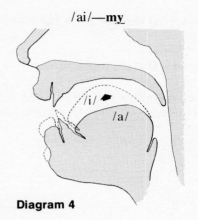

/ai/—my

Diagram 4

Part 2—Pronunciation Practice

Listen, watch, and practice. (Follow the linking lines (‿); shorten the unstressed weak words such as the, was, some.)

1.	nice night	It's‿a‿nice‿night.	3. bright light	We‿saw‿a‿bright‿light.
2.	I like fly	I‿like‿to‿fly.	4. nine lives	A‿cat‿has‿nine‿lives.

Practice each sentence again using natural rhythm, stress, and reductions. Exaggerate the /ai/ sounds slightly.

(Lab: Stop the tape for a few minutes of individual practice and self-monitoring.)

Part 3—Reading / Listening Practice (AK/TS)

Read each sentence silently. Find the words which you would guess are pronounced with Vowel 13. Draw a line under these words.

1. Why did he buy a white tie? (4 words)
2. Please buy nine pies. (3)
3. I can't find the right knife. (4)
4. I saw a bright light in the sky tonight. (5)

---

5. If /ai/ comes at the end of a word, the second part is more like Vowel 1, /iʸ/. If it comes in the middle of a word or the beginning of a word, particularly before a voiceless consonant, the second part is more like Vowel 2, /ɪ/.

(Lab: Stop the tape and ask students to give their answers. Then start the tape and have students check their work as the words for each line are given.)

Practice the sentences using natural rhythm, stress, and reductions. Exaggerate the /ai/ sounds slightly.

(Lab: Stop the tape for a few minutes of individual practice and self-monitoring.)

Part 4—Dictation (AK/TS)

Four sentences will be dictated. Listen and repeat. Listen and write. Listen and check. Underline each occurrence of Vowel 13. Check your spelling.

1. _____ (5 words)

2. _____ (5)

3. _____ (6)

4. _____ (6)

(Lab: Stop the tape and ask students to read their /ai/ words. Then start the tape and have students check their work as the words for each line are given.)

Practice the sentences again using natural rhythm, stress, and reductions. Exaggerate the /ai/ sounds slightly.

(Lab: Stop the tape for a few minutes of individual practice and self-monitoring.)

Part 5—Spelling (AK/TS)

The diphthong /ai/ is an open vowel. It can occur in all three word positions, initial, medial, and final. In spelling books /ai/ sometimes is called the "long *i*" sound. Many dictionaries use this symbol (ī) as the pronunciation guide for this sound. Listen and write. Repeat the words to yourself as you write.

Group 1	i				
find		_____	_____	_____	_____
Group 2	iC¢				
like		_____	_____	_____	_____
Group 3	y				
cry		_____	_____	_____	_____

Part 6—Test Sentences for Self-Monitoring and Self-Testing

Practice the following sentences using natural rhythm, stress, and reductions. Exaggerate the /ai/ sounds slightly. Record. Listen and monitor your pronunciation.

1. I'm flying to Miami on Friday.
2. A cat has nine lives.
3. It's a nice night.
4. I like to fly.

Part 7—Dictionary Homework

Look up the following words in your dictionary. Copy the pronunciation exactly. Include the syllable accent marks. Notice the symbol your dictionary uses as a pronunciation guide for this sound.

1. decide _____   3. quite _____   5. inquire _____

2. science _____   4. quiet _____   6. island _____

Summary—Pronunciation of /ai/

The /ai/ sound begins with the /a/ of Vowel 7 and ends with the /i/ of Vowel 1. Feel the difference between /a/ and /ai/: /a/ → /ai/   /a/ → /ai/   lot   light.

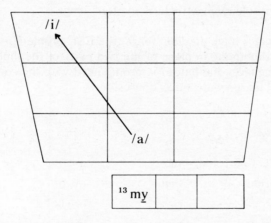

213

Resource Material

Part 1—Notes

The sound /ai/ is eleventh in general usage among the fifteen vowel sounds.

The following are the major spelling patterns for /ai/ with percentages for frequency of occurrence:

i	as in *I*	80% (including iCȼ, 37%)
y	as in *my*	14%
ie	as in *lie*	2%
yCȼ	as in *type*	2%

ESL interference / learning problems may include the following:

a. Sound: some languages have no diphthongs; the ESL problem may be one of using the first half of the diphthong in place of the two parts of the diphthong
b. Spelling: in many languages the letter *i* is pronounced with the sound /i/, as in *see*; this may lead to spelling/pronunciation confusion

Part 2—Major Spelling Patterns

Group 1   i, iCV, iCC (-igh, -ind, -imb)

climb	Fríday	high	might
mind	I	right	bright
kind	shíny	night	fright
find	spíral	sight	toníght

Group 2   iCȼ

nice	drive	nine	white
time	knife	while	life
smile	bride	live (*adjective*)	

Group 3   y

my	try	why	cry
by	dry	shy	fry
spy			

Group 4   ie

tie	tried	die	cried
lie	dried	pie	lied

Group 5   yCȼ, yClȼ

rhyme	type	style	cýcle

214

Part 3—Other Spelling Patterns

Group 1   y¢

    eye   dye   'bye

Group 2   uy

    buy   guy

Group 3   eight

    height

Group 4   g or q + uiC(¢)

    guide   quite   guidance

Part 4—Practice with /ai/ before Voiced / Voiceless Consonants

1. ri:de   right
2. si:de   sight
3. li:ve   life
4. bri:de   bright
5. hi:de   height
6. lie:d   light
7. tie:d   tight

Part 5—Practice with /ai/—/ɪ/ Pairs of Words

Vowel 13	*Vowel 2*
1. dine	dinner
2. decide	decision
3. five	fifth
4. child	children
5. wise	wisdom

Lesson 19

Intensive Practice with Vowel 14—c<u>ow</u> /au/

Part 1—Articulation

/au/—c<u>ow</u>

Vowel 14 is a diphthong made up of the sounds /a/
and /u/: /au/ → /au/.[6] Practice these words: c<u>ow</u>
d<u>ow</u>n   r<u>ou</u>nd.

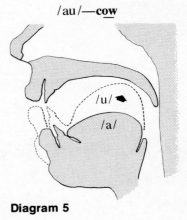

Diagram 5

Part 2—Pronunciation Practice

Listen, watch, and practice. (Follow the linking lines (‿); shorten the unstressed weak words such as ~~the~~,
~~was, some~~.)

1. thóusand   I‿learned‿a‿thousand‿nouns.
   n<u>ou</u>ns
2. l<u>ou</u>d   We‿heard‿a‿loud‿shout.
   sh<u>ou</u>t

3. flówers   She‿planted‿flowers‿around‿the‿house.
   aróund
   h<u>ou</u>se
4. d<u>ow</u>n   Please‿meet‿me‿down‿town.
   t<u>ow</u>n

Practice each sentence again using natural rhythm, stress, and reductions. Exaggerate the /au/ sounds
slightly.

(Lab: Stop the tape for a few minutes of individual practice and self-monitoring.)

Part 3—Reading / Listening Practice (AK/TS)

Read each sentence silently. Find the words which you would guess are pronounced with Vowel 14. Draw a
line under these words.

1. ~~The~~ mouse ran around ~~the~~ house. (3 words)
2. We found ~~a~~ brown cow on ~~the~~ mountain. (4)
3. I waited down town ~~for an~~ hour. (3)
4. Pronounce ~~the~~ vowel sounds. (3)

*(Lab: Stop the tape and ask students to give their answers. Then start the tape and have students check their
work as the words for each line are given.)*

---

6. If /au/ comes at the end of a word, the second part is more like Vowel 8, /u^w/. If it comes in the middle of a word or
   the beginning of a word, particularly before a voiceless consonant, the second part is more like Vowel 9, /ʊ/.

Practice the sentences using natural rhythm, stress, and reductions. Exaggerate the /au/ sounds slightly.

(Lab: Stop the tape for a few minutes of individual practice and self-monitoring.)

Part 4—Dictation (AK/TS)

Four sentences will be dictated. Listen and repeat. Listen and write. Listen and check. Underline each occurrence of Vowel 14. Check your spelling.

1. _____ (5 words)

2. _____ (5)

3. _____ (6)

4. _____ (6)

(Lab: Stop the tape and ask students to read their /au/ words. Then start the tape and have students check their work as the words for each line are given.)

Practice the sentences again using natural rhythm, stress, and reductions. Exaggerate the /au/ sounds slightly.

(Lab: Stop the tape for a few minutes of individual practice and self-monitoring.)

Part 5—Spelling (AK/TS)

The diphthong /au/ is an open vowel. It can occur in all three word positions, initial, medial, and final. Many dictionaries use this symbol (áu) as the pronunciation guide for this sound. Listen and write. Repeat the words to yourself as you write.

Group 1	ouC (C)		
shout	_____	_____	_____
Group 2	ow		
crowd	_____	_____	_____
Group 3	ouC¢		
route	_____	_____	
Group 4	ounc¢		
ounce	_____	_____	

Part 6—Test Sentences for Self-Monitoring and Self-Testing

Practice the following sentences using natural rhythm, stress, and reductions. Exaggerate the /au/ sounds slightly. Record. Listen and monitor your pronunciation.

1. I'll meet you down town in an hour.

2. A loud crowd was shouting his name.

3. We found a brown cow on the mountain.

4. We need a thousand pounds of flour.

Part 7—Dictionary Homework

Look up the following words in your dictionary. Copy the pronounciation exactly. Include the syllable accent marks. Notice the symbol your dictionary uses as a pronunciation guide for this sound.

1. pronounce _____ 3. mountain _____ 5. bough _____

2. announce _____ 4. compound _____ 6. spout _____

Summary—Pronunciation of /au/

The /au/ sound begins with the /a/ of Vowel 7 and ends with the /u/ of Vowel 8. Feel the difference between /a/ and /au/: /a/ → /au/   /a/ → /au/   shot shout.

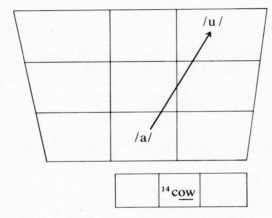

^{14} cow

Resource Material

Part 1—Notes

The sound /au/ is fourteenth in general usage among the fifteen vowel sounds.

The following are major spelling patterns for /au/ with percentages for frequency of occurrence:

ouC(C)	as in *loud*	56%
ow	as in *down*	29%
ouС¢	as in *house*	
ounС¢	as in *pronounce*	13%

ESL interference / learning problems may include the following:

a. Sound: some languages have no diphthongs; the ESL problem may be one of using the first half of the diphthong in place of the two parts of the diphthong.

Part 2—Major Spelling Patterns

Group 1 ouC(C)

loud	south	ground	cloud
foul	abóut	out	sound
withóut	douþt	found	aróund
noun	round	thóusand	
mouth	pound	móuntain	

Group 2 ow

how	brown	crowd	allów
now	town	owl	vówel
cow	down		tówel

Group 3 ouС¢, ounС¢

house	ounce
mouse	pronóunce
route	annóunce

Part 3—Practice with /au/ before Voiced / Voiceless Consonants

1. hou:se (verb; *s* = /z/)   house (noun; *s* = /s/)
2. clou:d   clout

Part 4—Practice with /au/—/ʌ/ Pairs of Words

Vowel 14	*Vowel 6*
1. south	southern
2. pronounce	pronunciation

Lesson 20

Intensive Practice with Vowel 15—b<u>oy</u> /ɔi/

Part 1—Articulation

/ɔi/—b<u>oy</u>

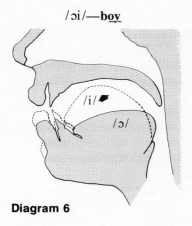

Diagram 6

Vowel 15 is a diphthong made up of the sounds /ɔ/
and /i/: /ɔi/ /ɔi/.[7] Practice these words:
b<u>oy</u>   n<u>oi</u>se   v<u>oi</u>ce.

Part 2—Pronunciation Practice

Listen, watch, and practice. (Follow the linking lines (‿); shorten the unstressed weak words such as ~~the,~~
~~was, some~~.)

1. <u>oi</u>l	The‿oil‿was‿boiling.	3. p<u>oi</u>nt	She‿pointed‿to‿the‿noisy‿boys.
b<u>oi</u>l		nóisy	
2. j<u>oi</u>n	He‿joined‿a‿coin‿club.	b<u>oy</u>s	
c<u>oi</u>n		4. vóices	The‿loud‿voices‿annoyed‿us.
		annóy	

Practice each sentence again using natural rhythm, stress, and reductions. Exaggerate the /ɔi/ sounds
slightly.

(Lab: Stop the tape for a few minutes of individual practice and self-monitoring.)

Part 3—Reading / Listening Practice (AK/TS)

Read each sentence silently. Find the words which you would guess are pronounced with Vowel 15. Draw a
line under these words.

1. The boys enjoyed their noisy toys. (4 words)
2. Their loud voices made too much noise! (2)
3. The boiling oil was destroyed. (3)
4. His loyal friends were appointed. (2)

*(Lab: Stop the tape and ask students to give their answers. Then start the tape and have the students check
their work as the words for each line are given.)*

---

7. If /ɔi/ comes at the end of a word, the second part is more like Vowel 1, /iʸ/. If it comes in the middle of a word or the
   beginning of a word, particularly before a voiceless consonant, the second part is more like Vowel 2, /ɪ/.

Practice the sentences using natural rhythm, stress, and reductions. Exaggerate the /ɔi/ sounds slightly.

(Lab: Stop the tape for a few minutes of individual practice and self-monitoring.)

Part 4—Dictation (AK/TS)

Four sentences will be dictated. Listen and repeat. Listen and write. Listen and check. Underline each occurrence of Vowel 15. Check your spelling.

1. _____ (5 words)

2. _____ (4)

3. _____ (4)

4. _____ (6)

(Lab: Stop the tape and ask students to read their /ɔi/ words. Then start the tape and have students check their work as the words for each line are given.)

Practice the sentences again using natural rhythm, stress, and reductions. Exaggerate the /ɔi/ sounds slightly.

(Lab: Stop the tape for a few minutes of individual practice and self-monitoring.)

Part 5—Spelling (AK/TS)

The diphthong /ɔi/ is an open vowel. It can occur in all three word positions, initial, medial, and final. Many dictionaries use this symbol (oi) as the pronunciation guide for this sound. Listen and write. Repeat the words to yourself as you write.

Group 1	oi		
join		_____	_____
Group 2	oy		
boy		_____	_____
Group 3	oiC¢		
noise		_____	

Part 6—Test Sentences for Self-Monitoring and Self-Testing

Practice the following sentences using natural rhythm, stress, and reductions. Exaggerate the /ɔi/ sounds slightly. Record. Listen and monitor your pronunciation.

1. The boys enjoyed their noisy toys.
2. The boiling oil was destroyed.
3. He pointed to the noisy boys.
4. The voices annoyed us.

Part 7—Dictionary Homework

Look up the following words in your dictionary. Copy the pronunciation exactly. Include the syllable accent marks. Notice the symbol your dictionary uses as a pronunciation guide for this sound.

1. annoyance _____   3. loyalty _____   5. decoy _____

2. voyage _____   4. envoy _____   6. poise _____

Summary—Pronunciation of /ɔi/

The /ɔi/ sound begins with the /ɔ/ of Vowel 11 and ends with the /i/ of Vowel 1. Feel the difference between /ɔ/ and /ɔi/: /ɔ/ → /ɔi/   /ɔ/ → /ɔi/   l<u>aw</u> b<u>oy</u>   t<u>a</u>ll t<u>oi</u>l.

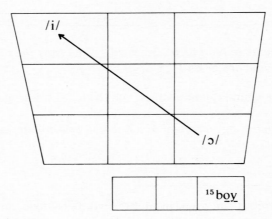

Resource Material

Part 1— Notes

The sound /ɔi/ is fifteenth in general usage among the fifteen vowel sounds.

The following are the major spelling patterns for /ɔi/ with percentages for frequency of occurrence:

oi	as in *join*	62%
oy	as in *joy*	32%
oiC¢	as in *voice*	
oyC¢	as in *Joyce*	6%

ESL interference / learning problems may include the following:

a. Sound: some languages have no diphthongs; the ESL problem may be one of using the first half of the diphthong in place of the two parts of the diphthong.

Part 2— Major Spelling Patterns

Group 1   oi

join	appóint	oil
coin	póison	boil
point	nóisy	toil
		soil

Group 2   oy

joy	enjóy	lóyal
toy	annóy	
boy	destróy	

Group 3   oiC¢, oyC¢

noise	Joyce
voice	
rejóice	

Lesson 21
Diphthong Tests

Part 1—Discrimination[8] (AK/TS)

Directions: Listen to the following sentences. Draw a circle around the word (and vowel number) you think you hear.

Examples: He bought a (tie—toy).   *Answer:* toy
               13 15   15

He bought a (toy—tie).   *Answer:* tie
               15 13   13

These sentences will be given once, only.

1. He loves to eat Hawaiian (pie—poi)!
                               13   15

2. She bought some new (tiles—towels).
                           13   14

3. The (boy—bough) fell down.
            15   14

4. They're afraid of the (mouse—mice)!
                       14   13

5. It's a steel (file—foil).
            13   15

6. Is it time to go (dine—down)?
                  13   14

7. That's a terrible (voice—vice)!
                 15   13

8. What a good (buy—boy—bow)!
                13   15   14

9. Did you find the (oil—owl—aisle)?
                  15   14   13

10. Spell the word (tile—towel—toil).
                 13   14   15

Part 2—Spelling[9] (AK/TS)

Directions: Put the following words in the correct column according to the vowel in their pronunciation. The teacher will *not* read the words.

(Lab: Stop the tape and complete part 2; allow 5 to 10 minutes.)

try	join	find	noun	climb
bright	south	voice	appoint	destroy
crowd	dime	annoy	hour	mountain

---

8. *Lab*: At the end of part 1 stop the tape and ask students to give their answers. Write them on the chalkboard and have students check their work. Replay this segment of the test for review.
9. *Lab*: At the end of part 2 stop the tape and ask students to give their answers. Write them on the chalkboard and have students check their work. Pronounce them and discuss the spelling patterns.

Vowel 13	*Vowel 14*	*Vowel 15*
m<u>y</u>	c<u>ow</u>	b<u>oy</u>
_____	_____	_____
_____	_____	_____
_____	_____	_____
_____	_____	_____
_____	_____	_____

Part 3—Test Sentences for Writing Vowel Numbers[10] (AK/TS)

Directions: Listen as the following words are pronounced. Write the number of the vowel below the line.

Vowel 13	/ai/	as in	m<u>y</u>
Vowel 14	/au/	as in	c<u>ow</u>
Vowel 15	/ɔi/	as in	b<u>oy</u>

Repeat and write the vowel numbers.

1. It took f<u>i</u>ve h<u>ours</u> to cl<u>i</u>mb the m<u>ou</u>ntain.

2. Wr<u>i</u>te the v<u>ow</u>el numbers on the l<u>i</u>nes as you pron<u>ou</u>nce them.

3. <u>I</u> heard l<u>ou</u>d n<u>oi</u>sy v<u>oi</u>ces <u>ou</u>tside m<u>y</u> h<u>ou</u>se!

4. The n<u>i</u>ne n<u>oi</u>sy b<u>oy</u>s spilled the <u>oi</u>l in the <u>ai</u>sle!

5. The b<u>oy</u> went to b<u>uy</u> some t<u>ie</u>s, some t<u>oy</u>s, and some fl<u>ow</u>ers.

6. There's an <u>oi</u>ly <u>ow</u>l in the <u>ai</u>sle!

Part 4—Test Sentences for Self-Monitoring and Self-Testing

Directions: Practice the sentences in part 3 using natural rhythm, stress, and reductions. Exaggerate the sounds slightly. Record. Listen and monitor your pronunciation.

---

10. *Lab*: At the end of part 3 stop the tape and ask students to give the vowel numbers they have written. Replay this segment of the test and have students check their work.

Section F—Rapid Review and Testing

Section Notes

Section F has three lessons. Lesson 22 presents a rapid review of the Vowel Chart and brief practice with the key words for each of the fifteen vowel sounds.

Lesson 23 presents rapid review of production, brief practice, and testing for the five front vowels and for the three central vowels.

Lesson 24 presents rapid review of production, brief practice, and testing for the four back vowels and for the three diphthongs.

Lesson 22

Rapid Review of the Vowels[1]

Part 1—Review: Five Basic Vowels, /i/, /e/, /a/, /o/, /u/

Most languages of the world have three basic vowel sounds. They are not exactly the same in all languages, but they are similar. In many languages these three sounds are pronounced as single pure sounds.

The three basic sounds are:

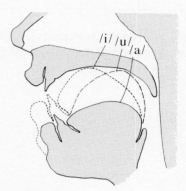

Diagram 1

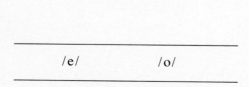

/i/		/u/
	/a/	

In English, however, /i/ and /u/ are not pronounced as single pure sounds but are lengthened and slightly diphthongized. That is, in addition to the pure sound, they also have a second shorter sound: /iʸ/, /uʷ/. Listen to the pronunciation of the following words.

/iʸ/	/a/	/uʷ/
s<u>ee</u>	m<u>a</u>	tw<u>o</u>
n<u>ee</u>d	f<u>a</u>ther	f<u>oo</u>d
b<u>ea</u>t	st<u>o</u>p	tr<u>u</u>th

Most languages of the world also have two additional basic vowel sounds. Again, in many languages these two sounds are pronounced as single pure sounds.

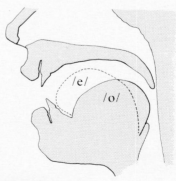

Diagram 2

/e/	/o/

---

1. Students who have just completed the lessons in Unit 1 may wish to go directly to lesson 23.

In English, however, like /iʸ/ and /uʷ/, they are lengthened and slightly diphthongized. That is, they have a second shorter sound: /eⁱ/, /oᵘ/. Listen to the following words.

/eⁱ/	/oᵘ/
s<u>ay</u>	n<u>o</u>
m<u>a</u>de	r<u>o</u>de
t<u>a</u>ke	h<u>o</u>pe

Look at diagram 3. Repeat: /iʸ/ /a/ /uʷ/. Notice these three vowels are connected and form a triangle on the Vowel Chart (Vowels 1, 7, and 8).

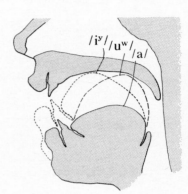

Diagram 3
THE THREE VOWELS

Look at Diagram 4. Repeat: /iʸ/ /eⁱ/ /a/ /oᵘ/ /uʷ/. Notice these five vowels are circled on the Vowel Chart. They are connected by a dotted line (Vowels 1, 3, 7, 10, and 8).

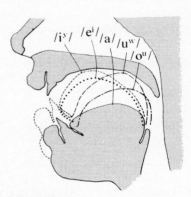

Diagram 4
THE FIVE VOWELS

Vowel Chart

	FRONT	CENTRAL	BACK
HIGH	① see / 2 it	12 bird	⑧ two / 9 books
MID	③ say / 4 yes	6 bus	⑩ no
LOW	5 fat	⑦ stop	11 law

DIPHTHONGS	13 my	14 cow	15 boy

Part 2—The Fifteen Vowel Sounds

Look at the Vowel Chart. Look at the front vowels. Notice there are two high front vowels: Vowels 1 and 2, /iʸ/ as in **see**, /ɪ/ as in **it**. Repeat: **see   it   see it.**

Notice there are two mid front vowels: vowels 3 and 4, /eⁱ/ as in **say**, /ɛ/ as in **yes**. Repeat: **say   yes   say yes.**

Notice there is one low front vowel: Vowel 5, /æ/ as in **fat**. Repeat: **fat   fat.** Repeat the front vowels: /iʸ/   /ɪ/   /eⁱ/   /ɛ/   /æ/   **see it   say yes   fat.**

Look at the central vowels. Notice there is one high central vowel: Vowel 12, /ɝ/ as in **bird**. Repeat: **bird   bird.**

Notice there is one mid central vowel: Vowel 6, /ʌ/ as in **bus**. Repeat: **bus   bus.**

Notice there is one low central vowel: Vowel 7, /a/ as in **stop**. Repeat: **stop   stop.** Repeat the central vowels: /ɝ/   /ʌ/   /a/   **bird   bus stop.**

Look at the back vowels. Notice there are two high back vowels: Vowels 8 and 9, /uʷ/ as in **two,** /ʊ/ as in **books**. Repeat: **two   books   two books.**

Notice there is one mid back vowel: Vowel 10, /oᵘ/ as in **no**. Repeat: **no   no.**

Notice there is one low back vowel: Vowel 11, /ɔ/ as in **law**. Repeat: **law   law.** Repeat the back vowels: /uʷ/   /ʊ/   /oᵘ/   /ɔ/   **two books   no law.**

Look at the diphthongs. Notice there are three diphthongs. Vowel 13 is /ai/ as in **my**. Vowel 14 is /au/ as in **cow**. Vowel 15 is /ɔi/ as in **boy**. Repeat: /ai/   /au/   /ɔi/   **my cowboy   my cowboy.**

Repeat the diphthongs: /ai/   /au/   /ɔi/   ·   **my cowboy.**

Repeat the key word phrases on the Vowel Chart.
see it   say yes   a fat bird   a bus stop   two books   no law   my cowboy

Lesson 23
Rapid Review and Testing of the Front and Central Vowels

Front Vowels

Part 1—Review

Many languages have only two front vowels, /i/ and /e/. As just reviewed in lesson 22, the /i/ and /e/ are two of the five basic vowels found in most languages of the world: /i/, /e/, /a/, /o/, and /u/. English has /i/ and /e/ and three additional front vowel sounds, making five front vowels.

Vowel 1 is a very high front vowel.

/iʸ/—s<u>ee</u>

Vowel 2 is a lower high front vowel.

/ɪ/—<u>i</u>t

Vowel 3 is a mid front vowel.

/eⁱ/—s<u>ay</u>

Vowel 4 is a lower mid front vowel.

/ɛ/—y<u>e</u>s

Vowel 5 is a low front vowel.

/æ/—f<u>a</u>t

Look at diagram 5. Repeat: /iʸ/   /ɪ/   /eⁱ/   /ɛ/   /æ/.

Look at diagram 6.

The large symbols represent the two basic front vowels: /i/ and /e/.

The small symbols represent the five English front vowels: /iʸ/, /ɪ/, /eⁱ/, /ɛ/, and /æ/.

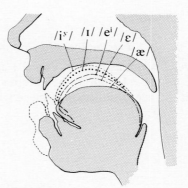

Diagram 5

¹s<u>ee</u> /iʸ/ ²<u>i</u>t /ɪ/	**i**		
³s<u>ay</u> /eⁱ/ ⁴y<u>e</u>s /ɛ/	**e**		
⁵f<u>a</u>t /æ/			

Diagram 6

Part 2—Production, Practice, and Pronunciation Review Tests

Directions: Read and review the production notes for Vowel 1 (column 1). Practice the review test words and sentences for Vowel 1 (column 2). Then record, listen, and analyze. Continue in the same way with Vowels 2, 3, 4, and 5.

VOWEL 1

Production and Practice		*Review Test*
Vowel 1 is the high front vowel. It is not a pure /i/ as in some languages.[2] It has a /y/ glide at the end: /iʸ/. Pronounce these words: s<u>ee</u> m<u>e</u> r<u>ea</u>d.	gr<u>ee</u>n	I want a green tree!
	tr<u>ee</u>	
	thr<u>ee</u>	I lost three keys!
	k<u>ey</u>s	
	r<u>ea</u>d	Read each book!
	<u>ea</u>ch	

VOWEL 2

Production and Practice		*Review Test*
Vowel 2 is not as high as Vowel 1 and it does not have a glide.[3] Listen to the difference: /iʸ/ → /ɪ/ s<u>ee</u> it s<u>ee</u> it. Pronounce these words: th<u>i</u>s d<u>i</u>d b<u>i</u>t.	th<u>i</u>s	This isn't his!
	<u>i</u>sn't	
	h<u>i</u>s	
	wh<u>i</u>ch	Which window?
	wíndow	

VOWEL 3

Production and Practice		*Review Test*
This is a mid front vowel. It is not a pure /e/ as in some languages. It has an /i/ glide at the end: /eⁱ/ s<u>ay</u>. Pronounce these words: w<u>ay</u> d<u>ay</u> c<u>a</u>me.	t<u>a</u>ke	Take it away!
	aw<u>á</u>y	
	tod<u>á</u>y	Today is the eighth of May.
	<u>ei</u>ghth	
	M<u>ay</u>	

VOWEL 4

Production and Practice		*Review Test*
Vowel 4 is a mid front vowel but it is lower than Vowel 3. It does not have a glide. Listen to the difference: /eⁱ/ → /ɛ/ l<u>a</u>te l<u>e</u>t. Pronounce these words: l<u>e</u>ss g<u>e</u>t m<u>e</u>n.	b<u>e</u>st	It's the best restaurant in town.
	r<u>é</u>staurant	
	r<u>é</u>ady	I'll be ready at ten-twenty!
	t<u>e</u>n	
	tw<u>é</u>nty	

---

2. Not pure as in French *oui* or Spanish *si*, French *les* or Spanish *de*.
3. See page 140 for notes on lax vowels and a centering glide tendency in some environments.

VOWEL 5

Production and Practice		*Review Test*

Vowel 5 is the lowest front vowel. The jaw is lowered and the tongue is arched forward a little so that it is not confused with Vowel 7. Listen to the difference: /æ/ → /a/. Pronounce these words: fa̱t   ca̱t   ba̱d.

há̱ppy

fá̱mily

há̱ndsome

ma̱n

da̱nced

sa̱ng

They're a happy family!

He's a handsome man!

They danced and sang.

Part 3—Front Vowel Tests

Test 1: Discrimination[4] (AK/TS)

Directions: Listen to the following sentences. Draw a circle around the word (and vowel number) you think you hear.

Examples: Who bought the ((paper—pepper)?   *Answer:* paper
                          3   4   3

              Who bought the (paper—(pepper)?   *Answer:* pepper
                          3   4   4

These sentences will be given only once.

1. I bought another (sheep—ship).
             1   2

2. Do you have a (pain—pen)?
             3   4

3. Who borrowed my (pan—pen)?
               5   4

4. She has a new (pen—pin).
             4   2

5. She's (sleeping—slipping).
          1   2

6. He (tasted—tested) it.
        3   4

7. I can smell the (leather—lather).
                4   5

8. The waiter gave me the (bill—bell).
                           2   4

9. Do you have a (pin—pain—pen—pan)?
             2   3   4   5

10. Spell the word (seat—sit—set—sat).
            1   2   4   5

---

4. *Lab*: At the end of test 1 stop the tape and ask students to give their answers. Write them on the chalkboard and have students check their work. You may want to replay this segment of the test for review.

Test 2: Spelling[5] (AK/TS)

Directions: Put the following words in the correct column according to the vowel in their pronunciation. The teacher will *not* read the words.

(Lab: Stop the tape and complete test 2; allow 5 to 10 minutes.)

cat	easy	black	last	fish
these	rain	red	get	letter
little	test	may	gate	sang
table	big	green	she	six

Vowel 1	*Vowel 2*	*Vowel 3*	*Vowel 4*	*Vowel 5*
s<u>ee</u>	<u>i</u>t	s<u>ay</u>	y<u>e</u>s	f<u>a</u>t
_____	_____	_____	_____	_____
_____	_____	_____	_____	_____
_____	_____	_____	_____	_____
_____	_____	_____	_____	_____

Test 3: Test Sentences for Writing Vowel Numbers[6] (AK/TS)

Directions: Listen as the following words are pronounced. Write the number of the vowel below the line.

Vowel 1	/iʸ/	as in	s<u>ee</u>
Vowel 2	/ɪ/	as in	<u>i</u>t
Vowel 3	/eⁱ/	as in	s<u>ay</u>
Vowel 4	/ɛ/	as in	y<u>e</u>s
Vowel 5	/æ/	as in	f<u>a</u>t

Repeat and write the vowel numbers.

1. The t<u>ea</u>cher g<u>a</u>ve us a sp<u>e</u>cial r<u>ea</u>ding t<u>e</u>st.

2. H<u>i</u>s l<u>i</u>ttle c<u>a</u>t ch<u>a</u>sed the b<u>i</u>g r<u>a</u>t.

3. I th<u>i</u>nk we'll t<u>a</u>ke a v<u>a</u>cation <u>i</u>n Nov<u>e</u>mber.

4. The l<u>a</u>st qu<u>e</u>stion on the t<u>e</u>st was <u>ea</u>sy to <u>a</u>nswer.

5. I g<u>ue</u>ss he'll w<u>ai</u>t unt<u>i</u>l W<u>e</u>dnesday.

6. M<u>a</u>ny l<u>a</u>nds h<u>a</u>ve a c<u>e</u>lebration on the first d<u>ay</u> of M<u>ay</u>.

---

5. *Lab*: At the end of test 2 stop the tape and ask students to give their answers. Write them on the chalkboard and have students check their work. Pronounce them and discuss the spelling patterns.
6. *Lab*: At the end of test 3 stop the tape and ask students to give the vowel numbers they have written. You may want to replay this segment of the test and have students check their work.

Test 4: Test Sentences for Self-Monitoring and Self-Testing

Directions: Practice the sentences in test 3 using natural rhythm, stress, and reductions. Exaggerate the sounds slightly. Record. Listen and monitor your pronunciation.

Central Vowels

Part 1—Review

Many languages have only one central vowel, the low central vowel /a/. The /a/ sound is one of the five basic vowels found in most languages of the world: /i/, /e/, /a/, /o/, and /u/. English has the /a/ sound and two additional central vowel sounds, making three central vowels.

Vowel 12 is a high central vowel.

/ɝ/—bird

Vowel 6 is a mid central vowel.

/ʌ/—bus

Vowel 7 is a low central vowel.

/a/—stop

Look at diagram 7. Repeat: /ɝ/   /ʌ/   /a/.

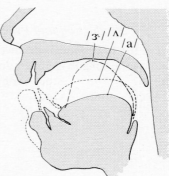

Diagram 7

Look at diagram 8.

The large symbol represents the one basic central vowel: /a/.

The small symbols represent the three English central vowels: /ɝ/, /ʌ/, and /a/.

¹²bird	/ɝ/	
⁶bus	/ʌ/	
⁷stop father	/a/ a	

Diagram 8

Part 2—Production, Practice, and Pronunciation Review Tests

Directions: Read and review the production notes for Vowel 12 (column 1). Practice the review test words and sentences for Vowel 12 (column 2). Then record, listen, and analyze. Continue in the same way with Vowels 6 and 7.

VOWEL 12

Production and Practice

Vowel 12 is the vowel-*r* sound. In these words the vowel before the *r* sound is silent: bird   work   her. They are pronounced as if they were spelled: b'rd   w'rk   h'r. The tongue is raised high and "bunched up" against the center part of the hard roof of the mouth: /ɝ/   /ɝ/   bird. Pronounce these words: bird   work   her.

Review Test

learn   Learn ten new words!
words
her   Her skirt was purple!
skirt
púrple
work   I can work on Thursday.
Thúrsday

VOWEL 6

Production and Practice		*Review Test*
Vowel 6 is the mid central vowel. The tongue is in the middle position and the jaw is partly raised: /ʌ/ /ʌ/ bu̱s. Pronounce these words: bu̱s su̱n ru̱n.	stúdy	I'll study on Monday!
	Mónday	
	cóusin	My cousin is coming to lunch!
	cóming	
	lunch	
	rúnning	He's running to catch the bus.
	bu̱s	

VOWEL 7

Production and Practice		*Review Test*
Vowel 7 is the lowest central vowel. The jaw is lowered and the tongue is pulled down from the rest position: /a/ /a/ sto̱p. Pronounce these words: sto̱p ho̱t clo̱ck.	fáther	My father forgot!
	forgót	
	cóllege	College opens in October.
	Octóber	
	go̱t	I got a spot on my collar.
	spot	
	collar	

Part 3—Central Vowel Tests

Test 1: Discrimination[7] (AK/TS)

Directions: Listen to the following sentences. Draw a circle around the word (and vowel number) you think you hear.

Examples: Who owns the (duck—dock)?   *Answer*: dock
6   7   7

Who owns the (dock—duck)?   *Answer*: duck
7   6   6

These sentences will be given only once.

1. The (bird—bud) is beautiful!
   12   6
2. Was it (hot—hurt)?
   7   12
3. My (lock—luck) was good!
   7   6
4. The (cub—curb) was black.
   6   12
5. Who (shut—shot) it?
   6   7

6. That was a good (shirt—shot)!
   12   7
7. Which (curlers—collars—colors) did she buy?
   12   7   6
8. Where are the (ducks—docks)?
   6   7
9. I didn't see the (cub—curb—cob).
   6   12   7
10. Spell the word (lock—lurk—luck).
    7   12   6

---

7. *Lab*: At the end of test 1 stop the tape and ask students to give their answers. Write them on the chalkboard and have students check their work. You may want to replay this segment of the test for review.

Test 2: Spelling[8] (AK/TS)

Directions: Put the following words in the correct column according to the vowel in their pronunciation. The teacher will *not* read the words.

(Lab: Stop the tape and complete test 2; allow 5 to 10 minutes.)

cot	work	luck	shut	church
shirt	drop	sun	shot	lunch
lock	fun	nurse	cut	clock
hurt	her	not	top	word
duck				

Vowel 12	*Vowel 6*	*Vowel 7*
bi<u>r</u>d	b<u>u</u>s	st<u>o</u>p
_____	_____	_____
_____	_____	_____
_____	_____	_____
_____	_____	_____
_____	_____	_____
_____	_____	_____
_____	_____	_____

Test 3: Test Sentences for Writing Vowel Numbers[9] (AK/TS)

Directions: Listen as the following words are pronounced. Write the number of the vowel below the line.

Vowel 12	/ɝ/	as in	bi<u>r</u>d
Vowel 6	/ʌ/	as in	b<u>u</u>s
Vowel 7	/a/	as in	st<u>o</u>p

Repeat and write the vowel numbers.

1. H<u>er</u> h<u>u</u>sband g<u>o</u>t h<u>er</u> an<u>o</u>ther f<u>ur</u> coat.

2. The g<u>ir</u>ls w<u>er</u>e st<u>u</u>dying the pr<u>o</u>blems on S<u>u</u>nday and M<u>o</u>nday.

3. The d<u>o</u>ct<u>or</u> and the n<u>ur</u>se left the h<u>o</u>spital at six o'cl<u>o</u>ck.

4. My <u>u</u>ncle and my c<u>ou</u>sin h<u>u</u>rried home from w<u>o</u>rk.

5. I g<u>o</u>t a new c<u>o</u>tton sh<u>ir</u>t with a c<u>o</u>lorful c<u>o</u>llar.

Test 4: Test Sentences for Self-Monitoring and Self-Testing

Directions: Practice the sentences in test 3 using natural rhythm, stress, and reductions. Exaggerate the sounds slightly. Record. Listen and monitor your pronunciation.

---

8. *Lab*: At the end of test 2 stop the tape and ask students to give their answers. Write them on the chalkboard and have students check their work. Pronounce them and discuss the spelling patterns.
9. *Lab*: At the end of test 3 stop the tape and ask students to give the vowel numbers they have written. You may want to replay this segment of the test and have students check their work.

Lesson 24

Rapid Review and Testing of the Back Vowels and Diphthongs

Back Vowels

Part 1—Review

Many languages have only two back vowels, /u/ and /o/. The /u/ and /o/ are two of the five basic vowels found in most languages of the world: /i/, /e/, /a/, /o/, and /u/. English has /u/ and /o/ and two additional back vowel sounds, making four back vowels.

Vowel 8 is a very high back vowel.

/u^w/—tw<u>o</u>

Vowel 9 is a lower high back vowel.

/ʊ/—b<u>oo</u>ks

Vowel 10 is a mid back vowel.

/o^u/—n<u>o</u>

Vowel 11 is a low back vowel.

/ɔ/—l<u>aw</u>

Look at diagram 9. Repeat: /u^w/ /ʊ/ /o^u/ /ɔ/.

Look at diagram 10.

The large symbols represent the two basic back vowels: /u/ and /o/.

The small symbols represent the four English back vowels: /u^w/, /ʊ/, /o^u/, and /ɔ/.

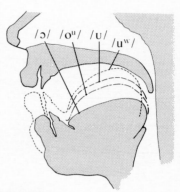

Diagram 9

		/u^w/ **u**
^{8}tw<u>o</u> ^{9}b<u>oo</u>ks		/ʊ/
^{10}n<u>o</u>		/o^u/ **o**
^{11}l<u>aw</u>		/ɔ/

Diagram 10

Part 2—Production, Practice, and Pronunciation Review Tests

Directions: Read and review the production notes for Vowel 8 (column 1). Practice the review test words and sentences for Vowel 8 (column 2). Then record, listen, and analyze. Continue in the same way with Vowels 9, 10, and 11.

VOWEL 8

Production and Practice

Vowel 8 is a high back vowel. It is not a pure /u/ as in some languages. It has a /w/ glide at the end: /uᵂ/. Pronounce these words: n<u>ew</u>   n<u>oo</u>n   t<u>oo</u>.

	### Review Test
n<u>ew</u>	She wants some new blue shoes!
bl<u>ue</u>	
sh<u>oe</u>s	
n<u>ew</u>	We have a new group of students.
gr<u>ou</u>p	
stúdents	
tw<u>o</u>	I want two bags of fruit.
fr<u>ui</u>t.	

VOWEL 9

Production and Practice

Vowel 9 is not as high as Vowel 8. Listen to the difference: /uᵂ/ → /ʊ/   tw<u>o</u>   b<u>oo</u>ks   tw<u>o</u> b<u>oo</u>ks. Pronounce these words: b<u>oo</u>k   st<u>oo</u>d p<u>u</u>t.

	### Review Test
t<u>oo</u>k	Someone took my book!
b<u>oo</u>k	
st<u>oo</u>d	He stood on one foot.
f<u>oo</u>t	
g<u>oo</u>d	She's a good cook!
c<u>oo</u>k	

VOWEL 10

Production and Practice

Vowel 10 is a mid back vowel. It is not a pure /o/ as in some languages. It has an /u/ glide at the end: /oᵘ/. Pronounce these words: n<u>o</u>   <u>ow</u>n   n<u>o</u>te.

	### Review Test
w<u>o</u>n't	I won't go!
g<u>o</u>	
s<u>o</u>ld	We sold the old stove.
<u>o</u>ld	
st<u>o</u>ve	
cl<u>o</u>se	Please close the window.
wínd<u>ow</u>	

VOWEL 11

Production and Practice

Vowel 11 is the low back vowel. The jaw is lowered more than for Vowel 10: /oᵘ/ → /ɔ/   l<u>ow</u>   l<u>aw</u>. Pronounce these words: l<u>aw</u>   s<u>aw</u>   c<u>au</u>ght.

	### Review Test
l<u>o</u>st	I lost my ball!
b<u>a</u>ll	
acr<u>ó</u>ss	It's across the hall!
h<u>a</u>ll	
t<u>au</u>ght	He taught us a song.
s<u>o</u>ng	
l<u>o</u>ng	How long was he gone?
g<u>o</u>ne	

Part 3—Back Vowel Tests

Test 1: Discrimination.[10] (AK/TS)

Directions: Listen to the following sentences. Draw a circle around the word (and vowel number) you think you hear.

Examples: I was (cold—called).   *Answer*: cold
                    10   11   10

I was (cold—called).   *Answer*: called
             10   11   11

These sentences will be given only once.

1. It was a golden (hawk—hook)!
            11   9

2. He's in the (low—law) school.
            10   11

3. It was a long (pull—pool).
             9   8

4. Who paid for the (wool—wall)?
             9   11

5. Mr. White is very (bold—bald)!
             10   11

6. The (suit—soot) was black.
        8   9

7. It isn't (Fall—full) yet!
             11   9

8. Whose (bowl—ball) is this?
             10   11

9. It looks (fullish—foolish)!
             9   8

10. Spell the word (pool—pull—pole—Paul).
                 8   9   10   11

11. Spell the word (cooed—could—code—cawed).
                 8   9   10   11

12. Spell the word (bull—bowl—ball).
                 9   10   11

Test 2: Spelling[11] (AK/TS)

Directions: Put the following words in the correct column according to the vowel in their pronunciation. The teacher will *not* read the words.

(Lab: Stop the tape and complete test 2; allow 5 to 10 minutes.)

school	caught	push	talk	pull
ball	could	pole	you	bold
bull	food	rule	long	taught
cold	code	rose	do	would

Vowel 8	*Vowel 9*	*Vowel 10*	*Vowel 11*
tw<u>o</u>	b<u>oo</u>ks	n<u>o</u>	l<u>aw</u>
_____	_____	_____	_____
_____	_____	_____	_____
_____	_____	_____	_____
_____	_____	_____	_____
_____	_____	_____	_____

---

10. *Lab*: At the end of test 1 stop the tape and ask students to give their answers. Write them on the chalkboard and have students check their work. You may want to replay this segment of the test for review.

11. *Lab*: At the end of test 2 stop the tape and ask students to give their answers. Write them on the chalkboard and have students check their work. Pronounce them and discuss the spelling patterns.

Test 3: Test Sentences for Writing Vowel Numbers[12] (AK/TS)

Directions: Listen as the following words are pronounced. Write the number of the vowel below the line.

Vowel 8	/u^w/	as in	two
Vowel 9	/ʊ/	as in	books
Vowel 10	/o^u/	as in	no
Vowel 11	/ɔ/	as in	law

Repeat and write the vowel numbers.

1. Who put the sugar in my orange juice?

2. It shouldn't snow in June, July, or August.

3. By November the woods ought to be full of snow.

4. She put the small blue coat in the lower drawer.

5. You were gone so long we thought you were lost.

6. He taught football at the local high school.

Test 4: Test Sentences for Self-Monitoring and Self-Testing

Directions: Practice the sentences in test 3 using natural rhythm, stress, and reductions. Exaggerate the sounds slightly. Record. Listen and monitor your pronunciation.

---

12. *Lab*: At the end of test 3 stop the tape and ask students to give the vowel numbers they have written. You may want to replay this segment of the test and have students check their work.

Diphthongs

Part 1—Review

Many languages do not have diphthongs. English has three diphthongs. Diphthongs are double sounds. Each of them is made up of two distinct parts, that is, two different sounds.

Vowel 13 is the diphthong /ai/, as in *my*. It begins with the low central sound /a/ and ends with a high front /i/ or /ɪ/.[13] Look at diagram 11. Repeat: /ai/   /ai/.

Vowel 14 is the diphthong /au/, as in *cow*. It begins with the low central sound /a/ and ends with a high back /u/ or /ʊ/.[14] Look at diagram 12. Repeat: /au/   /au/.

Vowel 15 is the diphthong /ɔi/, as in *boy*. It begins with the low back sound /ɔ/[15] and ends with a high front /i/ or /ɪ/.[16] Look at diagram 13. Repeat: /ɔi/   /ɔi/.

/ai/—**my**

/au/—**cow**

/ɔi/—**boy**

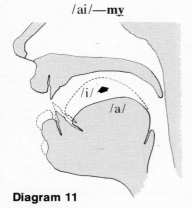

Diagram 11

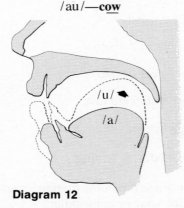

Diagram 12

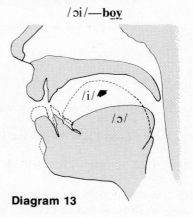

Diagram 13

Part 2—Production, Practice, and Pronunciation Review Tests

Directions: Read and review the production notes for Vowel 13 (column 1). Practice the review test words and sentences for Vowel 13 (column 2). Then record, listen, and analyze. Continue in the same way with Vowels 14 and 15.

VOWEL 13

Production and Practice

Vowel 13 is a diphthong made up of the sounds of /a/ and /i/. Notice the way the mouth closes and the tongue rises for /ai/   /ai/. Pronounce these words:
my   right   nice.

Review Test

nice   It's a nice night!
night

bright   There's a bright light in the sky!
light
sky

I   I like to fly.
like
fly

---

13. If this diphthong comes at the end of a word, the second part is more like Vowel 1. If it comes in the middle of a word, it is more like Vowel 2.
14. If this diphthong comes at the end of a word, the second part is more like Vowel 8. If it comes in the middle of a word, it is more like Vowel 9.
15. For some speakers the first part of Vowel 15 is more like the first part of Vowel 10, /o/, for the diphthong /oi/.
16. If this diphthong comes at the end of a word, the second part is more like Vowel 1. If it comes in the middle of a word, it is more like Vowel 2.

VOWEL 14

Production and Practice		*Review Test*

Vowel 14 is a diphthong made up of the sounds of /a/ and /u/. Notice the way the mouth closes and the lips round for /au/ → /au/. Pronounce these words: c<u>ow</u> d<u>ow</u>n r<u>ou</u>nd.

d<u>ow</u>n   Meet me down town in an hour.

t<u>ow</u>n

h<u>ou</u>r

m<u>ou</u>se   The mouse ran around the house.

ar<u>óu</u>nd

h<u>ou</u>se

cr<u>ow</u>d   The crowd was loud.

l<u>ou</u>d   It was a loud crowd!

VOWEL 15

Production and Practice		*Review Test*

Vowel 15 is a diphthong made up of the sounds of /ɔ/ and /i/. Notice the way the mouth closes, the tongue rises, and the lips spread for /ɔi/ → /ɔi/. Pronounce these words: b<u>oy</u> n<u>oi</u>se v<u>oi</u>ce.

n<u>ói</u>sy   What a noisy toy!

t<u>oy</u>

b<u>oy</u>   The boy joined a coin club.

j<u>oi</u>n

c<u>oi</u>n

j<u>óy</u>ous   What a joyous voice!

v<u>oi</u>ce

Part 3—Diphthong Tests

Test 1: Discrimination[17] (AK/TS)

Directions: Listen to the following sentences. Draw a circle around the word (and vowel number) you think you hear.

Examples: He bought a (tie—(toy)).   *Answer*: toy
            13   15   15

He bought a (toy—(tie)).   *Answer*: tie
            15   13   13

These sentences will be given only once.

1. He loves to eat Hawaiian (pie—poi)!
                      13   15

2. She brought some new (tiles—towels).
                      13   14

3. The (boy—bough) fell down.
          15   14

4. They're afraid of the (mouse—mice)!
                   14   13

5. It's a steel (file—foil).
            13   15

6. Is it time to go (dine—down)?
               13   14

7. That's a terrible (voice—vice)!
              15   13

8. What a good (buy—boy—bow)!
             13   15   14

9. Did you find the (oil—owl—aisle)?
               15   14   13

10. Spell the word (tile—towel—toil).
            13   14   15

---

17. *Lab*: At the end of test 1 stop the tape and ask students to give their answers. Write them on the chalkboard and have students check their work. You may want to replay this segment of the test for review.

Test 2: Spelling.[18] (AK/TS)

Directions: Put the following words in the correct column according to the vowel in their pronunciation. The teacher will *not* read the words.

(Lab: Stop the tape and complete test 2; allow 5 to 10 minutes.)

try	join	find	noun	climb
bright	south	voice	appoint	destroy
crowd	dime	annoy	hour	mountain

Vowel 13	*Vowel 14*	*Vowel 15*
m<u>y</u>	c<u>ow</u>	b<u>oy</u>
_____	_____	_____
_____	_____	_____
_____	_____	_____
_____	_____	_____
_____	_____	_____

Test 3: Test Sentences for Writing Vowel Numbers.[19] (AK/TS)

Directions: Listen as the following words are pronounced. Write the number of the vowel below the line.

Vowel 13	/ai/	as in	m<u>y</u>
Vowel 14	/au/	as in	c<u>ow</u>
Vowel 15	/ɔi/	as in	b<u>oy</u>

Repeat and write the vowel numbers.

1. The c<u>ow</u>b<u>oy</u>s f<u>ou</u>nd a br<u>ow</u>n and wh<u>i</u>te c<u>ow</u>.

2. We inv<u>i</u>ted the cl<u>ow</u>n to j<u>oi</u>n the cr<u>ow</u>d ins<u>i</u>de the h<u>ou</u>se.

3. Ab<u>ou</u>t m<u>i</u>dn<u>i</u>ght we dec<u>i</u>ded to dr<u>i</u>ve d<u>ow</u>n t<u>ow</u>n.

4. We enj<u>oy</u>ed fl<u>y</u>ing through the wh<u>i</u>te cl<u>ou</u>ds h<u>i</u>gh in the sk<u>y</u>.

5. His v<u>oi</u>ce is surpr<u>i</u>singly l<u>ou</u>d.

6. I c<u>ou</u>nted f<u>i</u>ve r<u>oy</u>al cr<u>ow</u>ns in the happy cr<u>ow</u>d.

Test 4: Test Sentences for Self-Monitoring and Self-Testing

Directions: Practice the sentences in test 3 using natural rhythm, stress, and reductions. Exaggerate the sounds slightly. Record. Listen and monitor your pronunciation.

---

18. *Lab*: At the end of test 2 stop the tape and ask students to give their answers. Write them on the chalkboard and have students check their work. Pronounce them and discuss the spelling patterns.
19. *Lab*: At the end of test 3 stop the tape and ask students to give the vowel numbers they have written. You may want to replay this segment of the test and have students check their work.

Supplement A
Practice in Context
for
Unit 1

Section A

Introduction

Twenty context practices are included in this supplement, four each for Sections B, C, D, E, and F of Unit 1. Some contexts are serious and some are lighthearted. Some are easy and some are difficult. Advanced students may be able to do the rapid review and testing lessons in Units 1 and 2 and proceed directly to Supplements A, B, and C for practice, recording, and self-monitoring of pronunciation.

These supplementary practices are included in *Improving Spoken English* for expanded practice beyond the pronunciation and perception work provided in Unit 1. They are *not* intended to substitute for real-life communicative activities which can be provided only by individual teachers in their specific teaching/learning situations. They *are* intended for continued practice of the features of stress, rhythm, and intonation introduced in Unit 1, in more interesting and realistic contexts. Students are urged to record themselves and to listen and monitor their pronunciation.

In addition to these twenty practices, the sixteen practices in Supplement B also may be used for stress, rhythm, and intonation practice as well as for vowel practice.

The number of practices provided here is limited. Teachers may want to add similar practices to meet the particular needs of specific classes.

Section B

Accented/Unaccented Syllables

Practice 1—English Idioms: Foods

These are a few idioms heard frequently in spoken English. The names of foods are used in these expressions. Practice reading them. Monitor syllable accent. Discuss the meanings with your teacher. Add new idioms with foods.

1. Don't spill the beans!	(tell the secret)
2. My car is a lémon!	(a defective product)
3. His yoúngest son is the ápple of his eye.	(his favorite)
4. Don't put all your eggs in one básket.	(all your hopes on one thing)
5. Give us your opínion in a nútshell.	(in very brief form)
6. That sounds físhy to me.	(probably not true)
7. That would be péachy keen.	(very good)
8. That súbject is a hot potáto.	(people have strong feelings about it)
9. Éverything was in ápple pie órder.	(in perfect order)
10. They were packed ínto the élevator like sardínes in a can.	(very crowded)
11. The new stúdents are the cream of the crop.	(the very best)
12. I'm all bútter fíngers todáy.	(my fingers seem slippery; I drop everything)
13. There is no use crýing over spilled milk.	(no use in worrying about something that has already happened)
14. She was as cool as a cúcumber.	(very self-assured)
15. He's as slow as molásses in Jánuary.	(very slow)

Practice 2—Recorded Telephone Message: Maplewood Movies

The following has been scripted from a real recorded telephone message. Practice reading the words in the word list with attention to monitoring the syllable accents as marked. Then read the message monitoring the accented syllables.

TELEPHONE VOICE: This is a recorded message from your Maplewood Movies which are located in the Maplewood Shopping Center. Our feature today in Theater One is *Murder on the Orient Express*. Our feature today in Theater Two is *The Sound of Music*. Show times are at one-thirty, three-thirty, five-fifty, seven-fifteen, and nine-thirty. All seats are two dollars for adults and one dollar for children under twelve. If you have any further questions, please call 689–4334. Thank you for calling your Maplewood Movies.

méssage	músic	todáy	recórded
móvies	dóllars	expréss	nine-thírty
shópping	chíldren	adúlts	one-thírty
cénter	únder		three-thírty
féature	fúrther	Máplewood	five-fífty
múrder	quéstions	lócated	
	cálling	théater	seven-fiftéen
		Órient	

Practice 3—Proverbs

A proverb is a folk saying which expresses a bit of folk truth or wisdom. Practice the following proverbs with attention to monitoring syllable accents as marked. Discuss the meanings of the proverbs. The ideas in most of these proverbs have been expressed in many languages.

1. A jóurney of a thóusand miles starts with a síngle step. (Chinese proverb)
2. I will side with my bróther agáinst my cóusin, but I will side with my cóusin agáinst a stránger. (Arabic proverb)
3. Blood is thícker than wáter. (German proverb)
4. Don't márry for móney; you can bórrow it chéaper. (Scottish proverb)
5. Necéssity is the móther of invéntion. (French proverb)
6. Hónesty is the best pólicy. (Benjamin Franklin)
7. Árguing and bórrowing cause tears and sórrowing. (Dutch proverb)
8. Mísery loves cómpany. (a proverb in many languages)
9. Próverbs give us the wísdom of mankínd. (Persian proverb)

Practice 4—Radio News Reading: Foreign Students

Read the passage aloud sentence by sentence. Mark the accented syllables. Then practice reading the passage with attention to monitoring syllable accents. Read for meaning so that the listener gets the sense or important points of information.

RADIO REPORTER: Good afternoon. Here is the first in our series of special news briefs brought to you by the International Trans-World Press. Subject: *Foreign Students Studying in the United States.*

Foreign students studying in the United States now number nearly one hundred and seventy-nine thousand. This figure for the academic year nineteen seventy-five, nineteen seventy-six (1975–1976) comes from the Ínstitute of Internátional Educátion. The major fields of study are the following: engineering, medicine, biology, the physical sciences, and teacher training. The country with the largest group of students is Irán. The continent of Ásia sends more students than any other continent. The ten largest enrollments are:

Irán	19,630 (nineteen thousand, six hundred thirty)
Hóng Kong	11,746 (eleven thousand, seven hundred forty-six)
Nigéria	11,282 (eleven thousand, two hundred eighty-two)
Taiwán	10,071 (ten thousand, seventy-one)
Índia	9,497 (nine thousand, four hundred ninety-seven)

249

Cánada	9,289 (nine thousand, two hundred eighty-nine)
Tháiland	7,300 (seven thousand, three hundred)
Japán	6,974 (six thousand, nine hundred seventy-four)
Venezuéla	4,616 (four thousand, six hundred sixteen)
México	4,553 (four thousand, five hundred fifty-three)

Tune in next week for the next in our series of special news briefs.

Section C

Syllables and Suffixes

Practice 5—English Idioms: Animals, Birds, Insects

These are a few idioms heard frequently in spoken English. The names of animals are used in these expressions. Practice reading them. Monitor the suffixes as marked. Discuss the meanings. Add new idioms.

1. Don't count your chicken<u>s</u> before they are hatch<u>ed</u>.

   (don't depend on something before it is a fact)

2. He dogg<u>ed</u> my footstep<u>s</u>.

   (followed me everywhere)

3. They were running like hors<u>es</u> head<u>ed</u> for the barn.

   (very fast)

4. Children are terrible copy cat<u>s</u>.

   (they copy what they see others doing)

5. He wasn't suppos<u>ed</u> to monkey around with his father'<u>s</u> tool<u>s</u>.

   (wasn't supposed to play with them)

6. My goose was cook<u>ed</u>.

   (someone found out about my plans and exposed me)

7. I always have butterflie<u>s</u> in my stomach when I give speech<u>es</u>.

   (I am nervous)

8. They are as clever as fox<u>es</u>.

   (very clever and crafty)

9. Their action<u>s</u> show<u>ed</u> they were snake<u>s</u> in the grass.

   (not to be trusted)

10. It's too late to lock the barn door<u>s</u> after the hors<u>es</u> are stolen.

    (too late to prevent something after it has happened)

11. The early bird catch<u>es</u> the worm.

    (people who get an early start on something will get the best result)

12. You can't teach an old dog new trick<u>s</u>.

    (people are slow to change to new things)

13. It was raining cat<u>s</u> and dog<u>s</u>.

    (heavy rainfall)

Practice 6—Recorded Telephone Message: National Weather Service

The following has been scripted from a real recorded telephone message. Practice reading it with attention to the suffixes as marked. Then practice the words in the word list with attention to monitoring the syllable accents as marked. Read the message again monitoring *both* suffixes and syllable accents.

TELEPHONE VOICE: The National Weather Service present<u>s</u> a two-day abbreviat<u>ed</u> forecast for five principal cit<u>ies</u> of the Eastern Unit<u>ed</u> State<u>s</u>. *Boston*—partly cloudy today; high, sixty-five degrees; tonight'<u>s</u> low, fifty; sunny on We*d*n*e*sday; high, sixty-eight. *Miami*—partly sunny today and tomorrow; high both day<u>s</u>, in the upper eight<u>ies</u>; night low<u>s</u>, in the high seven<u>ties</u>. *New York City*—partly cloudy with scatter<u>ed</u> rain shower<u>s</u>; today'<u>s</u> high, in the mid six<u>ties</u>; tonight'<u>s</u> low, in the high fif<u>ties</u>. *Pittsburgh*—thunder shower<u>s</u> today with high wind<u>s</u> expect<u>ed</u>; high<u>s</u> both day<u>s</u>, in the high six<u>ties</u>; low<u>s</u>, in the high for<u>ties</u>. *New Orleans*—today'<u>s</u> high, eighty-seven; tonight'<u>s</u> low, eighty; We*d*n*e*sday, heavy rainstorm<u>s</u>, with moderate wind<u>s</u>; high, ninety; low, eighty-two.

251

pártly	fórties	tonígt	Miámi
clóudy	fífties	todáy	Uníted
súnny	síxties	degrées	New Órleans
wéather	éighties	presénts	tomórrow
fórecast	nínety		
sérvice	Éastern	nátional	New York Cíty
thúnder	Píttsburgh	séventies	
shówers	Bóston	móderate	abbréviated
scáttered	Wédnesday	príncipal	
cíties			

Practice 7—Proverbs

A proverb is a folk saying which expresses a bit of folk truth or wisdom. Practice the following proverbs with attention to monitoring suffixes as marked. Then read them again with attention to monitoring both suffixes and syllable accents. Discuss the meanings of the proverbs. The ideas in most of these proverbs have been expressed in many languages. Proverbs 5 through 10 are found in several languages.

1. April showers bring May flowers. (English proverb)
2. He who laughs last, laughs best! (French, Italian, Danish proverb)
3. Where there's life, there's hope. (Italian and Portuguese proverb)
4. All things come to him who waits. (French proverb)
5. Nothing ventured; nothing gained.
6. A penny saved is a penny earned.
7. Actions speak louder than words.
8. Fools rush in where angels fear to tread.
9. It never rains but it pours.
10. If wishes were horses, beggars would ride.

Practice 8—Radio News Reading: Structure of the U.S. Government

Practice the following passage with attention to syllable accent and suffixes. Read for meaning so that the listener gets the sense or important points of information. Discuss the various structures of governments.

RADIO REPORTER: Good afternoon. Here is another in our series of special news briefs brought to you by the International Trans-World Press. Subject: *Structure of the U.S. Government*.

The government of the United States has a three-part organization. This structure of government sometimes is called "separation of power." The theory of "separation of power" is this: it makes sure that no one branch of government becomes more powerful than the other two.

The first branch of government described in the Constitution is the Legislative branch. This provides for the Congress of the United States which is divided into two parts. One part is the upper house which is called the Senate. Each of the fifty states has two senators regardless of population. The one hundred senators are elected for six-year terms. The other house is called the

252

lower house, the House of Representatives. Each state has representatives in proportion to its population. The present House of Representatives has four hundred and thirty-five members, who are elected for two-year terms.

The second of the three branches of government is the Executive branch. This branch is headed by the President who is elected for a term of four years. The President appoints his cabinet of department officials.

The third of the three branches of the United States government is the Judicial branch. The Judicial branch is headed by a group of nine judges called the Supreme Court. These nine judges are appointed for life by the President after the senators have approved the President's choice or choices.

Tune in next week for the next in our series of special news briefs.

Section D

Sentence Sense: Rhythm and Stress

Practice 9—Proverbs and Wise Words

Proverbs and wise words express a special bit of truth or wisdom. Practice reading the following with attention to monitoring the rhythm and sentence stresses. Sentence stresses are underlined. Read for meaning so the listener gets the exact meaning of the message.

1. It is better to be a nobody who accomplishes something, than a somebody who accomplishes nothing. (A. Pundit)
2. Iron rusts from disuse; water loses its purity from stagnation and in cold weather becomes frozen; and so does inaction sap the vigors of the mind. (Leonardo da Vinci)
3. Heaven helps those, who help themselves. (Benjamin Franklin)
4. Cleanliness is next to godliness. (a proverb in many languages)
5. Patience is the key to joy; but haste is the key to sorrow. (Arabic proverb)
6. Soldiers win the battles; generals get the credit. (Napoleon Bonaparte)
7. If he is indeed wise he does not bid you enter the house of his wisdom, but rather leads you to the threshold of your own mind. (Kahlil Gibran, in *The Prophet*, speaking of teaching and teachers)

Practice 10—Recorded Telephone Message: Passports

The following has been scripted from a real recorded telephone message. Read the message aloud sentence by sentence. Mark pauses. Mark any added sentence stresses which you wish to make. Then practice reading the message. Read it for meaning, that is, with as much sentence sense as possible so that the listener gets the important parts of the message.

TELEPHONE VOICE: This is Donald M. Anderson, Jefferson County Clerk, bringing you a recorded message regarding applications for passports. Application may be made in the County Clerk's Office, County Building, corner of Main Street and Second Avenue. This office is open from eight-thirty A.M. to five-thirty P.M., Monday through Friday. Applicants must appear in person and present the following:

One: Two duplicate photographs taken within six months of the date of application. These must be full face of the applicant, no smaller than two-and-a-half by two-and-a-half inches, and no larger than three by three inches. Color photographs meeting the foregoing requirements are acceptable. Snapshots, vending machine photographs, or polaroid prints are not acceptable.
Two: Proof of citizenship. This may be a certified record of birth, a previous U.S. passport, or a naturalization certificate.
Three: Personal identification. This may be a driver's license, a recently expired passport, or a government or military I.D. card.
Four: Fees. A ten dollar money order or your personal check made out to the passport office, and three dollars and forty cents in cash, for local fees.

Your <u>pass</u>port will be <u>rea</u>dy in three or four <u>weeks</u>. For additional information, please call 884–<u>3</u>415 between the hours of ten <small>A.M.</small> and four <small>P.M.</small> Information regarding innocula<u>t</u>ions may be ob<u>tain</u>ed by calling your local Board of <u>Health</u>.

<u>Thank</u> you for <u>call</u>ing. Have a <u>good</u> trip.

Practice 11—Old Irish Good Luck Saying

Practice the following lines with attention to monitoring the rhythm and sentence stresses. Sentence stresses are underlined. Discuss the meaning of the lines.

> May there <u>al</u>ways be work for your <u>hands</u> to do.
>
> May your <u>purse</u> always hold a <u>coin</u> or two.
>
> May the <u>sun</u> always shine on your <u>win</u>dow pane.
>
> May a <u>rain</u>bow be certain to <u>fol</u>low each rain.
>
> May the <u>heart</u> of a friend <u>al</u>ways be near you.
>
> May your <u>heart</u> be filled with <u>glad</u>ness to cheer you.

(author unknown)

Practice 12—Radio News Reading: Ocean Sciences and Engineering

Read the following passage aloud sentence by sentence. Mark pauses; add sentence stresses wherever you wish. Then read it monitoring syllable accent, suffixes, rhythm, and stress. Read for meaning so that the listener gets the sense or important points of information. Discuss the reading.

RADIO REPORTER: Good after<u>noon</u>. Here is a<u>nother</u> in our series of special news briefs brought to you by the International Trans-World <u>Press</u>. Subject: *The Expan<u>ding</u> Field of Ocean Science and Engi<u>neer</u>ing*.

The a<u>bun</u>dance of <u>water</u> on earth makes it u<u>nique</u> among the <u>plan</u>ets of our <u>solar</u> system. The <u>o</u>ceans cover over <u>seven</u>ty percent of its <u>sur</u>face, <u>and</u>, although Earth's <u>land</u> has been explored <u>thor</u>oughly, the <u>o</u>ceans still keep most of their <u>secrets</u>.

As the world popu<u>la</u>tion continues to ex<u>pand</u>, man must turn to the <u>o</u>ceans to meet many basic <u>needs</u>—<u>food</u>, <u>min</u>erals, <u>chem</u>icals, and drinkable <u>water</u>. <u>These</u> are present in the <u>o</u>cean in unbe<u>lie</u>vable quantities. Man must ex<u>plore</u> and learn to <u>use</u> these resources of the seas and must <u>al</u>so learn how to con<u>serve</u> them.

With<u>in</u> the past ten <u>years</u> the field of ocean science and engi<u>neer</u>ing has expanded far be<u>yond</u> the dreams of <u>scientists</u>. Re<u>searchers</u> have moved ahead to <u>new</u> horizons which <u>now</u> rival the explorations of outer <u>space</u>. Advances in pre<u>ci</u>sion and auto<u>ma</u>tion—particularly in hy<u>drog</u>raphy and in <u>chart</u>making—have <u>added</u> to our knowledge of ocean ter<u>rain</u> and have prepared the path for <u>o</u>ther oceanographic <u>sciences</u>. Developments in the <u>fol</u>lowing fields are moving ahead <u>rap</u>idly: <u>phys</u>ical oceanography, <u>chem</u>ical oceanography, marine bi<u>o</u>logy, and <u>sub</u>marine ge<u>o</u>logy.

To keep such a <u>vast</u> scientific effort moving <u>for</u>ward, <u>large</u> numbers of <u>scientists</u> and trained per<u>son</u>nel are needed. The promise of <u>new</u> wealth from the <u>sea</u> has created an e<u>nor</u>mous demand for <u>scientists</u> and engi<u>neers</u> to study the <u>nature</u> of the ocean and the po<u>ten</u>tial of its <u>resources</u>.

<u>Tune</u> in <u>next</u> week for the <u>next</u> in our series of <u>special news briefs</u>.[1]

---

1. Adapted from *The Water Planet*, U.S. Oceanographic Office, Washington, D.C., pp. ii and 30.

Section E

Elisions and Assimilations

Practice 13—English Idioms: Anatomy

Below are a few idioms heard frequently in spoken English. The names of different parts of the body are used in these expressions. Practice reading them. Monitor the contractions and the plural and past tense suffixes. Discuss the meanings.

1. I'd help you but my hands're tied.   (circumstances make it impossible)

2. He's up to his neck in trouble.   (a lot of trouble)

3. They're on the last leg of the trip.   (the last part)

4. That's a real slap in the face.   (very insulting)

5. He isn't from this neck of the woods.   (this part of the country)

6. He doesn't have a leg to stand on.   (nothing to support his idea)

7. We're driving into the teeth of the storm.   (the worst part)

8. They'd escaped by the skin of their teeth.   (just barely escaped)

9. We'll need someone to back us up.   (to support us)

10. We'll cross our fingers that he'll be safe.   (wish for good luck)

11. His left hand doesn't know what his right hand's doing.   (his behavior is contradictory)

12. I don't think his heart's in his work.   (isn't really interested)

13. This cake is so delicious it'll melt in your mouth.   (very good to the taste)

14. He's a person who likes a lot of elbow room.   (likes space; doesn't want to be crowded)

15. He isn't dry behind the ears.   (is very inexperienced in life)

Practice 14—Telephone Conversation: Ordering Breakfast

The following has been scripted from a real telephone conversation. It is a real-life conversational dialogue. Practice reading the lines of the conversation with attention to the contractions and contractions with sound changes, rhythm, and stress. (This telephone conversation is nearly the same as one which might take place person-to-person in a restaurant.)

(Ring.)
WAITER'S VOICE: Good morning. Room service.
CUSTOMER'S VOICE: Good morning. I'd like to order breakfast please.
WAITER: Yes Ma'am, and what's your room number.
CUSTOMER: Room seven twenty-four.
W: All right, what'll you have?
C: I'd like orange juice . . .
W: Regular or large?
C: Mmm, large, I guess.
W: All right (spoken slowly, as if writing the order).
C: . . . and I'd like two eggs . . .
W: How d'ya want your eggs?

256

C: Oh . . . scrambled, please.
W: All right.
C: . . . ~~and~~ bacon . . .
W: All right.
C: . . . ~~and~~ toast . . .
W: D'ya want ~~your~~ toast buttered ~~or~~ plain?
C: Buttered.
W: All right.
C: . . . ~~and~~ coffee.
W: D'ya take ~~your~~ coffee with cream?
C: No, black.
W: Anything else?
C: No, thank you. That's all.
W: Okay. That'll be 'bout twenty minutes.
C: Thank you.
W: ~~You're~~ welcome.

Practice 15—Rhymalogues

The following two-line dialogues are called rhymalogues. Practice reading the rhymalogues with attention to the contractions, sound changes, rhythm, and stress. The sentence stresses are underlined.

1. *Pat*:   Wouldja like a piece of <u>can</u>dy, <u>An</u>dy?

   Andy: No thanks <u>Pat</u>. I don't wanna get <u>fat</u>.

   (*Wouldja* is a contracted form of *would + you*.
   Wanna is a contracted form of *want + to*.)

2. *Jane*:   Howdja get <u>back</u>, <u>Jack</u>?

   Jack: I came on the <u>train</u>, Jane.

   (*Howdja* is a contracted form of *how + did + you*.)

3. *Sue*:   Whendja get <u>in</u>, <u>Lynn</u>?

   Lynn: I got in about <u>two</u>, <u>Sue</u>.

   (*Whendja* is a contracted form of *when + did + you*).

4. *Mr. Devon*: When's the next <u>bus</u>, <u>Gus</u>?

   Gus: It'll leave around <u>seven</u>, Mr. <u>De</u>von.

5. *Mack*:   Where's your dog <u>Pal</u>, <u>Al</u>?

   Al: He's out in the <u>back</u>, <u>Mack</u>.

Practice 16—Radio Weather Report

The following has been scripted from a real weather report. Practice this passage with attention to contractions, rhythm, and stress. Read for meaning so that the listener gets the sense or important points of information.

ANNOUNCER: And <u>now</u> for our <u>noon</u>time report from the <u>Weath</u>er Bureau, here's our <u>weath</u>er reporter <u>Joan</u> <u>Jack</u>son.

REPORTER: Thanks Dick Davis, and good afternoon everyone. Here's the weather news for today. Winter is not over yet! Two storm systems, one from the Gulf, and the other from the Northern Rockies, will move through the area today. This'll give us snow, but only in light accumulations of an inch or less. Tonight these storms will join forces off the East Coast. Then the snow will stop but the temperatures will drop sharply. Highs today'll be thirty-one to thirty-six; lows tonight'll be eighteen to twenty-three. Wednesday will be partly sunny with a chance of snow showers and temperatures near thirty.

ANNOUNCER: Thanks Joan, and now back to our music—"There's a Bluebird on My Shoulder."

Section F

Intonation

Practice 17—Telephone Conversation: Flower Shop

The following has been scripted from a real telephone conversation. Practice reading the lines of the conversation with attention to intonation, rhythm, and stress.

A: Good afternoon. Johnson's Flower Shop.

B: Hello. Is this a bad time to call for some information on prices?

A: No, I can help you.

B: Thank you. Do you carry the long-stem roses?

A: Yes we do.

B: How much are they?

A: They're twelve dollars a dozen.

B: And what colors do they come in?

A: They come in red, pink, white, orange, and yellow.

B: All right. Thank you very much.

A: You're very welcome.

Practice 18—Telephone Conversation: Car Rental Information

The following has been scripted from a real telephone conversation. Practice reading the lines of the conversation with attention to intonation, rhythm, and stress.

A: Good morning. Rapid Rent-a-Car.

B: Good morning. I'd like some information.

A: All right.

B: Could you tell me how much it costs per day to rent a car?

A: Did you have any special size in mind?

B: No. Not really.

A: All right. Our smallest cars are subcompacts. They rent for eight dollars a day and eight cents a mile.

B: Let me write that down.

A: Okay (pause).

B: What's the next size?

A: The next size up is our standard size car . . . at nine dollars a day and nine cents a mile.

B: M-hm (spoken slowly, as if writing the information).

A: Next we have our full size car . . . at twelve dollars a day and twelve cents a mile.

B: M-hm (spoken slowly, as if writing the information).

A: And last we have our luxury cars . . . at fourteen dollars a day and fourteen cents a mile.

B: All right. Thanks for your help.

A: That's okay. Thanks for calling.

Practice 19—Telephone Conversation: Travel Information

The following has been scripted from a real telephone conversation. Practice reading the lines of the conversation with attention to intonation, rhythm, and stress.

A: Three A Motoring Services.

B: Hello. Could you give me some information?

A: Yes, ma'am.

B: I'd like driving distances to three cities.

A: Okay. What are they?

B: New York City, downtown . . .

A: All right.

B: . . . Miami, downtown . . .

A: All right.

B: . . . and Chicago.

A: All right. Hold on please.

B: Okay (pause).

A: Here we go. New York City is two hundred thirty-nine miles via the Lincoln Tunnel . . .

B: M-hm (spoken slowly, as if writing the information).

A: . . . two hundred thirty-eight miles via the Holland Tunnel, and two hundred forty-seven via the George Washington Bridge.

B: Could you repeat the last one?

A: Two hundred forty-seven via the George Washington Bridge.

B: Thank you (pause).

A: Miami is one thousand ninety-eight miles . . .

B: M-hm (spoken slowly, as if writing the information).

A: . . . and Chicago is six hundred ninety-nine miles.

B: Thank you very much. I appreciate your help.

A: You're entirely welcome.

Practice 20—Radio News Reading: UNICEF

Read the following passage aloud sentence by sentence. Mark pauses. Practice reading the passage with attention to intonation, rhythm, and stress.

REPORTER: Good afternoon. Here is another in our series of special news briefs brought to you by the International Trans-World Press. Subject: *UNICEF (The United Nations International Children's Emergency Fund)*.

Long before the organization of UNICEF, more than thirty years ago, Abraham Lincoln had this to say about children. "A child is a person who is going to carry on what you have started. He is going to sit where you are sitting, and when you are gone, attend to those things which you think are important. You may adopt all the policies you please, but how they are carried out depends on him. He will assume control of your cities, states, and nations. He is going to move in and take over your churches, schools, universities, and corporations. All your books are going to be judged, praised, or condemned by him. The fate of humanity is in his hands."

UNICEF helps children throughout the world, regardless of race, religion, or nationality.

Caring, planning, and working for the future of the world's children is a year-round job for UNICEF. It has spent over thirty years helping to improve children's services in the most deprived areas of the world, where three-fourths of the world child population currently lives. Today UNICEF is working in over a hundred countries to give children a good start in life, the good start every child deserves.

Who will take over the world tomorrow? The children.

Tune in next week for the next in our series of special news briefs.[2]

---

2. Adapted from the UNICEF brochure, 1976.

Supplement B
Practice in Context
for
Unit 2

Section A

Introduction

Sixteen practices in context are included in this supplement, four each for sections B, C, D, and E of Unit 2. Some contexts are serious and some are lighthearted. Some are easy and some are difficult. Advanced students may be able to do the rapid review and testing lessons in Units 1 and 2 and proceed directly to Supplements A, B, and C for practice, recording, and self-monitoring of pronunciation.

These supplementary practices are included in *Improving Spoken English* for expanded practice beyond the pronunciation and perception work provided in Unit 2. They are *not* intended to substitute for real-life communicative activities which can be provided only by individual teachers in their specific teaching/learning situations. They *are* intended for continued practice of the fifteen vowel sounds presented in Unit 2, in more interesting and realistic contexts. Students are urged to record themselves and to listen and monitor their pronunciation.

In addition to these sixteen practices, the twenty practices in Supplement A also may be used for vowel practice as well as for stress, rhythm, and intonation practice.

The number of practices provided here is limited. Teachers may want to add similar practices to meet the particular needs of specific classes.

Section B

Front Vowels

Practice 1—Tongue Twisters

Tongue twisters are folk sayings in which a few sounds are repeated many times. They may seem difficult to pronounce at first. Practice the following tongue twisters slowly, at first, and then more rapidly. Practice with attention to monitoring the front vowels as marked: 1 (as in s<u>ee</u>), 2 (as in <u>it</u>), 3 (as in s<u>ay</u>), 4 (as in y<u>e</u>s), and 5 (as in f<u>a</u>t).

1. Peter Piper picked a peck of pickled peppers.
   1   2   4   2   4

   If Peter Piper picked a peck of pickled peppers,
   2 1   2   4   2   4

   Where is the peck of pickled peppers Peter Piper picked?
   2   4   2   4   1   2

2. Tina Taylor the ticket-taker takes tea at ten past ten.
   1 3   2   3   3   1   4   5   4

   If Tina Taylor is taking tea, who's taking tickets at ten past ten?
   2 1 3 2 3   1   3   2   4   5   4

(In these two tongue twisters, attention to the aspiration of prevocalic plosives may be helpful for some students.)

Practice 2—Old English Rhyme

In this rhyme, lines one, two, and five rhyme; lines three and four rhyme. Practice with attention to monitoring the front vowels, as marked. Monitor rhythm and stress as you read. Sentence stresses are underlined and reduced words have a line through them.

My Friend Gladys

Oh the <u>sad</u>ness of her <u>sad</u>ness, when she's <u>sad</u>!
     5   5   4   1   5

Oh the <u>glad</u>ness of her <u>glad</u>ness, when she's <u>glad</u>!
     5   5   4   1   5

But the <u>sad</u>ness of her <u>sad</u>ness,
     5   5

And the <u>glad</u>ness of her <u>glad</u>ness,
     5   5

Are nothing like her <u>mad</u>ness—when she's <u>mad</u>!
             5   4   1   5

(author unknown)

Practice 3—Rhymalogues

The following two-line dialogues are called rhymalogues. The last two words in each line rhyme, and each receives a sentence stress. Practice the rhymalogues with attention to the front vowels, as marked. Notice the spelling for each.

1. *Jack*:   It's starting to <u>rain</u>, <u>Jane</u>.
                2   3   3

   Jane: Then we'd better go <u>back</u>, <u>Jack</u>.
                4   1   4   5   5

2. *Mr. Dix*:   I'll meet you at the <u>bank</u>, <u>Frank</u>.
                  1   5   5

   Frank: I'll be there at <u>six</u>, <u>Mr. Dix</u>.
                1   2   2

3. *Ben*:   How long should we <u>wait</u>, <u>Kate</u>?
                         1   3   3

   Kate: Let's wait 'til <u>ten</u>, <u>Ben</u>.
               4   3   2   4   4

4. *Lou*:   You really look <u>sick</u>, <u>Dick</u>.
                 1   2   2

   Dick: I think I have the <u>flu</u>, <u>Lou</u>.
               2   5

5. *Mabel*:   Where do you want the <u>fan</u>, <u>Dan</u>?
                       5   5

   Dan: Please put it on the <u>table</u>, <u>Mabel</u>.
            1   2   3   3

Practice 4—Radio News Reading: International Ice Patrol

Practice the following short radio news report. Mark the front vowels and monitor them as you read. Mark pauses and monitor stress. Read for meaning so that the listener gets the sense or important points of information.

     REPORTER: Good afternoon. Here is another in our series of special news briefs, brought to you by the International Trans-World Press. Subject: *The International Ice Patrol.*

     In April, nineteen twelve (1912), the ship Titanic hit an iceberg off the coast of Canada. Fifteen hundred (1500) people drowned in the icy cold waters of the North Atlantic. As a direct result of this tragedy, the International Ice Patrol was organized. It monitors icebergs and reports any which move into the North Atlantic shipping lanes.

     Seventeen countries contribute money to finance the International Ice Patrol. Ships and planes keep a twenty-four hour watch. They report any icebergs which move into the North Atlantic shipping lanes. The patrol begins in early March and continues through late July.

     The icebergs break off from the glaciers of the Greenland Icecap. Ocean currents carry them into the Atlantic shipping lanes. Some years as many as a thousand may be seen; some years less than a dozen. The average each year is around four hundred.

     Since the beginning of the International Ice Patrol the tragedy of the Titanic has not been repeated; not a single life has been lost through collision with icebergs.

Tune in next week for the next in our series of special news briefs.[1]

---

1. Adapted from Dubach, Harold W., and Taber, Robert W., *Questions about the Oceans*, National Oceanographic Data Center, U.S. Naval Oceanographic Office, Washington, D.C., pp. 110–11.

Section C

Back Vowels

Practice 5—Old Irish Good Luck Saying

Practice the following lines with attention to monitoring the back vowels as marked: 8 (as in tw<u>o</u>), 9 (as in b<u>oo</u>ks), 10 (as in n<u>o</u>), and 11 (as in l<u>aw</u>). Then mark any front vowels and practice a second time monitoring *both* back and front vowels. Discuss the meaning of the lines.

> May the road rise with you,
>   10   8
>   And the wind be always at your back.
>   11

> May the sun shine warm upon your face,
>   11   11
>   And the rain fall soft upon your fields.
>   11   11   11

> And until we meet again . . .

> May the good lord hold you in the hollow of his hand.
>   9   11   10   8   10

> (author unknown)

Practice 6—Limerick

Limericks are a special kind of rhyme. Lines one, two, and five have three sentence stresses and the last words in these lines rhyme. Lines three and four have two sentence stresses and the last words rhyme. Practice the limerick with attention to monitoring the back vowels and the rhythm and stress of each line. Then mark any front vowels and practice a second time monitoring *both* back and front vowels. Discuss the meaning of the limerick.

> There was a young man named McCall,
>   11
> Who fell in the spring in the Fall,
>   8   11
>   'twould have been a sad thing,
>   9
>   If he'd died in the spring,
> But he didn't, he died in the fall.
>   11

Practice 7—Rhymalogues

The following two-line dialogues are called rhymalogues. The last two words in each line rhyme, and each receives a sentence stress. Practice the rhymalogues with attention to the back vowels, as marked. Notice the spelling for each.

1. *Lou*:   What time is the show, Joe?
                     10   10

   Joe: I think it starts at two, Lou.
                     8   8

2. *Mr. Drew*: You really are tall, Paul.
                  8   11   11

   Paul: I'm six foot, two, Mr. Drew.
                  9   8   8

3. *Mrs. Wood*: Have you seen the new play, Ray?
                  8   8

   Ray: Yes, it's very good, Mrs. Wood.
                  9   9

4. *Mr. Rost*: Here are your books, Mrs. Brooks.
                  9   9

   Mrs. Brooks: How much do they cost, Mr. Rost?
                  11   11

5. *Ben*:   What time did he call, Mr. Hall?
                  11   11

   Mr. Hall: He called around ten, Ben.
                  11

Practice 8—Radio News Reading: Population Explosion

Practice the following short radio news report. Mark back vowels and monitor them as you read. Mark pauses and monitor rhythm and sentence stress. Read for meaning so that the listener gets the sense or important points of information.

REPORTER: Good afternoon. Here is another in our series of special news briefs, brought to you by the International Trans-World Press. Subject: *Population Explosion.*

The people who study population growth are called demographic experts. They believe that a total of seventy-six billion people have lived on earth since the dawn of civilization. At that time, approximately six thousand B. C., the world population probably was around eight million people. It was not until the year eighteen-twenty (1820) that one *billion* people were living on the earth at the same time. Today the population is over *three-and-a-half* billion. The population of the earth is increasing now at the rate of doubling the population every thirty years. By the year two thousand (2000) the population will be over *six-and-a-half* billion.

Larger and larger numbers of people are living in smaller and smaller areas. Half of today's population is crowded into Western Europe and South Asia. In fact, half of the world's population lives on one-tenth of the earth's land surface. The most densely populated country is the Netherlands with nine hundred twenty-four people per square mile. England is second with eight hundred and seventy-two. In contrast, Australia has a population density of approximately five people per square mile.

Tune in next week for another in our series of special news briefs.

Section D

Central Vowels

Practice 9—Tongue Twisters

Tongue twisters are folk sayings in which a few sounds are repeated many times. They may seem difficult to pronounce at first. Practice the following tongue twisters slowly, at first, and then more rapidly. Practice with attention to monitoring the central vowels as marked: 12 (as in bird), 6 (as in bus), and 7 (as in stop), and back vowel 9 (as in books).

1. Fuzzy Wuzzy was a bear.
   6   6   6   4 + 12

   Fuzzy Wuzzy had no hair.
   6   6   4 + 12

   Fuzzy Wuzzy wasn't fuzzy,
   6   6   6   6

   Was 'e?
   6   1

2. How much wood could a woodchuck chuck
   6   9   9   9   6   6

   if a woodchuck could chuck wood?
   9   6   9   6   9

Practice 10—Limerick

Limericks are a special kind of rhyme. Lines one, two, and five have three sentence stresses and the last words in these lines rhyme. Lines three and four have two sentence stresses and the last words rhyme. Practice the limerick with attention to monitoring the central vowels and the rhythm and stress of each line. Then mark other vowels (front and back) and practice a second time. Discuss the meaning of the limerick.

There once was a woman named Bunny,
4 + 12 6   6   6

Whose smile was so happy and sunny.
                 6   6

People's names she forgot,
                 12 7

But that worried her not.
6   12   12 7

She simply called all of them Honey!
                              6

Practice 11—Rhymalogues

The following two-line dialogues are called rhymalogues. The last two words in each line rhyme, and each receives a sentence stress. Practice the rhymalogues with attention to the central vowels, as marked. Notice the spelling for each.

1. *Bobby*:   Did you ever play soccer, Mr. Crocker?
                    12   7   12   12   7   12

   Mr. Crocker: Only as a hobby, Bobby.
                    7   7

2. *Vern*: Who's the new girl, Earl?
               12   12

   Earl: I think her name is Fern, Vern.
            12   12   12

3. *Mr. Kirk*: Can you come to the party, Marty?
                6   7 + 12 7 + 12

   Marty: No, I have to work, Mr. Kirk.
             12   12   12

4. *Mr. Farr*: Did you come on the bus, Gus?
                6   6   6

   Gus: No, I drove my car, Mr. Farr.
           7+12 12 7 + 12

5. *Mr. Rucker*: What's your new job, Bob?
                6   12   7   7

   Bob: I'm working as a trucker, Mr. Rucker.
          12   6   12   12 6   12

Practice 12—Radio News Reading: Food from the Sea

Practice the following short radio news report. Mark the central vowels and monitor them as you read. Mark pauses and monitor rhythm and sentence stress. Read for meaning so that the listener gets the sense or important points of information.

REPORTER: Good afternoon. Here is another in our series of special news briefs, brought to you by the International Trans-World Press. Subject: *Food from the Sea*.

The waters of the oceans of the earth are full to overflowing with all kinds of food. Under careful scientific management, the sea alone could supply enough food for roughly seven times the present world population. This is more than enough to end starvation among men.

Nearly a third of the world's population suffers from lack of protein. Millions live in hunger and die from malnutrition, while enough food for all abounds in the sea. If starvation is to be avoided among the underfed peoples of the world in the closing years of the twentieth century, positive steps must be taken now to improve their food supply. The food resources of the seas must be handled scientifically and protected from pollution.

Oceanographers are working on these problems. A fish protein concentrate (FPC) has been produced. It could do much to combat dietary deficiencies among the underfed population. Problems of pollution are being attacked by both government officials and operators of industrial plants. Steps are being taken to remedy some of the more serious problems.

Feeding the hungry of the earth from the resources of the sea—while protecting the waters from the waste products of a highly technological world—is one of the most important challenges facing the world scientists of today and tomorrow.

Tune in next week for another in our series of special news briefs.[2]

_____

2. Adapted from *The Water Planet*, U.S. Naval Oceanographic Office, Washington, D.C., pp. 14–15.

Section E

Diphthongs

Practice 13—Rhyme

Practice the following rhyme with attention to monitoring the diphthongs as marked: 13 (as in m<u>y</u>), 14 (as in c<u>ow</u>), and 15 (as in b<u>oy</u>). Monitor rhythm and stress as you read. Sentence stresses are underlined.

Methuselah

Methuselah ate what he found on his plate,

14

And never, as people do now,

14

Did he know the amount of the calorie count.

14

He ate it because it was chow.

14

He cheerfully ate all kinds of food,

13

Without any troubles or fears,

14

And what do you think? How long did he live?

14

He lived over nine hundred years!

13

(author unknown)

Practice 14—Limerick

Limericks are a special kind of rhyme. Lines one, two, and five have three sentence stresses and the last words in these lines rhyme. Lines three and four have two sentence stresses and the last words rhyme. Practice the limerick with attention to monitoring the diphthongs and the rhythm and stress of each line. Then mark other vowels (front, back, central) and practice a second time. Discuss the meaning of the limerick.

There is a young fellow in Troy,

15

Who is looking for folks to employ.

15

They'll make fruited ices.

13

For very low prices.

13

This work should bring everyone joy.

15

Practice 15—Rhymalogues

The following two-line dialogues are called rhymalogues. The last two words in each line rhyme and each receives a sentence stress. Practice the rhymalogues with attention to the diphthongs, as marked. Notice the spelling for each.

1. *Jean*:   What's your first choice, Joyce?
         15 15

 Joyce: I think I'll buy the green, Jean.
        13   13   13

2. *Mrs. Price*: What would you like, Mike?
          13   13

 Mike: I'd like some lemon ice, Mrs. Price.
       13 13   13   13

3. *Clyde*:   Are you going downtown, Mr. Brown?
         14 14   14

 Mr. Brown: Yes, would you like a ride, Clyde?
         13   13   13

4. *Mrs. White*: Who's the new boy, Roy?
          15   15

 Roy: I think his name is Dwight, Mrs. White.
       13   13   13

5. *Dr. Gray*:   What beautiful flowers, Mrs. Bowers!
          14   14

 Mrs. Bowers: Would you like a bouquet, Dr. Gray?
          13

Practice 16—Radio News Reading: Earthquake Safety Rules

Practice the following short radio news report. Mark the diphthongs and monitor them as you read. Mark pauses and monitor rhythm and sentence stress. Read for meaning so that the listener gets the sense or important points of information.

REPORTER: Good afternoon. Here is another in our series of special news briefs, brought to you by the International Trans-World Press. Subject: *Earthquake Safety Rules*.

An earthquake strikes your area and for a minute or two the "solid" earth moves like the deck of a ship. What you do during and immediately after the tremor may make life-and-death differences for you, your family, and your neighbors. These rules will help you survive. During the shaking:

One: Don't panic. The motion is frightening, but unless it shakes something down on top of you, it is harmless. Keep calm and ride it out.

Two: If you are indoors, stay indoors. Take cover under a desk, table, bench, or in doorways, halls, and against inside walls. Stay away from glass.

Three: Don't use candles, matches, or other open flames. Put out all fires.

Four: If you are outside, move away from buildings and utility wires. Once in the open, stay there until the shaking stops.

Five: Don't run through or near buildings. The greatest danger from falling debris is just outside doorways and close to outer walls.

Six: If you are in a moving car, stop as quickly as safety permits, but stay in the car. A car is an excellent seismometer; it will jiggle fearsomely on its springs during the earthquake; but it is a good place to stay until the shaking stops.

Tune in next week for another in our series of special news briefs.[3]

---

3. Adapted from *Earthquakes*, U.S. Department of Commerce, Environmental Science Services Administration, Washington, D.C., p. 15.

Supplement C
Vowel Contrasts
for Unit 2

Using the Vowel Contrast Lessons

Sixteen vowel contrast lessons are included to supplement the intensive vowel lessons in Unit 2 and the sixteen vowel practices in Supplement B. Advanced students may be able to do the rapid review and testing lessons in Units 1 and 2 and proceed directly to Supplements A, B, and C for practice, recording, and self-monitoring of pronunciation.

As with Supplements A and B, these supplementary vowel contrast lessons are included in *Improving Spoken English* in order to meet individual needs of students by providing additional practice beyond the pronunciation and perception work in Unit 2. Many students prefer to do all sixteen contrast lessons, even though some are easy; they feel that the careful attention to vowel contrasts as presented in these lessons is important in the overall improvement of their spoken English. Each contrast lesson has two divisions. The first division provides four phases of pronunciation practice. Students are urged to record practice 3 and practice 4 and to listen and monitor their pronunciation. The second division provides three phases of discrimination testing.

The number of vowel contrast lessons included here is limited. Teachers may want to add similar lessons to meet the particular needs of specific classes.

Contrast 1: Vowel 1 and Vowel 2—s<u>ee</u> /iʸ/ and <u>i</u>t /ɪ/

Practice 1

Repeat the items in column 1. The lips are rather thin and spread and the lower jaw is raised for /iʸ/. The tongue is arched upward and forward in the highest front articulatory position for English vowels. The /iʸ/ is not a pure sound. That is, it has two parts; the tongue is pulled up a little closer to the front of the roof of the mouth from /i/ toward /y/. Repeat: /iʸ/   /iʸ/   s<u>ee</u>   s<u>ee</u>.

Column 1	Column 2
s<u>ea</u>t	s<u>i</u>t
<u>ea</u>t	<u>i</u>t
<u>ea</u>ch	<u>i</u>tch
f<u>ee</u>t	f<u>i</u>t
gr<u>ee</u>n	gr<u>i</u>n
sh<u>ee</u>p	sh<u>i</u>p
l<u>ea</u>ving	l<u>i</u>ving
f<u>ee</u>l	f<u>i</u>ll
st<u>ee</u>l	st<u>i</u>ll
h<u>ee</u>l	h<u>i</u>ll

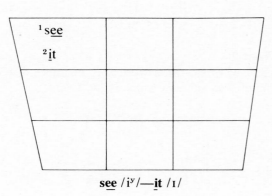

s<u>ee</u> /iʸ/—<u>i</u>t /ɪ/

Practice 2

Repeat the items in column 2. The jaw and the tongue are both lowered a little for /ɪ/. There is more space between the upper and lower teeth. The /ɪ/ does not have the /y/ glide of /iʸ/. Repeat: /ɪ/   /ɪ/   <u>i</u>t   <u>i</u>t.

Practice 3

Repeat the pairs of items in columns 1 and 2. Then repeat the pairs of sentences below.

He bought a sh<u>ee</u>p.	He bought a sh<u>i</u>p.
When did he l<u>ea</u>ve here?	When did he l<u>i</u>ve here?
I'll f<u>ee</u>l it.	I'll f<u>i</u>ll it.
It's st<u>ee</u>l.	It's st<u>i</u>ll.

Practice 4

Stop the tape. Read each sentence silently. Write the vowel number for each underlined vowel letter below it: Vowel 1 (as in s<u>ee</u>) or Vowel 2 (as in <u>i</u>t). Check your answers in the Answer Key. Practice in class and discuss with your teacher.

1. H<u>e</u>'s s<u>i</u>tting <u>i</u>n my s<u>ea</u>t!

2. Sh<u>e</u> d<u>i</u>dn't f<u>i</u>n<u>i</u>sh the cl<u>ea</u>ning?

3. H<u>e</u> put h<u>i</u>s sh<u>ee</u>p on the sh<u>i</u>p.

4. I have a f<u>ee</u>ling th<u>e</u>se shoes won't f<u>i</u>t my big f<u>ee</u>t!

Supplement C
Contrast 1

Test 1

You will hear pairs of words or sentences using items from the teacher's list. As you listen, decide whether they are the same (S) or different (D). Circle S or D.

Examples:	eat	eat		steel	still
	(S) circled	D		S	(D) circled
1.	S	D	5.	S	D
2.	S	D	6.	S	D
3.	S	D	7.	S	D
4.	S	D	8.	S	D

Test 2

You will hear three words or sentences. Two of them will be the same. One will be different. Circle the number of the one which is *different.*

Examples:	steel	steel	still		feel	fill	fill
	1	2	(3) circled		(1) circled	2	3
1.	1	2	3	5.	1	2	3
2.	1	2	3	6.	1	2	3
3.	1	2	3	7.	1	2	3
4.	1	2	3	8.	1	2	3

Test 3

You will hear six items from the teacher's list. Decide if each contains Vowel 1 (see) or Vowel 2 (it). Write the vowel number and the word (or sentence). Check your spelling.

1. ______________________
2. ______________________
3. ______________________
4. ______________________
5. ______________________
6. ______________________

Check your answers in the Answer Key.

Teacher's List

bead	bid	peel	pill	sleep	slip
seat	sit	steel	still	he's	his
sheep	ship	read	rid	easy	is he
leaving	living	deep	dip	heel	hill
feel	fill	each	itch		

She's sleeping.	She's slipping.
I need another sheep.	I need another ship.
He's leaving here.	He's living here.
Was it steel?	Was it still?
I'll feel it.	I'll fill it.
There's the heel.	There's the hill.
When did he leave here?	When did he live here?

Contrast 2: Vowel 3 and Vowel 4—s<u>ay</u> /eⁱ/ and y<u>es</u> /ɛ/

Practice 1

Repeat the items in column 1. The /eⁱ/ sound is not a pure sound. That is, it is made up of two parts. The lower jaw is raised from half-open for /e/ to a higher position for /i/. It is important to make the two parts clearly, although the first part is stronger than the second part. Repeat: /eⁱ/   /eⁱ/   s<u>ay</u>   s<u>ay</u>.

Column 1   *Column 2*

late   let

g<u>a</u>te   g<u>e</u>t

w<u>ai</u>t   w<u>e</u>t

t<u>a</u>ste   t<u>e</u>st

p<u>ai</u>n   p<u>e</u>n

<u>a</u>ge   <u>e</u>dge

l<u>a</u>ce   l<u>e</u>ss

p<u>a</u>per   p<u>e</u>pper

f<u>ai</u>l   f<u>e</u>ll

s<u>a</u>le   s<u>e</u>ll

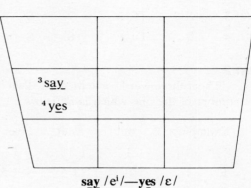

s<u>ay</u> /eⁱ/—y<u>es</u> /ɛ/

Practice 2

Repeat the items in column 2. The jaw and the tongue are both lowered a little for /ɛ/. There is more space between the upper and lower teeth. It does not have the /i/ glide of /eⁱ/. Repeat: /ɛ/ /ɛ/   yes   yes.

Practice 3

Repeat the pairs of items in columns 1 and 2. Then repeat the pairs of sentences below.

Do you have a p<u>ai</u>n?   Do you have a p<u>e</u>n?

I need some more p<u>a</u>per.   I need some more p<u>e</u>pper.

He t<u>a</u>sted it.   He t<u>e</u>sted it.

I have a d<u>a</u>te.   I have a d<u>e</u>bt.

Practice 4

Stop the tape. Read each sentence silently. Write the vowel number for each underlined vowel letter below it: Vowel 3 (as in s<u>ay</u>) or Vowel 4 (as in y<u>es</u>). Check your answers in the Answer Key. Practice in class and discuss with your teacher.

1. <u>A</u>pril w<u>ea</u>ther is w<u>e</u>t and r<u>ai</u>ny.

2. The l<u>a</u>dy s<u>e</u>t the p<u>e</u>pper on the p<u>a</u>per.

3. Wh<u>e</u>n it g<u>e</u>ts l<u>a</u>te, I w<u>ai</u>t by the g<u>a</u>te.

4. The r<u>e</u>d l<u>a</u>ce dr<u>e</u>ss was on s<u>a</u>le.

Test 1

You will hear pairs of words or sentences using items from the teacher's list. As you listen, decide whether they are the same (S) or different (D). Circle S or D.

Examples: late   let   edge   edge
           S   (D)   (S)   D

1. S   D   5. S   D
2. S   D   6. S   D
3. S   D   7. S   D
4. S   D   8. S   D

Test 2

You will hear three words or sentences. Two of them will be the same. One will be different. Circle the number of the one which is *different*.

Examples: wet   wait   wet   age   age   edge
           1   (2)   3   1   2   (3)

1. 1   2   3   5. 1   2   3
2. 1   2   3   6. 1   2   3
3. 1   2   3   7. 1   2   3
4. 1   2   3   8. 1   2   3

Test 3

You will hear six items from the teacher's list. Decide if each contains Vowel 3 (s<u>ay</u>) or Vowel 4 (y<u>es</u>). Write the vowel number and the word (or sentence). Check your spelling.

1. _____   4. _____

2. _____   5. _____

3. _____   6. _____

Check your answers in the Answer Key.

Teacher's List

main	men	late	let	lace	less
tale	tell	gate	get	paper	pepper
mate	met	wait	wet	fail	fell
date	debt	taste	test	sale	sell
		pain	pen		
		age	edge		

Who bought the paper?   Who bought the pepper?

It's my date.   It's my debt.

He tasted it.   He tested it.

I have a date.   I have a debt.

I need some more paper.   I need some more pepper.

Do you have a pain?   Do you have a pen?

Contrast 3: Vowel 5 and Vowel 7—f<u>a</u>t /æ/ and st<u>o</u>p /a/

Practice 1

Repeat the items in column 1. The lower jaw and the tongue are lowered for /æ/. The tongue is rounded a little and arched forward a little. The tip of the tongue touches the insides of the lower front teeth. Repeat: /æ/   /æ/   f<u>a</u>t   f<u>a</u>t.

Column 1	*Column 2*
h<u>a</u>t	h<u>o</u>t
c<u>a</u>p	c<u>o</u>p
t<u>a</u>p	t<u>o</u>p
<u>a</u>dd	<u>o</u>dd
c<u>a</u>ts	c<u>o</u>ts
bl<u>a</u>ck	bl<u>o</u>ck
s<u>a</u>ck	s<u>o</u>ck
c<u>a</u>b	c<u>o</u>b
b<u>a</u>cks	b<u>o</u>x
b<u>a</u>ttle	b<u>o</u>ttle

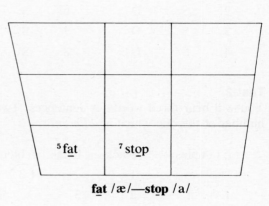

f<u>a</u>t /æ/—st<u>o</u>p /a/

Practice 2

Repeat the items in column 2. The jaw and the tongue also are lowered for /a/. In contrast to /æ/, however, the tongue is pulled down and back from the position of /æ/. In contrast to the rounding and forward arching for /æ/, the tongue is concave (i.e., rounded inward.) Repeat: /a/   /a/   st<u>o</u>p   st<u>o</u>p.

Practice 3

Repeat the pairs of items in columns 1 and 2. Then repeat the pairs of sentences below.

It was a big b<u>a</u>ttle.	It was a big b<u>o</u>ttle.
I have two little c<u>a</u>ts.	I have two little c<u>o</u>ts.
She dropped the s<u>a</u>ck.	She dropped the s<u>o</u>ck.
Is that a new c<u>a</u>p?	Is that a new c<u>o</u>p?

Practice 4

Stop the tape. Read each sentence silently. Write the vowel number for each underlined vowel letter below it: Vowel 5 (f<u>a</u>t) or Vowel 7 (st<u>o</u>p). Check your answers in the Answer Key. Practice in class and discuss with your teacher.

1. Who dr<u>o</u>pped the c<u>a</u>t into the bl<u>a</u>ck b<u>o</u>x?

2. Put the b<u>o</u>ttle on the bl<u>a</u>ck bl<u>o</u>ck in the l<u>a</u>b.

3. Gr<u>a</u>ndf<u>a</u>ther put my new s<u>o</u>cks in the s<u>a</u>ck.

4. The bl<u>a</u>ck c<u>a</u>t s<u>a</u>t on t<u>o</u>p of the r<u>o</u>ck.

Supplement C
Contrast 3

Test 1

You will hear pairs of words or sentences using items from the teacher's list. As you listen, decide whether they are the same (S) or different (D). Circle S or D.

Examples: hat   hot   cat   cat
             S   (D)   (S)   D

1.	S	D	5.	S	D
2.	S	D	6.	S	D
3.	S	D	7.	S	D
4.	S	D	8.	S	D

Test 2

You will hear three words or sentences. Two of them will be the same. One will be different. Circle the number of the one which is *different*.

Examples: black   black   block   battle   bottle   battle
             1   2   (3)   1   (2)   3

1.	1	2	3	5.	1	2	3
2.	1	2	3	6.	1	2	3
3.	1	2	3	7.	1	2	3
4.	1	2	3	8.	1	2	3

Test 3

You will hear six items from the teacher's list. Decide if each contains Vowel 5 (f<u>a</u>t) or Vowel 7 (st<u>o</u>p). Write the vowel number and the word (or sentence). Check your spelling.

1. _____   4. _____

2. _____   5. _____

3. _____   6. _____

Check your answers in the Answer Key.

Teacher's List

lack	lock	cap	cop	sack	sock
map	mop	tap	top	cab	cob
pat	pot	add	odd	backs	box
rack	rock	cats	cots	battle	bottle
hat	hot	black	block		

Whose map is this?   Whose mop is this?

It was a big battle.   It was a big bottle.

She dropped the sack.   She dropped the sock.

I have two little cats.   I have two little cots.

Is that a new cap?   Is that a new cop?

That's a big rack.   That's a big rock.

Contrast 4: Vowel 7 and Vowel 6—stop /a/ and bus /ʌ/

Practice 1
Repeat the items in column 1. The lower jaw and the tongue are lowered for /a/. The tongue is pulled down from the neutral or rest position and it is concave (i.e., rounded inward). Repeat: /a/   /a/   stop   stop.

Column 1	Column 2
pop	pup
cop	cup
not	nut
cot	cut
lock	luck
shot	shut
robber	rubber
dock	duck
doll	dull
collar	color

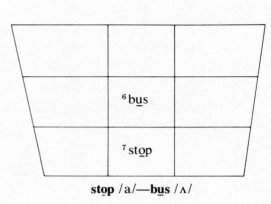

stop /a/—bus /ʌ/

Practice 2
Repeat the items in column 2. The jaw is partially raised for /ʌ/. There is much less space between the upper and lower teeth. The tongue is rather flat in the neutral or rest position. It is only slightly concave (i.e., rounded inward). Repeat: /ʌ/   /ʌ/   bus   bus.

Practice 3
Repeat the pairs of items in columns 1 and 2. Then repeat the pairs of sentences below.

Where is the dock?	Where is the duck?
Which collar do you want?	Which color do you want?
My lock was good.	My luck was good.
Who shot it?	Who shut it?

Practice 4
Stop the tape. Read each sentence silently. Write the vowel number for each underlined vowel letter below it: Vowel 7 (stop) or Vowel 6 (bus). Check your answers in the Answer Key. Practice in class and discuss with your teacher.

1. He won a watch and a lot of money.

2. My brother is studying at another college.

3. The summer months are too hot for comfort.

4. The doctor promised to come on Sunday or Monday.

Test 1

You will hear pairs of words or sentences using items from the teacher's list. As you listen, decide whether they are the same (S) or different (D). Circle S or D.

Examples:	cup	cop		luck	luck
	S	Ⓓ		Ⓢ	D

1.	S	D		5.	S	D
2.	S	D		6.	S	D
3.	S	D		7.	S	D
4.	S	D		8.	S	D

Test 2

You will hear three words or sentences. Two of them will be the same. One will be different. Circle the number of the one which is *different*.

Examples:	luck	luck	lock		doll	dull	dull
	1	2	③		①	2	3

1.	1	2	3		5.	1	2	3
2.	1	2	3		6.	1	2	3
3.	1	2	3		7.	1	2	3
4.	1	2	3		8.	1	2	3

Test 3

You will hear six items from the teacher's list. Decide if each contains Vowel 6 (b<u>u</u>s) or Vowel 7 (st<u>o</u>p). Write the vowel number and the word (or sentence). Check your spelling.

1. _____   4. _____

2. _____   5. _____

3. _____   6. _____

Check your answers in the Answer Key.

Teacher's List

hot	hut	not	nut	robber	rubber
bomb	bum	cot	cut	dock	duck
pop	pup	lock	luck	doll	dull
cop	cup	shot	shut	collar	color

Which collar do you like?	Which color do you like?
Where is the dock?	Where is the duck?
Who shot it?	Who shut it?
My lock was good.	My luck was good.
Which collar did you want?	Which color did you want?
It's a rubber dock.	It's a rubber duck.

Contrast 5: Vowel 12 and Vowel 6—bird /ɝ/ and bus /ʌ/

Practice 1
Repeat the items in column 1. The lower jaw is raised for /ɝ/. The tongue is pulled up high and bunched close to the center of the hard roof of the mouth. The sides of the tongue touch the insides of the upper back teeth. The front and the tip of the tongue are pointed upward, and, for some speakers a little backward. Repeat: /ɝ/ /ɝ/ bird bird.

Column 1	Column 2
bird	bud
burn	bun
fern (Fern)	fun
shirt	shut
hurt	hut
Curt	cut
Burt	but
turn	ton
lurk	luck
curb	cub

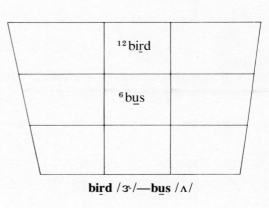

bird /ɝ/—bus /ʌ/

Practice 2
Repeat the items in column 2. The jaw is partially lowered from /ɝ/ to /ʌ/. The tongue is lowered and is flattened, not bunched, as for /ɝ/. It is in the neutral or rest position. The tongue is slightly concave (i.e., rounded inward). Repeat: /ʌ/ /ʌ/ bus bus.

Practice 3
Repeat the pairs of items in columns 1 and 2. Then repeat the pairs of sentences below.

The bird was yellow.	The bud was yellow.
The curb was black.	The cub was black.
It was Fern!	It was fun!
He took a turn.	He took a ton.

Practice 4
Stop the tape. Read each sentence silently. Write the vowel number for each underlined vowel letter below it: Vowel 12 (bird) or Vowel 6 (bus). Check your answers in the Answer Key. Practice in class and discuss with your teacher.

1. Curt shut his shirt in the door!

2. Worst luck! Someone burned the buns!

3. Uncle Burt! Can you come to supper?

4. Lunch will be served in the other room.

Test 1

You will hear pairs of words or sentences using items from the teacher's list. As you listen, decide whether they are the same (S) or different (D). Circle S or D.

Examples A:	turn	turn		ton	turn
	Ⓢ	D		S	Ⓓ

1.	S	D	5.	S	D
2.	S	D	6.	S	D
3.	S	D	7.	S	D
4.	S	D	8.	S	D

Test 2

You will hear three words or sentences. Two of them will be the same. One will be different. Circle the number of the one which is *different*.

Examples:	fern	fern	fun		bird	bud	bud
	1	2	③		①	2	3

1.	1	2	3	5.	1	2	3
2.	1	2	3	6.	1	2	3
3.	1	2	3	7.	1	2	3
4.	1	2	3	8.	1	2	3

Test 3

You will hear six items from the teacher's list. Decide if each contains Vowel 6 (b<u>u</u>s) or Vowel 12 (b<u>ir</u>d). Write the vowel number; and the word (or sentence). Check your spelling.

1. _____   4. _____

2. _____   5. _____

3. _____   6. _____

Check your answers in the Answer Key.

Teacher's List

bird	bud	lurk	luck	Curt	cut
fern (Fern)	fun	burn	bun	turn	ton
hurt	hut	shirt	shut	curb	cub
Bert	but				

The bird was yellow.	The bud was yellow.
The curb was black.	The cub was black.
It was Fern!	It was fun!
Come and see the birds!	Come and see the buds!
He took a turn.	He took a ton.
I didn't see the curb!	I didn't see the cub!

288

Contrast 6: Vowel 8 and Vowel 9—tw<u>o</u> /u^w/ and b<u>oo</u>ks /ʊ/

Practice 1
Repeat the items in column 1. The lips are tightly rounded and the lower jaw is raised for /u^w/. The tongue is pulled upward and backward in the highest back articulatory position for English vowels. The /u^w/ is not a pure sound. That is, it has two parts; the tongue is pulled up a little closer to the back of the roof of the mouth from /u/ to /w/. Repeat: /u^w/   /u^w/   tw<u>o</u>   tw<u>o</u>.

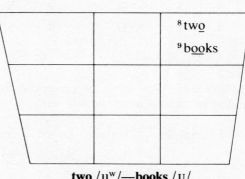

Column 1	*Column 2*
s<u>ui</u>t	s<u>oo</u>t
p<u>oo</u>l	p<u>u</u>ll
f<u>oo</u>l	f<u>u</u>ll
f<u>oo</u>lish	f<u>u</u>llish
wh<u>o</u>'d	h<u>oo</u>d
L<u>u</u>ke	l<u>oo</u>k
c<u>oo</u>ed	c<u>ou</u>ld

tw<u>o</u> /u^w/—b<u>oo</u>ks /ʊ/

Practice 2
Repeat the items in column 2. The jaw and the tongue are both lowered a little for /ʊ/. The lips are more loosely rounded for /ʊ/ and there is less tension in the lip musculature. The /ʊ/ does not have the /w/ glide. Repeat: /ʊ/   /ʊ/   b<u>oo</u>ks   b<u>oo</u>ks.

Practice 3
Repeat the pairs of items in columns 1 and 2. Then repeat the pairs of sentences below.

The s<u>ui</u>t was black.	The s<u>oo</u>t was black.
It was a long p<u>oo</u>l.	It was a long p<u>u</u>ll.
It's f<u>oo</u>lish.	It's f<u>u</u>llish.
I went to L<u>u</u>ke!	I went to l<u>oo</u>k!

Practice 4
Stop the tape. Read each sentence silently. Write the vowel number for each underlined vowel letter below it: Vowel 8 (tw<u>o</u>) or Vowel 9 (b<u>oo</u>ks). Check your answers in the Answer Key. Practice in class and discuss with your teacher.

1. I sh<u>ou</u>ld buy some s<u>u</u>gar, some s<u>ou</u>p, some c<u>oo</u>kies, and some fr<u>ui</u>t.

2. R<u>u</u>thy! Don't p<u>u</u>t your f<u>oo</u>t on the n<u>ew</u> bl<u>ue</u> c<u>u</u>shion!

3. W<u>oo</u>dy p<u>u</u>shed L<u>ou</u>ie int<u>o</u> the p<u>oo</u>l! Wh<u>o</u> did it? W<u>oo</u>dy did it!

4. Wh<u>o</u> t<u>oo</u>k my g<u>oo</u>d n<u>ew</u> cookbook? S<u>u</u>zy t<u>oo</u>k it.

Supplement C
Contrast 6

Test 1

You will hear pairs of words or sentences using items from the teacher's list. As you listen, decide whether they are the same (S) or different (D). Circle S or D.

	Examples:	stood	stood		pull	pool
		(S)	D		S	(D)
1.	S	D		5.	S	D
2.	S	D		6.	S	D
3.	S	D		7.	S	D
4.	S	D		8.	S	D

Test 2

You will hear three words or sentences. Two of them will be the same. One will be different. Circle the number of the one which is *different*.

	Examples:	cooed	cooed	could		pool	pull	pull
		1	2	(3)		(1)	2	3
1.	1	2	3		5.	1	2	3
2.	1	2	3		6.	1	2	3
3.	1	2	3		7.	1	2	3
4.	1	2	3		8.	1	2	3

Test 3

You will hear six items from the teacher's list. Decide if each contains Vowel 8 (tw<u>o</u>) or Vowel 9 (b<u>oo</u>ks). Write the vowel number and the word (or sentence). Check your spelling.

1. _____   4. _____

2. _____   5. _____

3. _____   6. _____

Check your answers in the Answer Key.

Teacher's List

suit	soot		foolish	fullish
fool	full		pool	pull
who'd	hood		Luke	look
cooed	could			

The suit was black.	The soot was black.
It's foolish.	It's fullish.
It was a long pool.	It was a long pull.
I went to Luke!	I went to look!

Contrast 7: Vowel 10 and Vowel 11—no /oᵘ/ and law /ɔ/

Practice 1

Repeat the items in column 1. The /oᵘ/ is not a pure sound. That is, it is made up of two parts. The lower jaw is raised from half-open for /o/ to a higher position for /u/. It is important to make the two parts clearly, although the first part is stronger than the second part. Repeat: /oᵘ/   /oᵘ/   no   no.

Column 1	Column 2
low	law
Joe	jaw
so	saw
coat	caught
boat	bought
bowl	ball
pole	Paul
whole	hall
bold	bald
cold	called

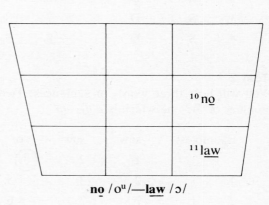

no /oᵘ/—law /ɔ/

Practice 2

Repeat the items in column 2. The jaw is lowered for /ɔ/ and the tongue is pulled down and back into the lowest back articulatory position for English vowels. The /ɔ/ is followed by a slight centering glide toward /ə/, whereas the movement in /oᵘ/ is upward for /u/. Repeat: /ɔ/   /ɔ/   law   law.

Practice 3

Repeat the pairs of items in columns 1 and 2. Then repeat the pairs of sentences below.

He's in the low school.	He's in the law school.
Whose bowl is this?	Whose ball is this?
Mr. White is bold.	Mr. White is bald.
I was cold.	I was called.

Practice 4

Stop the tape. Read each sentence silently. Write the vowel number for each underlined vowel letter below it: Vowel 10 (no) or Vowel 11 (law). Check your answers in the Answer Key. Practice in class and discuss with your teacher.

1. Moe and Joe taught us the wrong song!

2. Don't go 'til the lawyer calls!

3. I thought Paul was going home!

4. We won't know the cost 'til we talk to Mr. Shaw.

Test 1

You will hear pairs of words or sentences using items from the teacher's list. As you listen, decide whether they are the same (S) or different (D). Circle S or D.

Examples: boat   bought   law   law
             S   (D)   (S)   D

1. S   D   5. S   D
2. S   D   6. S   D
3. S   D   7. S   D
4. S   D   8. S   D

Test 2

You will hear three words or sentences. Two of them will be the same. One will be different. Circle the number of the one which is *different*.

Examples: saw   saw   so   jaw   Joe   Joe
             1   2   (3)   (1)   2   3

1. 1   2   3   5. 1   2   3
2. 1   2   3   6. 1   2   3
3. 1   2   3   7. 1   2   3
4. 1   2   3   8. 1   2   3

Test 3

You will hear six items from the teacher's list. Decide if each contains Vowel 10 (n<u>o</u>) or Vowel 11 (l<u>aw</u>). Write the vowel number and the word (or sentence). Check your spelling.

1. _____   4. _____

2. _____   5. _____

3. _____   6. _____

Check your answers in the Answer Key.

Teacher's List

low	law	cold	called	pole	Paul
so	saw	row	raw	bold	bald
boat	bought	Joe	jaw	toast	tossed
whole	hall	coat	caught	coal	call
show	Shaw				

Please give me a blue bowl.   Please give me a blue ball.

He's getting bolder!   He's getting balder!

Was he cold?   Was he called?

Mr. Lewis is bold.   Mr. Lewis is bald.

I'm in the low school.   I'm in the law school.

Where's my red bowl?   Where's my red ball?

Contrast 8: Vowel 7 and Vowel 11—st<u>o</u>p /a/ and l<u>aw</u> /ɔ/

Practice 1
Repeat the items in column 1. The lower jaw and the tongue are lowered for /a/. The tongue is pulled down from the neutral or rest position and is concave (i.e., rounded inward). Repeat: /a/ /a/ st<u>o</u>p st<u>o</u>p.

Column 1	Column 2
c<u>o</u>t	c<u>au</u>ght
c<u>o</u>llar	c<u>a</u>ller
D<u>o</u>n	d<u>aw</u>n
y<u>o</u>n	y<u>aw</u>n
t<u>o</u>t	t<u>au</u>ght
s<u>o</u>d	s<u>aw</u>ed
f<u>a</u>r	f<u>ou</u>r*
c<u>a</u>r	c<u>o</u>re*
f<u>a</u>rm	f<u>o</u>rm*
b<u>a</u>rn	b<u>o</u>rn*
m<u>a</u>r	m<u>o</u>re*

st<u>o</u>p /a/—l<u>aw</u> /ɔ/

Practice 2
Repeat the items in column 2. The jaw and the tongue are raised a little from /a/ to /ɔ/. There is less space between the upper and lower teeth. The lower lip is raised, tensed, and protruded a little. The upper lip and the muscle in the center of the chin may be tensed slightly. The tongue shape is nearly the same as for /a/ except for a slight upward and backward arching. Repeat: /ɔ/ /ɔ/ l<u>aw</u> l<u>aw</u>. Notice the words in column 2 which are marked with an asterisk. The pronunciation of /ɔ/ before the vowel-*r* is variable; for some speakers /oᵘ/ is used instead of /ɔ/.

Practice 3
Repeat the pairs of items in columns 1 and 2. Then repeat the pairs of sentences below.

Is it f<u>a</u>r?	Is it f<u>ou</u>r?
Where's the c<u>o</u>llar?	Where's the c<u>a</u>ller?
It's an old c<u>a</u>r.	It's an old c<u>o</u>re.

Practice 4
Stop the tape. Read each sentence silently. Write the vowel number for each underlined vowel letter below it: Vowel 7 (st<u>o</u>p) or Vowel 11 (l<u>aw</u>). Check your answers in the Answer Key. Practice in class and discuss with your teacher.

1. D<u>o</u>ctor Sh<u>aw</u> gave my f<u>a</u>ther a d<u>o</u>g.

2. P<u>au</u>l b<u>ou</u>ght a new c<u>o</u>llar for his d<u>o</u>g.

3. The c<u>a</u>ller c<u>au</u>ght his c<u>o</u>llar in the c<u>a</u>r d<u>oo</u>r!

Test 1
You will hear pairs of words or sentences using items from the teacher's list. As you listen, decide whether they are the same (S) or different (D). Circle S or D.

Examples: cot   cot   Don   dawn

          (S)   D   S   (D)

1.   S   D   5.   S   D
2.   S   D   6.   S   D
3.   S   D   7.   S   D
4.   S   D   8.   S   D

Test 2
You will hear three words or sentences. Two of them will be the same. One will be different. Circle the number of the one which is *different*.

Examples: tot   tot   taught   core   car   car

          1   2   (3)   (1)   2   3

1.   1   2   3   5.   1   2   3
2.   1   2   3   6.   1   2   3
3.   1   2   3   7.   1   2   3
4.   1   2   3   8.   1   2   3

Test 3
You will hear six items from the teacher's list. Decide if each contains Vowel 7 (st<u>o</u>p) or Vowel 11 (l<u>aw</u>). Write the vowel number and the word (or sentence). Check your spelling.

1. _____   4. _____

2. _____   5. _____

3. _____   6. _____

Check your answers in the Answer Key.

Teacher's List

cot	caught	farm	form	sod	sawed
Don	dawn	mar	more	car	core
tot	taught	collar	caller	barn	born
far	four	yon	yawn		

Is it far?   Is it four?

Where's the collar?   Where's the caller?

It's Don.   It's dawn.

It's just an old car.   It's just an old core.

Contrast 9: Vowel 6 and Vowel 11—bus /ʌ/ and law /ɔ/

Practice 1
Repeat the items in column 1. The lower jaw is partially raised for /ʌ/ and the tongue is rather flat in the neutral rest position. The tongue is slightly concave (i.e., rounded inward). The lips are not tensed. Repeat: /ʌ/   /ʌ/   bus   bus.

Column 1	Column 2
gun	gone
cut	caught
but	bought
color	caller
sung	song
rung	wrong
bus	boss
cuff	cough
Chuck	chalk
mud	Maude

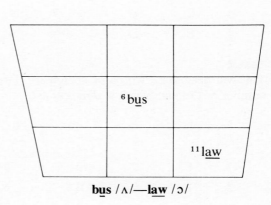

bus /ʌ/—law /ɔ/

Practice 2
Repeat the items in column 2. The jaw is lowered only a little from /ʌ/ to /ɔ/. The tongue is pulled down and back and the shape is more concave (i.e., rounded inward) for /ɔ/ than for /ʌ/. The lower lip is raised, tensed, and protruded a little. The upper lip and the muscle in the center of the chin may be tensed slightly. Repeat: /ɔ/   /ɔ/   law   law.

Practice 3
Repeat the pairs of items in columns 1 and 2. Then repeat the pairs of sentences.

Here comes my bus.	Here comes my boss.
That color was beautiful.	That caller was beautiful.
He cut it.	He caught it.
I'll get Chuck.	I'll get chalk.

Practice 4
Stop the tape. Read each sentence silently. Write the vowel number for each underlined vowel letter below it: Vowel 6 (bus) or Vowel 11 (law). Check your answers in the Answer Key. Practice in class and discuss with your teacher.

1. My cousin has gone abroad to study law.

2. Paul wants a cup of coffee and a doughnut.

3. His daughter taught us a dozen songs.

4. I called the bus company, but I got a wrong number!

Test 1

You will hear pairs of words or sentences using items from the teacher's list. As you listen, decide whether they are the same (S) or different (D). Circle S or D.

Examples: caught caught   song sung
          Ⓢ   D   S   Ⓓ

1. S   D   5. S   D
2. S   D   6. S   D
3. S   D   7. S   D
4. S   D   8. S   D

Test 2

You will hear three words or sentences. Two of them will be the same. One will be different. Circle the number of the one which is *different*.

Examples: boss boss bus   bought but but
          1   2   ③   ①   2   3

1. 1   2   3   5. 1   2   3
2. 1   2   3   6. 1   2   3
3. 1   2   3   7. 1   2   3
4. 1   2   3   8. 1   2   3

Test 3

You will hear six items from the teacher's list. Decide if each contains Vowel 6 (b<u>u</u>s) or Vowel 11 (l<u>aw</u>). Write the vowel number and the word (or sentence). Check your spelling.

1. _____   4. _____

2. _____   5. _____

3. _____   6. _____

Check your answers in the Answer Key.

Teacher's List

gun	gone	Chuck	chalk	rung	wrong
but	bought	done	dawn	cuff	cough
sung	song	cut	caught	mud	Maude
bus	boss	color	caller	tongue	tong

Here comes my bus.	Here comes my boss.
She cut the apple.	She caught the apple.
Which color did you like?	Which caller did you like?
My bus is never late!	My boss is never late!
That color is beautiful!	That caller is beautiful!
I need Chuck.	I need chalk.
I'll get Chuck.	I'll get chalk.
He cut it.	He caught it.

Contrast 10: Vowel 6 and Vowel 9—b<u>u</u>s /ʌ/ and b<u>oo</u>ks /ʊ/

Practice 1
Repeat the items in column 1. The lower jaw is partially raised for /ʌ/ and the tongue is rather flat in the neutral rest position. The tongue is slightly concave (i.e., rounded inward). The lips are not rounded. Repeat: /ʌ/   /ʌ/   b<u>u</u>s   b<u>u</u>s.

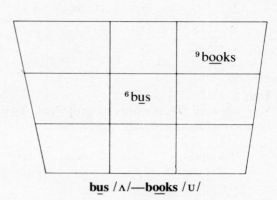

bus /ʌ/—b<u>oo</u>ks /ʊ/

Column 1	*Column 2*
l<u>u</u>ck	l<u>oo</u>k
b<u>u</u>ck	b<u>oo</u>k
t<u>u</u>ck	t<u>oo</u>k
p<u>u</u>tt	p<u>u</u>t
r<u>ou</u>gh	r<u>oo</u>f
h<u>u</u>ff	h<u>oo</u>f
st<u>u</u>d	st<u>oo</u>d
c<u>u</u>d	c<u>ou</u>ld

Practice 2
Repeat the items in column 2. The jaw is raised for /ʊ/. In contrast to /ʌ/, the tongue is bunched quite high toward the back of the roof of the mouth. The lips are loosely rounded. Repeat: /ʊ/   /ʊ/   b<u>oo</u>ks b<u>oo</u>ks.

Practice 3
Repeat the pairs of items in columns 1 and 2. Then repeat the pairs of sentences below.

Can you loan me a b<u>u</u>ck?	Can you loan me a b<u>oo</u>k?
Where did he p<u>u</u>tt the ball?	Where did he p<u>u</u>t the ball?
How do you spell "r<u>ou</u>gh"?	How do you spell "r<u>oo</u>f"?

Practice 4
Stop the tape. Read each sentence silently. Write the vowel number for each underlined vowel letter below it: Vowel 6 (b<u>u</u>s) or Vowel 9 (b<u>oo</u>ks). Check your answers in the Answer Key. Practice in class and discuss with your teacher.

1. We said, "G<u>oo</u>dbye and g<u>oo</u>d l<u>u</u>ck!" when the j<u>u</u>dge left the c<u>ou</u>ntry.

2. Next m<u>o</u>nth the w<u>oo</u>ds will be f<u>u</u>ll of h<u>u</u>nters.

3. W<u>ou</u>ld you p<u>u</u>t the m<u>o</u>ney in my b<u>u</u>s?

4. My br<u>o</u>ther p<u>u</u>t a new r<u>oo</u>f on his st<u>u</u>dy.

Test 1

You will hear pairs of words or sentences using items from the teacher's list. As you listen, decide whether they are the same (S) or different (D). Circle S or D.

Examples: bus   bus   luck   look

(S)   D   S   (D)

1.	S	D		5.	S	D
2.	S	D		6.	S	D
3.	S	D		7.	S	D
4.	S	D		8.	S	D

Test 2

You will hear three words or sentences. Two of them will be the same. One will be different. Circle the number of the one which is *different*.

Examples: tuck   tuck   took   putt   put   put

1   2   (3)   (1)   2   3

1.	1	2	3		5.	1	2	3
2.	1	2	3		6.	1	2	3
3.	1	2	3		7.	1	2	3
4.	1	2	3		8.	1	2	3

Test 3

You will hear six items from the teacher's list. Decide if each contains Vowel 6 (b<u>u</u>s) or Vowel 9 (b<u>oo</u>ks). Write the vowel number and the word (or sentence). Check your spelling.

1. _____   4. _____

2. _____   5. _____

3. _____   6. _____

Check your answer in the Answer Key.

Teacher's List

luck	look	stud	stood	putt	put
buck	book	tuck	took	cud	could
huff	hoof	rough	roof		

I need two bucks.   I need two books.

He loaned me a buck.   He loaned me a book.

He will putt the golf ball into the cup.   He will put the golf ball into the cup.

How do you spell "rough"?   How do you spell "roof"?

Where did he putt the ball?   Where did he put the ball?

Contrast 11: Vowel 12 and Vowel 9—bird /ɝ/ and books /ʊ/

Practice 1

Repeat the items in column 1. The lower jaw is raised for /ɝ/. The tongue is pulled up high and bunched close to the center of the hard roof of the mouth. The sides of the tongue touch the insides of the upper back teeth. The front and the tip of the tongue are pointed upward, and, for some speakers, a little backward. Repeat: /ɝ/   /ɝ/   bird   bird.

Column 1	*Column 2*
word	wood (Wood)
herd	hood
lurk	look
Kirk	cook (Cook)
Turk	took
Burke	book
pert	put
purse	puss
shirk	shook
stirred	stood

bird /ɝ/—books /ʊ/

Practice 2

Repeat the items in column 2. The /ʊ/ sound is pronounced with the jaw raised. In contrast to /ɝ/, the tongue is bunched toward the back of the roof of the mouth instead of toward the center. The tongue is pulled back and there is little if any contact with the upper teeth. The lips are loosely rounded. Repeat: /ʊ/ /ʊ/   books   books.

Practice 3

Repeat the pairs of items in columns 1 and 2. Then repeat the pairs of sentences below.

It's a big herd.	It's a big hood.
I saw the words.	I saw the woods.
His name is Kirk.	His name is Cook.
The Burkes will be late.	The books will be late.

Practice 4

Stop the tape. Read each sentence silently. Write the vowel number for each underlined vowel letter below it: Vowel 12 (bird) or Vowel 9 (books). Check your answers in the Answer Key. Practice in class and discuss with your teacher.

1. The woman put the birdbook in her purse.

2. The cook should return to work on Thursday.

3. If Burt would push it and Curt would pull it, they could move it!

Test 1

You will hear pairs of words or sentences using items from the teacher's list. As you listen, decide whether they are the same (S) or different (D). Circle S or D.

Examples: look   look   lurk   look
           (S)   D   S   (D)

1.	S	D	5.	S	D
2.	S	D	6.	S	D
3.	S	D	7.	S	D
4.	S	D	8.	S	D

Test 2

You will hear three words or sentences. Two of them will be the same. One will be different. Circle the number of the one which is *different*.

Examples: stirred   stirred   stood   word   wood   wood
           1   2   (3)   (1)   2   3

1.	1	2	3	5.	1	2	3
2.	1	2	3	6.	1	2	3
3.	1	2	3	7.	1	2	3
4.	1	2	3	8.	1	2	3

Test 3

You will hear six items from the teacher's list. Decide if each contains Vowel 12 (b<u>ir</u>d) or Vowel 9 (b<u>oo</u>ks). Write the vowel number and the word (or sentence). Check your spelling.

1. _____   4. _____

2. _____   5. _____

3. _____   6. _____

Check your answers in the Answer Key.

Teacher's List

word	wood (Wood)	shirk	shook	Burke	book
lurk	look	herd	hood	purse	puss
Turk	took	Kirk	cook (Cook)	stirred	stood
pert	put				

He has a big herd.	He has a big hood.
Can you see the words?	Can you see the woods?
My last name is Kirk.	My last name is Cook.
The Burkes are coming tomorrow.	The books are coming tomorrow.
The Burkes will be here today.	The books will be here today.
He sold his herd.	He sold his hood.

Contrast 12: Vowel 6 and Vowel 10—b<u>u</u>s /ʌ/ and n<u>o</u> /oᵘ/

Practice 1
Repeat the items in column 1. The lower jaw is partially raised for /ʌ/ and the tongue is rather flat in the neutral rest position. The tongue is slightly concave (i.e., rounded inward). The lips are not rounded. Repeat: /ʌ/   /ʌ/   b<u>u</u>s   b<u>u</u>s.

Column 1	*Column 2*
c<u>u</u>t	c<u>oa</u>t
n<u>u</u>t	n<u>o</u>te
b<u>u</u>t	b<u>oa</u>t
c<u>o</u>me	c<u>o</u>mb
m<u>u</u>st	m<u>o</u>st
n<u>o</u>ne	kn<u>ow</u>n
f<u>u</u>n	ph<u>o</u>ne
b<u>u</u>n	b<u>o</u>ne
t<u>o</u>n	t<u>o</u>ne
str<u>u</u>ck	str<u>o</u>ke
Ch<u>u</u>ck	ch<u>o</u>ke

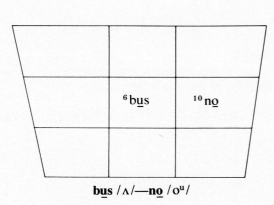

b<u>u</u>s /ʌ/—n<u>o</u> /oᵘ/

Practice 2
Repeat the items in column 2. The /oᵘ/ sound is not a pure sound. That is, it is made up of two parts. The lower jaw is raised from partially raised for /o/ to a higher position for /u/. It is important to make the two parts clearly, although the first part is stronger than the second part. Repeat: /oᵘ/   /oᵘ/   n<u>o</u>   n<u>o</u>.

Practice 3
Repeat the pairs of items in columns 1 and 2. Then repeat the pairs of sentences below.

He wants a n<u>u</u>t.	He wants a n<u>o</u>te.
It was a little c<u>u</u>t.	It was a little c<u>oa</u>t.
The dog was chewing a b<u>u</u>n.	The dog was chewing a b<u>o</u>ne.
He bought a two-t<u>o</u>n truck.	He bought a two-t<u>o</u>ne truck.

Practice 4
Stop the tape. Read each sentence silently. Write the vowel number for each underlined vowel letter below it: Vowel 6 (b<u>u</u>s) or Vowel 10 (n<u>o</u>). Check your answers in the Answer Key. Practice in class and discuss with your teacher.

1. Before it sn<u>ow</u>s, we m<u>u</u>st cl<u>o</u>se our s<u>u</u>mmer h<u>o</u>me in the c<u>ou</u>ntry.

2. Ch<u>u</u>ck c<u>u</u>t his elb<u>ow</u> when he sh<u>u</u>t the br<u>o</u>ken wind<u>ow</u>.

3. I d<u>o</u>n't kn<u>ow</u>, and I w<u>o</u>n't kn<u>ow</u> until the j<u>u</u>dges v<u>o</u>te on M<u>o</u>nday.

4. J<u>oe</u> s<u>o</u>ld <u>o</u>ne b<u>oa</u>t to his <u>u</u>ncle and the <u>o</u>ther b<u>oa</u>t to his br<u>o</u>ther.

Test 1

You will hear pairs of words or sentences using items from the teacher's list. As you listen, decide whether they are the same (S) or different (D). Circle S or D.

	Examples:	hum	hum		comb	come
		(S)	D		S	(D)

1.	S	D		5.	S	D
2.	S	D		6.	S	D
3.	S	D		7.	S	D
4.	S	D		8.	S	D

Test 2

You will hear three words or sentences. Two of them will be the same. One will be different. Circle the number of the one which is *different*.

	Examples:	Chuck	Chuck	choke		fun	phone	phone
		1	2	(3)		(1)	2	3

1.	1	2	3		5.	1	2	3
2.	1	2	3		6.	1	2	3
3.	1	2	3		7.	1	2	3
4.	1	2	3		8.	1	2	3

Test 3

You will hear six items from the teacher's list. Decide if each contains Vowel 6 (b<u>u</u>s) or Vowel 10 (n<u>o</u>). Write the vowel number and the word (or sentence). Check your spelling.

1. _____   4. _____

2. _____   5. _____

3. _____   6. _____

Check your answers in the Answer Key.

Teacher's List

cut	coat	struck	stroke	none	known
but	boat	rub	robe	fun	phone
hum	home	nut	note	ton	tone
must	most	come	comb	Chuck	choke
bun	bone				

The cut was black and blue.	The coat was black and blue.
The dog was chewing a bun.	The dog was chewing a bone.
He bought a two-ton truck.	He bought a two-tone truck.
She gave him some nuts.	She gave him some notes.
The hum was very quiet.	The home was very quiet.
Where did you get that cut?	Where did you get that coat?
He wants a nut.	He wants a note.
It was a little cut.	It was a little coat.

Contrast 13: Vowel 9 and Vowel 11—b<u>oo</u>ks /ʊ/ and l<u>aw</u> /ɔ/

Practice 1
Repeat the items in column 1. The /ʊ/ sound is pronounced with the jaw raised and the back of the tongue bunched quite high toward the back of the roof of the mouth. The lips are loosely rounded. Repeat: /ʊ/ /ʊ/ b<u>oo</u>ks b<u>oo</u>ks.

Column 1
b<u>u</u>ll
p<u>u</u>ll
f<u>u</u>ll
w<u>oo</u>l
t<u>oo</u>k
h<u>oo</u>k
f<u>oo</u>t
s<u>oo</u>t

Column 2
b<u>a</u>ll
P<u>au</u>l
f<u>a</u>ll (Fall)
w<u>a</u>ll
t<u>a</u>lk
h<u>aw</u>k
f<u>ou</u>ght
s<u>ou</u>ght

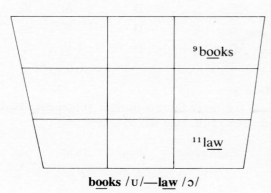

⁹b<u>oo</u>ks

¹¹l<u>aw</u>

b<u>oo</u>ks /ʊ/—l<u>aw</u> /ɔ/

Practice 2
Repeat the items in column 2. The jaw and the tongue are both lowered for /ɔ/. The tongue is pulled down and back into the lowest back articulatory position for English vowels. The lower lip and the muscle in the center of the chin may be slightly tensed. Repeat: /ɔ/ /ɔ/ l<u>aw</u> l<u>aw</u>.

Practice 3
Repeat the pairs of items in columns 1 and 2. Then repeat the pairs of sentences below.

The w<u>oo</u>l was yellow.
The b<u>u</u>ll was brown.
It was a golden h<u>oo</u>k.
It was f<u>u</u>ll.

The w<u>a</u>ll was yellow.
The b<u>a</u>ll was brown.
It was a golden h<u>aw</u>k.
It was F<u>a</u>ll.

Practice 4
Stop the tape. Read each sentence silently. Write the vowel number for each underlined vowel letter below it: Vowel 9 (b<u>oo</u>ks) and Vowel 11 (l<u>aw</u>). Check your answers in the Answer Key. Practice in class and discuss with your teacher.

1. P<u>au</u>l p<u>u</u>lled the h<u>oo</u>k out of the dog's p<u>aw</u>.

2. My l<u>aw</u>yer's d<u>au</u>ghter is a g<u>oo</u>d c<u>oo</u>k!

3. The b<u>o</u>ss t<u>oo</u>k a str<u>o</u>ng cup of c<u>o</u>ffee and two sugar c<u>oo</u>kies.

4. We t<u>oo</u>k a l<u>o</u>ng w<u>a</u>lk in the w<u>oo</u>ds.

Test 1
You will hear pairs of words or sentences using items from the teacher's list. As you listen, decide whether they are the same (S) or different (D). Circle S or D.

Examples: talk   talk   hook   hawk

                Ⓢ   D   S   Ⓓ

1.	S	D		5.	S	D
2.	S	D		6.	S	D
3.	S	D		7.	S	D
4.	S	D		8.	S	D

Test 2
You will hear three words or sentences. Two of them will be the same. One will be different. Circle the number of the one which is *different*.

Examples: Paul   Paul   pull   foot   fought   fought

                1   2   Ⓐ③   Ⓐ①   2   3

1.	1	2	3		5.	1	2	3
2.	1	2	3		6.	1	2	3
3.	1	2	3		7.	1	2	3
4.	1	2	3		8.	1	2	3

Test 3
You will hear six items from the teacher's list. Decide if each contains Vowel 9 (b<u>oo</u>ks) or Vowel 11 (l<u>aw</u>). Write the vowel number and the word (or sentence). Check your spelling.

1. _____   4. _____

2. _____   5. _____

3. _____   6. _____

Check your answers in the Answer Key.

Teacher's List

foot	fought	pull	Paul	full	fall
hook	hawk	soot	sought	bull	ball
wool	wall	took	talk		

The wool was yellow.	The wall was yellow.
The new bull was black.	The new ball was black.
It was a golden hook.	It was a golden hawk.
It was full.	It was Fall.
Who paid for the wool?	Who paid for the wall?
We don't need another bull!	We don't need another ball!
The hook hit my arm.	The hawk hit my arm.
It isn't full yet.	It isn't Fall yet.

Contrast 14: Vowel 2 and Vowel 4—it /ɪ/ and yes /ɛ/

Practice 1
Repeat the items in column 1. The lower jaw is raised for /ɪ/ and the tongue is held quite high. There is very little space between the upper and lower teeth. Repeat: /ɪ/ /ɪ/ it it.

Column 1	Column 2
bit	bet
mitt	met
lid	led
did	dead
wrist	rest
spill	spell
fill	fell
chick	check
big	beg
pin	pen
tin	ten
bitter	better

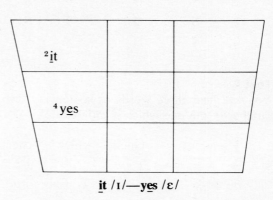

it /ɪ/—yes /ɛ/

Practice 2
Repeat the items in column 2. The lower jaw and the tongue are both lowered for /ɛ/. There is more space between the upper and lower teeth. Repeat: /ɛ/ /ɛ/ yes yes.

Practice 3
Repeat the pairs of items in columns 1 and 2. Then repeat the pairs of sentences below.

Does that taste bitter?	Does that taste better?
He had a little chick.	He had a little check.
I like your pin.	I like your pen.
She spilled it.	She spelled it.

Practice 4
Stop the tape. Read each sentence silently. Write the vowel number for each underlined vowel letter below it: Vowel 2 (it) or Vowel 4 (yes). Check your answers in the Answer Key. Practice in class and discuss with your teacher.

1. I met six French singers.

2. Which letter did Ted write?

3. Ken wrote six checks on the fifth of September.

4. Six friendly children were sitting next to the president.

Test 1
You will hear pairs of words or sentences using items from the teacher's list. As you listen, decide whether they are the same (S) or different (D). Circle S or D.

Examples: desk desk   tin ten
    (S) D   S (D)

1.	S	D		5.	S	D
2.	S	D		6.	S	D
3.	S	D		7.	S	D
4.	S	D		8.	S	D

Test 2
You will hear three words or sentences. Two of them will be the same. One will be different. Circle the number of the one which is *different*.

Examples: chick chick check   rest wrist wrist
     1   2 (3)   (1) 2   3

1.	1	2	3	5.	1	2	3
2.	1	2	3	6.	1	2	3
3.	1	2	3	7.	1	2	3
4.	1	2	3	8.	1	2	3

Test 3
You will hear six items from the teacher's list. Decide if each contains Vowel 2 (<u>i</u>t) or Vowel 4 (y<u>e</u>s). Write the vowel number and the word (or sentence). Check your spelling.

1. _____   4. _____

2. _____   5. _____

3. _____   6. _____

Check your answers in the Answer Key.

Teacher's List

bit	bet	big	beg	spill	spell
lid	led	tin	ten	chick	check
wrist	rest	mitt	met	pin	pen
fill	fell	did	dead	bitter	better

Does that taste bitter?   Does that taste better?

He had a little chick.   He had a little check.

I like your pin.   I like your pen.

She spilled it.   She spelled it.

That's a big chick.   That's a big check.

Is your pin new?   Is your pen new?

The taste was bitter.   The taste was better.

Contrast 15: Vowel 5 and Vowel 4—f<u>a</u>t /æ/ and y<u>e</u>s /ɛ/

Practice 1
Repeat the items in column 1. The jaw and the tongue are lowered for /æ/. In fact, the tongue is in the lowest front articulatory position for English vowels. It is rounded and arched forward a little. The tip of the tongue touches the backs of the lower front teeth. Repeat: /æ/   /æ/   f<u>a</u>t   f<u>a</u>t.

Column 1	*Column 2*
b<u>a</u>nd	b<u>e</u>nd
m<u>a</u>t	m<u>e</u>t
s<u>a</u>t	s<u>e</u>t
p<u>a</u>n	p<u>e</u>n
m<u>a</u>n	m<u>e</u>n
c<u>a</u>ttle	k<u>e</u>ttle
l<u>a</u>ther	l<u>ea</u>ther
p<u>a</u>ddle	p<u>e</u>dal
<u>a</u>dd	<u>E</u>d
t<u>a</u>n	t<u>e</u>n
l<u>a</u>nd	l<u>e</u>nd

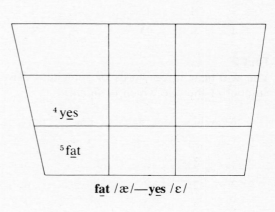

f<u>a</u>t /æ/—y<u>e</u>s /ɛ/

Practice 2
Repeat the items in column 2. The /ɛ/ is made with the lower jaw and the tongue both raised from their position for /æ/. There is less space between the upper and lower teeth. Repeat: /ɛ/   /ɛ/   y<u>e</u>s   y<u>e</u>s.

Practice 3
Repeat the pairs of items in columns 1 and 2. Then repeat the pairs of sentences below.

L<u>a</u>ther smells good.	L<u>ea</u>ther smells good.
Who paid for the c<u>a</u>ttle?	Who paid for the k<u>e</u>ttle?
He broke the p<u>a</u>ddle.	He broke the p<u>e</u>dal.
Did the m<u>a</u>n come yet?	Did the m<u>e</u>n come yet?
I found an old p<u>a</u>n.	I found an old p<u>e</u>n.

Practice 4
Stop the tape. Read each sentence silently. Write the vowel number for each underlined vowel letter below it: Vowel 5 (f<u>a</u>t) or Vowel 4 (y<u>e</u>s). Check your answers in the Answer Key. Practice in class and discuss with your teacher.

1. Let's <u>a</u>sk <u>E</u>dna to l<u>e</u>nd us a p<u>a</u>n.

2. I h<u>a</u>ve to move t<u>e</u>n h<u>ea</u>vy l<u>ea</u>ther s<u>a</u>ddles.

3. The w<u>ea</u>ther will be b<u>e</u>tter <u>a</u>fter January.

4. He <u>a</u>sked for t<u>e</u>n s<u>a</u>ndwiches and el<u>e</u>ven <u>a</u>pples.

Test 1
You will hear pairs of words or sentences using items from the teacher's list. As you listen, decide whether they are the same (S) or different (D). Circle S or D.

Examples: mat   mat   cattle   kettle
            (S)   D   S   (D)

1. S   D   5. S   D
2. S   D   6. S   D
3. S   D   7. S   D
4. S   D   8. S   D

Test 2
You will hear three words or sentences. Two of them will be the same. One will be different. Circle the number of the one which is *different*.

Examples: ten   ten   tan   band   bend   bend
            1   2   (3)   (1)   2   3

1. 1   2   3   5. 1   2   3
2. 1   2   3   6. 1   2   3
3. 1   2   3   7. 1   2   3
4. 1   2   3   8. 1   2   3

Test 3
You will hear six items from the teacher's list. Decide if each contains Vowel 5 (f<u>a</u>t) or Vowel 4 (y<u>e</u>s). Write the vowel number and the word (or sentence). Check your spelling.

1. _____   4. _____

2. _____   5. _____

3. _____   6. _____

Check your answers in the Answer Key.

Teacher's List

mat	met	tan	ten	lather	leather
pan	pen	band	bend	add	Ed
cattle	kettle	sat	set	land	lend
paddle	p<u>e</u>dal	man	men	lad	led

New lather smells good.   New leather smells good.
The man didn't come.   The men didn't come.
He broke the paddle.   He broke the p<u>e</u>dal.
Who bought the cattle?   Who bought the kettle?
I found an old pan.   I found an old pen.
Which man got the job?   Which men got the job?
Did the man come yet?   Did the men come yet?
I found the band.   I found the bend.

Contrast 16: Vowel 5 and Vowel 6—f<u>a</u>t /æ/ and b<u>u</u>s /ʌ/

Practice 1

Repeat the items in column 1. The lower jaw and the tongue are lowered for /æ/. The tongue is rounded a little and arched forward a little. The tip of the tongue touches the insides of the lower front teeth. Repeat: /æ/   /æ/   f<u>a</u>t   f<u>a</u>t.

Column 1

<u>a</u>nkle

c<u>a</u>p

m<u>a</u>tch

d<u>a</u>m

h<u>a</u>t

c<u>a</u>t

b<u>a</u>t

f<u>a</u>n

D<u>a</u>n

t<u>a</u>n

r<u>a</u>n

g<u>a</u>l

Column 2

<u>u</u>ncle

c<u>u</u>p

m<u>u</u>ch

d<u>u</u>mb

h<u>u</u>t

c<u>u</u>t

b<u>u</u>t

f<u>u</u>n

d<u>o</u>ne

t<u>o</u>n

r<u>u</u>n

g<u>u</u>ll

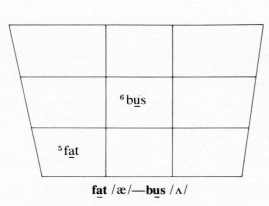

f<u>a</u>t /æ/—b<u>u</u>s /ʌ/

Practice 2

Repeat the items in column 2. The jaw is partially raised for /ʌ/. There is much less space between the upper and lower teeth. The tongue is rather flat in the neutral or rest position. In contrast to the rounding and forward arching for /æ/, the tongue is slightly concave (i.e., rounded inward). Repeat: /ʌ/   /ʌ/   b<u>u</u>s b<u>u</u>s.

Practice 3

Repeat the pairs of items in columns 1 and 2. Then repeat the pairs of sentences below.

He wants a new c<u>a</u>p.

It was D<u>a</u>n.

The little h<u>a</u>t was green.

It hurt my <u>a</u>nkle.

He has a little c<u>a</u>t.

He wants a new c<u>u</u>p.

It was d<u>o</u>ne.

The little h<u>u</u>t was green.

It hurt my <u>u</u>ncle.

He has a little c<u>u</u>t.

Practice 4

Stop the tape. Read each sentence silently. Write the vowel number for each underlined vowel letter below it: Vowel 5 (f<u>a</u>t) or Vowel 6 (b<u>u</u>s). Check your answers in the Answer Key. Practice in class and discuss with your teacher.

1. The cl<u>a</u>ss h<u>a</u>d l<u>u</u>nch <u>a</u>t h<u>a</u>lf p<u>a</u>st <u>o</u>ne.

2. Some<u>o</u>ne ordered a d<u>o</u>zen h<u>a</u>mburgers <u>a</u>nd a d<u>o</u>zen <u>a</u>pples.

3. My <u>au</u>nt and <u>u</u>ncle will leave for the c<u>ou</u>ntry on S<u>a</u>turday, S<u>u</u>nday, or M<u>o</u>nday.

4. My y<u>ou</u>ng c<u>ou</u>sin h<u>a</u>d a b<u>a</u>d <u>a</u>ccident.

Test 1
You will hear pairs of words or sentences using items from the teacher's list. As you listen, decide whether they are the same (S) or different (D). Circle S or D.

Examples: fan   fan   ankle   uncle
            (S)   D   S   (D)

1.   S   D   5.   S   D
2.   S   D   6.   S   D
3.   S   D   7.   S   D
4.   S   D   8.   S   D

Test 2
You will hear three words or sentences. Two of them will be the same. One will be different. Circle the number of the one which is *different*.

Examples: ran   ran   run   match   much   much
            1   2   (3)   (1)   2   3

1.   1   2   3   5.   1   2   3
2.   1   2   3   6.   1   2   3
3.   1   2   3   7.   1   2   3
4.   1   2   3   8.   1   2   3

Test 3
You will hear six items from the teacher's list. Decide if each contains Vowel 5 (f<u>a</u>t) or Vowel 6 (b<u>u</u>s). Write the vowel number and the word (or sentence). Check your spelling.

1. _____   4. _____

2. _____   5. _____

3. _____   6. _____

Check your answers in the Answer Key.

Teacher's List

cap	cup	cab	cub	Dan	done
dam	dumb	sang	sung	ran	run
cat	cut	match	much	gal	gull
fan	fun	hat	hut	ankle	uncle
tan	ton	bat	but		

Someone hurt my ankle!   Someone hurt my uncle!

The cab was black and white.   The cub was black and white.

I bought a little green hat.   I bought a little green hut.

She had a little cat on her arm.   She had a little cut on her arm.

It was Don on the phone.   It was done on the phone.

I saw a beautiful gal!   I saw a beautiful gull!

310

Vowel Contrast Chart

	Front Vowels					Central Vowels and Diphthongs					Back Vowels and Diphthongs				
	1	2	3	4	5	12	6	7	13	14	8	9	10	11	15
	/iʸ/	/ɪ/	/eⁱ/	/ɛ/	/æ/	/ɜ/	/ʌ/	/a/	/aɪ/	/au/	/uʷ/	/ʊ/	/oᵘ/	/ɔ/	/ɔɪ/
1.	leak	lick	lake	—	lack	lurk	luck	lock	like	—	Luke	look	—	—	—
2.	—	kit	Kate	—	cat	curt	cut	cot	kite	—	coot	—	coat	caught	—
3.	beat	bit	bait	bet	bat	Bert	but	bot	bite	bout	boot	—	boat	bought	—
4.	eat	it	ate	—	at	—	—	—	—	out	—	—	—	ought	—
5.	cheek	chick	—	check	—	—	Chuck	—	—	—	—	—	choke	chalk	—
6.	deed	did	—	dead	dad	—	dud	—	died	—	dude	—	—	—	—
7.	bead	bid	bayed	bed	bad	bird	bud	—	bide	bowed	booed	—	—	—	—
8.	—	fin	—	—	fan	fern	fun	—	fine	—	—	—	phone	fawn	—
9.	see	—	say	—	—	sir	—	—	sigh	sow	Sue	—	sew so	saw	soy
10.	weed we'd	—	wade	wed	—	word	—	wad	wide	—	wooed	would wood	—	—	—
11.	teal	till	tale	tell	—	—	—	—	tile	towel	tool	—	toll	tall	toil
12.	she'd	—	shade	shed	shad	—	—	shod	shied	—	shooed	should	showed	—	—
13.	heat	hit	hate	—	hat	hurt	hut	hot	height	—	hoot	—	—	—	—
14.	heed	hid	—	head	had	heard	—	—	hide	how'd	who'd	—	—	—	—
15.	neat	knit	Nate	net	gnat	—	nut	not	night	—	—	—	note	—	—
16.	seat	sit	—	set	sat	—	—	—	sight	—	suit	soot	—	sought	—
17.	feel	fill	fail	fell	—	furl	—	—	file	foul	fool	full	—	fall	foil
18.	peel	pill	pail	—	pal	pearl	—	—	pile	—	pool	pull	pole	Paul	—
19.	seek	sick	sake	—	sack	—	suck	sock	—	—	—	—	soak	—	—

Answer Key/Teacher Script

Unit 1

Lesson 1

Part 1 (page 4)

    1. I forgot my pencil.

    2. Tomorrow is Saturday.

    3. Call me tonight around seven.

Part 2 (page 4)

    4. I closed the door and waited for the bus.

    5. I bought four books for my two classes.

Part 3 (page 4)

    6. I ate a chicken-salad sandwich.

    7. The students are going to Chicago.

    8. He was waiting at the bus stop.

Part 4 (page 5)

    9. He isn't coming.

   10. The boys 'n' girls were late.

   11. I'm gonna study at the lab.

Part 5 (page 5)

   12. I'm hungry.

   13. Am I late?

   14. I bought hotdogs, French fries, apples, and candy.

Lesson 2   No dictation in this lesson.

Lesson 3

Part 3 (page 11)

1. becáuse	4. mysélf	7. asléep
2. todáy	5. néver	8. kítchen
3. bróther	6. arríve	9. sándwich

Part 3 (page 11)

    1. The téacher was late.   3. The báby was asléep.

    2. He arríved at ten.   4. Perháps I should do it mysélf.

Part 4 (pages 11–12)

    1. I was asléep.

    2. They will arríve at ten.

    3. I néver drink cóffee.

    4. I ate a chícken sándwich.

Resource Material

Part 3 (page 14)

Group 1.	afráid	Mónday	mysélf	decíde
Group 2.	dóllar	mídnight	guitár	sóftly
Group 3.	thirtéen	ballóon	scíence	agrée
Group 4.	hersélf	cóusin	máybe	vísit
Group 5.	sóldier	ártist	móney	escápe
Group 6.	políte	acróss	pópcorn	expénse

Part 4 (page 15)

1. I forgót to set my alárm.
2. My bróther is a fámous dóctor.
3. I bought a hótdog and some pópcorn.

4. The púppy was húngry and thírsty.
5. The sínger had a new guitár.

Lesson 4

Part 3 (pages 16–17)

1. Sómebody took my óvercoat.
2. She's a wónderful musícian.

3. We bought some béautiful fúrniture.
4. We can buy the médicine at the hóspital.

Part 4 (page 17)

1. I have a béautiful gárden.
2. Sómebody is at the door.
3. I have a wónderful idéa.
4. We will próbably go togéther.

Resource Material

Part 7 (page 19)

Group 1.	président	redúction	appéarance	impórtant
Group 2.	áccident	hóspital	tomórrow	énemy
Group 3.	enginéer	afternóon	cápital	overlóok
Group 4.	tomáto	Cánada	Chicágo	Ohío
Group 5.	ánimal	Flórida	ávenue	exámple
Group 6.	advénture	potáto	idéa	underpáid

Part 8 (page 20)

1. I understánd that gasolíne is very expénsive.
2. The accóuntant gave us the fináncial repórt.
3. I flew from Chicágo to Flórida and then to México Cíty.
4. My apártment is near the hóspital.
5. Tomórrow they will vísit the cápital in Wáshington.

Lesson 5

Part 3 (page 22)

1. todáy
   x
   1 2

2. toníght
   x
   1 2

3. agaín
   x
   1 2

4. tomórrow
   x
   1 2 3

5. télegram
   x
   1 2 3

6. disappéar
   x
   1 2 3

Resource Material

Part 5 (page 24)

1. I eat bréakfast at séven o'clock every morning.
2. The first word in the séntence is accented on the last sýllable.
3. I sent a télegram to the président.
4. He ate a léttuce and tomáto sálad for lunch.
5. There are no classes tomórrow because it's a hóliday.
6. The state góvernment of Téxas is very pówerful.
7. My landlord colléects the rent páyment on the first of the month.
8. There was a térrible car áccident on the corner.

Lesson 6

Part 3 (page 27)

Column 1	Column 2
1.	needed
2. want	
3. attend	
4.	talked
5.	liked
6. wash	
7.	played
8. live	
9.	studied

Part 4 (page 28)

Column 2	Column 3	Column 4
/t/	/d/	/ɪd/ or /əd/
danced	called	loaded
worked	lived	added
wished	played	wanted
liked	closed	needed
		waited

317

Part 5 (page 28)

1. She ordered a sandwich.
2. They arrived at ten.
3. We decided to wait for Bob.
4. We washed the windows and cleaned the house.

Resource Material

Part 1 (pages 29–30)

Column 1	Column 2	Column 3
/t/	/d/	/ɪd/ or /əd/
worked	stayed	decided
danced	snowed	added
liked	rained	wanted
washed	called	loaded
talked	opened	invited
	closed	tested
	lived	
	ordered	
	agreed	

Lesson 7

Part 3 (page 32)

Column 1	Column 2
1.	roses
2.	suitcases
3. bus	
4.	books
5. student	
6.	notes
7.	teachers
8. name	
9.	windows

Part 4 (page 33)

Column 2	Column 3	Column 4
/s/	/z/	/ɪz/ or /əz/
lamps	doors	dishes
cats	chairs	classes
lakes	names	roses
ropes	keys	boxes
		watches

318

Part 5 (page 33)

1. The <u>students</u> have four <u>classes</u>.
2. The <u>tests</u> are given on <u>Fridays</u>.
3. The <u>teachers</u> gave us the <u>answers</u>.
4. They have two <u>cats</u> and three <u>dogs</u>.

Resource Material

Part 1 (pages 35–36)

Column 1	Column 2	Column 3
/s/	/z/	/ɪz/ or /əz/
books	tables	nurses
lakes	names	buzzes
students	teachers	suitcases
ropes	gloves	watches
months	windows	dishes
	toys	boxes
		classes
		corsages
		languages

Lesson 8

Part 4 (pages 39–40)

1. I'd like some <u>pop</u>corn.
2. I'd like some <u>pop</u>corn, | and a <u>Coke</u>.
3. I'd like some <u>pop</u>corn, | a <u>Coke</u>, | and a <u>can</u>dy bar.

Lesson 9

Part 4 (page 44)

1. I ~~was~~ hungry ~~and~~ thirsty.
2. ~~The~~ students ~~are going to~~ class.
3. Bill ~~and~~ Sam ~~are from~~ Chicago.
4. I ~~must~~ go ~~to~~ class ~~at~~ two.

Lesson 10

Part 4 (page 49)

1. They were : ready for class.
2. Jeff : found a penny.
3. I wish : she would wait.
4. I gave Jane : nine dollars.

Lesson 11

Part 6 (page 56)

1. We're late to class.
2. I haven't seen him.
3. How've you been.
4. I should've called him.

Resource Material

Part 1—Chart 8 (page 57)

1. 1a.—1	9. 8a.—7
2. 5a.—3	10. 2a.—8
3. 2a.—2	11. 7a.—3
4. 1a.—5	12. 7a.—7
5. 2a.—7	13. 4a.—6
6. 3a.—6	14. 4a.—8
7. 3a.—8	15. 6a.—3
8. 9a.—3	

Part 1—Chart 9 (page 58)

1. 12a.—2	9. 5a.—1
2. 6a.—1	10. 1a.—1
3. 4a.—1	11. 7a.—1
4. 11a.—1	12. 10a.—1
5. 2a.—1	13. 15a.—2
6. 3a.—1	14. 14a.—2
7. 15a.—1	15. 8a.—1
8. 16a.—2	

Lesson 12

Part 3 (page 61)

1. What is your name?
2. Where are you from?
3. It is time for lunch.
4. Is he from France or from Spain?
5. Do you want tea or coffee?

Part 4 (page 62)

1. Did he ask her to come?
2. It is time for class.
3. I would like some cake and some ice cream.
4. Please give me a cup of coffee.

Resource Material

Part 2 (page 63)

1. I have waited for almost an hour.
2. Does he want the red car?
3. No, he wants the blue one.
4. Did he order a hamburger or a hotdog?
5. He was waiting for his friend.

Lesson 13

Part 4 (page 67)

Group 1	Group 2	Group 3	Group 4	Group 5
1. b	1. c	1. b	1. d	1. c
2. c	2. a	2. d	2. c	2. a
3. a	3. b	3. a	3. e	3. e
		4. c	4. b	4. b
			5. a	5. d

Lesson 14

Part 4 (page 75)

1a. ₂What would you like?³ ↘₁

1b. ₂I'd like a sandwich and a glass of milk.³ ↘₁

2a. ₂Where are you living?³ ↘₁

2b. ₂I have an apartment.³ ↘₁

3a. ₂Where are you from?³↘₁

3b. ₂I'm from Canada.³↘₁

4a. ₂How long have you been here?³ →₁

4b. ₂I've been here a month.³↘₁

5a. ₂What are you studying?³→₁

5b. ₂I'm in law school.³→₁

Lesson 15

Part 4 (page 82)

1a. ₂Are you going to the picnic?↗³

1b. ₂I can't.³↘₁ ₂I have an appointment.³→₁

2a. ₂Have all the students gone?↗³

2b. ₂All but John.³↘₁

3a. ₂Isn't John going?↗³

3b. ₂He's waiting for a friend.³→₁

4a. ₂Can they catch a bus later?↗³

4b. ₂Sure, they run every half hour.³→₁

Lesson 16

Part 4 (page 89)

1a. ₂What sports do you like?³→₁

1b. ₂I like baseball,↗³ ₂football,↗³ ₂basketball,³–––³ ₂and hockey.→₁

2a. ₂Have all the students gone?↗³

2b. ₂No, I saw John,↗³ ₂and Bill,↗³ ₂and Jack,³–––³ ₂and Mary.→₁

3a. ₂What did you have?³↘₁

3b. ₂I had some soup and crackers,↗³ ₂a salad,↗³ ₂a hotdog,³–––³ ₂and a Coke.↘₁

4a. ₂Where have you lived?³↘₁

4b. ₂I've lived in Boston,↗³ ₂in Detroit,↗³ ₂in New York,↗³–––––³ ₂and in Miami.→₁

Lesson 17   No dictation in this lesson.

Lesson 18   No dictation in this lesson.

Lesson 19   No dictation in this lesson.

Lesson 20

Part 1 (page 102)

1. understánd
   1 2 3

2. téacher
   1 2

3. président
   1 2 3

4. télephone
   1 2 3

5. musícian
   1 2 3

6. perháps
   1 2

7. mysélf
   1 2

8. discóver
   1 2 3

9. afternóon
   1 2 3

10. Septémber
    1 2 3

11. tomórrow
    1 2 3

12. yésterday
    1 2 3

Part 2 (page 102)

1. churches _____2_____

2. dimes _____1_____

3. kisses _____2_____

4. judges _____2_____

5. hills _____1_____

6. wanted _____2_____

7. missed _____1_____

8. lived _____1_____

9. landed _____2_____

10. laughed _____1_____

11. sounded _____2_____

12. gloves _____1_____

Part 3 (page 103)

1. I'd like a <u>sand</u>wich. (1 sentence stress)

2. I'd like a <u>sand</u>wich and a cup of <u>cof</u>fee. (2)

3. I'd like a <u>sand</u>wich, a cup of <u>cof</u>fee, and some <u>ice</u> cream. (3)

4. The <u>chil</u>dren <u>danced</u> and <u>sang</u>. (3)

5. Get <u>rea</u>dy for the <u>test</u>. (2)

6. I'm <u>going</u> to Chi<u>ca</u>go on <u>Mon</u>day. (3)

Part 4 (page 103)

1. I _must_ go _to_ class.

2. He _can_ come _at_ ten.

3. _The_ students _are_ going _to_ Chicago.

4. Get ready _for_ _the_ test.

5. I _was_ hungry _and_ thirsty.

6. They _can_ come _from_ four _to_ five.

Part 5 (page 103)

1. I won some : money.

2. I bought a silver : ring.

3. He's my favorite : teacher.

4. Meet me at the bus : stop.

5. We can help : Paul.

6. He's a bad : dog.

322

Part 6 (page 104)

1. He _doesn't_ work here.

2. _Why's_ he crying?

3. She _wasn't_ invited.

4. _How's_ your mother?

5. We _can't_ leave until ten.

6. _Isn't_ he coming?

Part 7 (page 104)

1. I _have to_ study.

2. I'll _meet you_ after class.

3. We're _going to_ study.

4. _What are you_ doing?

5. I don't _want to_ go.

6. Please _give me_ a cup of coffee.

Part 8 (pages 104–5)

1. ₂What would you like?

2. ₂I'd like a sandwich and a glass of milk.

3. ₂Where are you from?

4. ₂I'm from Canada.

5. ₂What are you studying?

6. ₂I'm in law school.

Part 9 (page 105)

1. ₂Have all the students gone?

2. ₂Isn't John going?

3. ₂Are you coming later?

Part 10 (page 105)

1. ₂I bought some soap, ₂some toothpaste, ₂and some Kleenex.

2. ₂I've lived in Boston, ₂in Detroit, ₂in New York, ₂and in Miami.

3. ₂I had some soup and crackers, ₂a salad, ₂a hotdog, ₂and a Coke.

323

Unit 2

Lesson 1   No dictation in this lesson.

Lesson 2   No dictation in this lesson.

Lesson 3

Part 3 (page 131)

1. We must leave at three.
2. These books seem easy to read.
3. Does he need these keys?
4. Please meet me at the beach.

Part 4 (page 131)

1. She was leaving for the beach.
2. These books seem easy to read.
3. The teacher needs the keys.
4. Please meet me at three.

Part 5 (pages 131–32)

1. be   she   meter   these   complete
2. see   three   between   week   cheese
3. tea   each   teacher   easy   please   leave
4. field   believe   thief

Lesson 4

Part 3 (page 136)

1. We were waiting for the train in the rain.
2. He ate eighty-eight cakes!
3. Jane Taylor is a famous lady.
4. The rain in Spain is mainly on the plain.

Part 4 (page 136)

1. He ate a great big steak.
2. Today is the eighth of April.
3. The lady was waiting by the gate.
4. The baby weighs eight pounds.

Part 5 (pages 136–37)

1. famous   baby   paper   late   came   place   gave
2. train   wait   rain   praise   raise
3. day   way   say   today
4. weight   eight   neighbor
5. great   break   steak

Lesson 5

Part 3 (page 141)

1. Let's have dinner at six.
2. I put four big fish in the dish.
3. Snow is the kiss of winter; rain is the kiss of spring!
4. Which picture is in the window?

Part 4 (page 142)

1. He caught <u>fifty</u> <u>big</u> <u>fish</u>.
2. My <u>sister</u> was <u>sitting</u> by the <u>river</u>.
3. I <u>live</u> at <u>sixteen</u> <u>sixteen</u> <u>Fifth</u> Avenue.
4. She wore a <u>big</u> <u>ring</u> on her <u>little</u> <u>finger</u>.

Part 5 (page 142)

1. big   sick   dish   listen   spring
2. giggle   middle   little   will   miss   dinner
3. bicycle   syllable   rhythm
4. business   busy   build   building   quit   quick

Lesson 6

Part 3 (page 146)

1. It's <u>twenty</u> past <u>ten</u>.
2. I <u>met</u> my <u>best</u> <u>friend</u> at the <u>restaurant</u>.
3. <u>Every</u> <u>lesson</u> will <u>end</u> with a <u>test</u>.
4. I <u>left</u> my <u>pencil</u> on the <u>desk</u>.

Part 4 (page 147)

1. I <u>left</u> my <u>red</u> <u>pencil</u> on the <u>desk</u>.
2. Winter <u>weather</u> is <u>never</u> <u>pleasant</u>.
3. <u>Get</u> <u>ready</u> for the <u>test</u>.
4. Study the <u>next</u> <u>seven</u> <u>lessons</u>.

Part 5 (page 147)

1. red   desk   forget   ever   never   pencil
2. better   letter   sell   yellow   lesson   egg
3. ready   head   bread   heavy   meant   weather
4. friend   friendly
5. guest   guess   question

Lesson 7

Part 3 (page 151)

1. Please <u>pass</u> the <u>apples</u>.
2. The <u>fat</u> <u>cat</u> <u>sat</u> on the <u>hat</u>.
3. <u>Sam</u> took the <u>last</u> <u>sandwich</u>.
4. The <u>classes</u> will <u>travel</u> by <u>taxi</u>.

Part 4 (page 152)

1. The <u>taxi</u> driver was a <u>handsome</u> <u>man</u>.
2. <u>Classes</u> <u>began</u> <u>last</u> week.
3. I <u>can't</u> <u>answer</u> the <u>last</u> question.
4. The <u>accident</u> <u>happened</u> <u>after</u> <u>class</u>.

Part 5 (page 152)

1. bad   sad   man   ask   last   basket
2. class   add   happy   happen   apple   battle
3. at   an   and   that   than   has
4. áfter   sándwich   práctice   perháps   reláx   understánd
5. laugh   laughter   aunt

Lesson 8

Part 1 (page 156)

1. I bought another (sheep — (ship)).
                 1   2

2. Do you have a ((pain) — pen)?
               3   4

3. Who borrowed my ((pan) — pen)?
               5   4

4. She has a new ((pen) — pin).
              4   2

5. She's ((sleeping) — slipping).
           1   2

6. He ((tasted) — tested) it.
         3   4

7. I can smell the (leather — (lather)).
                   4   5

8. The waiter gave me the (bill — (bell)).
                       2   4

9. Do you have a ((pin) — pain — pen — pan)?
               2   3   4   5

10. Spell the word (seat — sit — (set) — sat).
                 1   2   4   5

Part 2 (page 156)

Vowel 1	Vowel 2	Vowel 3	Vowel 4	Vowel 5
see	it	say	yes	fat
these	little	table	test	cat
easy	big	rain	red	black
green	fish	may	get	last
she	six	gate	letter	sang

Part 3 (page 157)

1. He's sitting in my seat!
      1   2 2 2   1

2. The lady set the pepper on the paper.
           3   4   4   3

3. Which letter did Ted leave on the desk?
      2   4   2 4   1   4

4. Betty would rather have a leather hat.
     4   5   5   4   5

5. He put his ten sheep on the red ship.
     1   2 4   1   4 2

6. Jim went to get six sandwiches and ten apples.
     2   4   4 2 5   2   4 5

Lesson 9

Part 3 (page 162)

1. I need a new blue suit.
2. Lou likes his new room.
3. We met a group of students at the zoo.
4. Sue wants some soup and some fruit.

Part 4 (page 163)

1. His new blue shoe fell in the pool.
2. A new group of students will arrive in June.
3. He threw a rock through the window.
4. Lou bought a new blue suit.

Part 5 (pages 163–64)

1. zoo   soon   room   school   boot   tooth   roof   loose
2. ruler   students   junior   July   June   rule
3. to   do   who

4. you   group   soup

5. threw   grew   flew

6. avenue   blue   true

Lesson 10

Part 3 (page 167)

1. Let's <u>go</u> to the <u>show</u>.
2. Who <u>owns</u> that <u>old</u> <u>yellow</u> <u>boat</u>?
3. I <u>know</u> <u>those</u> <u>fellows</u> <u>stole</u> the <u>gold</u>!
4. <u>Don't</u> <u>go</u> swimming <u>alone</u>.

Part 4 (page 168)

1. He <u>broke</u> his <u>shoulder</u> and his <u>toe</u>.
2. They <u>sold</u> the <u>old</u> <u>stove</u>.
3. My <u>window</u> <u>overlooks</u> the <u>ocean</u>.
4. I <u>hope</u> she likes <u>yellow</u> <u>roses</u>.

Part 5 (page 168)

1. so   radio   no   open   gold   both
2. wrote   home   broke   rose
3. slow   belów   yellów   wíndow
4. road   load   soap   boat

Lesson 11

Part 3 (pages 172–73)

1. They went for a <u>long</u> <u>walk</u>.
2. The teacher <u>taught</u> us the <u>wrong</u> <u>song</u>.
3. His <u>daughter's</u> <u>office</u> is <u>across</u> the <u>hall</u>.
4. Be careful! Don't <u>fall</u> <u>off</u> the <u>wall</u>.

Part 4 (page 173)

1. It was a <u>long</u> <u>song</u>.
2. His <u>daughter</u> is <u>tall</u>.
3. I <u>saw</u> them <u>talking</u> in the <u>hall</u>.
4. He <u>caught</u> the <u>ball</u>.

Part 5 (pages 173–74)

1. dog   fog   cost   off   song
2. call   hall   walk   bald   also
3. caught   taught   because
4. saw   draw   lawyer
5. ought   fought   bought

Lesson 12

Part 3 (page 178)

1. He <u>shouldn't</u> <u>put</u> his <u>foot</u> on the table.
2. Where <u>should</u> I <u>put</u> the <u>wood</u>?
3. The boy <u>stood</u> on one <u>foot</u>.
4. <u>Put</u> the <u>books</u> on the table.

Part 4 (page 179)

1. We <u>would</u> like to walk in the <u>woods</u>.
2. He bought a <u>good</u> <u>wool</u> sweater.
3. <u>Put</u> the <u>cookies</u> and the <u>sugar</u> on the table.
4. We <u>shook</u> hands and said <u>goodbye</u>.

Part 5 (page 179)

   1. put   pull   full   push   bush

   2. good   stood   took   cook

   3. should   could   would   shouldn't   couldn't

Lesson 13

Part 1 (page 182)

   1. It was a golden (hawk – hook)!
                 11   9

   2. He's in the (low – law) school.
              10   11

   3. It was a long (pull – pool).
              9   8

   4. Who paid for the (wool – wall)?
                 9   11

   5. Mr. White is very (bold – bald)!
                10   11

   6. The (suit – soot) was black.
          8   9

   7. It isn't (Fall – full) yet!
              .11   9

   8. Whose (bowl – ball) is this?
            10   11

   9. It looks (fullish – foolish)!
             9   8

  10. Spell the word (pool – pull – pole – Paul).
                 8   9   10   11

  11. Spell the word (cooed – could – code – cawed).
                  8   9   10   11

  12. Spell the word (bull – bowl – ball).
                 9   10   11

Part 2 (page 182)

Vowel 8	*Vowel 9*	*Vowel 10*	*Vowel 11*
tw<u>o</u>	b<u>oo</u>ks	n<u>o</u>	l<u>a</u>w
school	*bull*	*cold*	*ball*
boot	*could*	*code*	*caught*
rule	*push*	*pole*	*talk*
you	*pull*	*rose*	*long*
do	*would*	*bold*	*taught*

Part 3 (page 183)

   1. Who took my good new cookbook?
        8 9   9 8 9   9

   2. The lawyer's daughter is a good cook!
          11   11   9   9

   3. We took a long walk in the woods.
         9   11   11   9

   4. I thought Paul was going home.
          11   11   10   10

   5. Woody pushed Louie into the pool!
         9   9   8   8

   6. Don't go 'til the lawyer calls!
         10   10   11   11

Lesson 14

Part 3 (page 187)

   1. The <u>nurse</u> <u>burned</u> the <u>shirt</u>.

   2. It's a <u>modern</u> <u>church</u>.

   3. <u>Learn</u> <u>thirty</u> new <u>words</u>.

   4. <u>Thirty</u> <u>purple</u> <u>birds</u> <u>were</u> sitting on the <u>curb</u>.

Part 4 (page 188)

   1. I <u>never</u> <u>work</u> on <u>Thursday</u>.

   2. My <u>sister</u> wants a <u>purple</u> <u>skirt</u>.

   3. I washed my <u>brother's</u> <u>dirty</u> <u>shirt</u>.

   4. I <u>heard</u> a <u>bird</u> singing.

Part 5 (page 188)

1. her   fern   over   sister
2. fur   hurt   turn   purse
3. sir   bird   girl   first

4. world   work   worse   color
5. heard   learn   early   earth

Lesson 15

Part 3 (page 195)

1. The <u>Number</u> <u>One</u> <u>bus</u> <u>comes</u> at <u>one</u>.
2. His <u>brother</u> can't <u>come</u> <u>until</u> <u>Monday</u>.

3. June is a <u>lovely</u> <u>summer</u> <u>month</u>.
4. Her <u>mother</u> cooked a <u>wonderful</u> <u>supper</u>.

Part 4 (page 196)

1. <u>What</u> <u>color</u> is the <u>bus</u>?
2. My <u>uncle</u> is <u>coming</u> for <u>supper</u>.

3. Her <u>husband</u> was eating his <u>lunch</u>.
4. I <u>studied</u> on <u>Sunday</u> and <u>Monday</u>.

Part 5 (page 196)

1. sun   jump   butter   summer
2. son   money   come   Monday
3. cousin   young   double   trouble

Lesson 16

Part 3 (page 202)

1. <u>John</u> <u>forgot</u> his <u>promise</u>.
2. Is the <u>doctor</u> at the <u>hospital</u>?

3. I <u>got</u> a <u>spot</u> on my <u>collar</u>.
4. We <u>stopped</u> at the <u>shop</u> for a <u>bottle</u> of <u>pop</u>.

Part 4 (page 203)

1. He <u>forgot</u> his <u>promise</u>.
2. I <u>got</u> a <u>hotdog</u> and a <u>bottle</u> of <u>pop</u>.

3. I'm <u>sorry</u> I <u>dropped</u> the <u>clock</u>.
4. He <u>got</u> a <u>job</u> at a big <u>college</u>.

Part 5 (page 203)

1. not   hot   job   bottle   collar
2. father   watch   wash

Lesson 17

Part 1 (page 207)

1. The (bird — bud) is beautiful!
    12   6
2. Was it (hot — hurt)?
      7   12
3. My (lock — luck) was good!
     7   6
4. The (cub — curb) was black.
     6   12
5. Who (shut — shot) it?
      6   7

6. That was a good (shirt — shot)!
           12   7
7. Which (curlers — collars — colors) did she buy?
        12   7   6
8. Where are the (ducks — docks)?
           6   7
9. I didn't see the (cub — curb — cob).
           6   12   7
10. Spell the word (lock — lurk — luck).
          7   12   6

329

Part 2 (pages 207–8)

Vowel 12	*Vowel 6*	*Vowel 7*
b<u>ir</u>d	b<u>u</u>s	st<u>o</u>p
shirt	duck	cot
hurt	fun	lock
work	luck	drop
her	sun	not
nurse	shut	shot
church	cut	top
word	lunch	clock

Part 3 (page 208)

1. Worst luck! Someone burned ~~the~~ buns!
   12   6   6   6   12   6

2. ~~The~~ robber dropped ~~the~~ rubber duck!
        7   12   7   6   12 6

3. Bob's collar is ~~a~~ funny color!
    7   7   12   6   6   12

4. ~~The~~ robber shut his shirt in ~~the~~ locker.
        7   12   6   12   7   12

5. Dirk's duck ~~was~~ on ~~the~~ dock.
    12   6   7

6. ~~The~~ curler ~~and the~~ collar were ~~the~~ same color!
        12 12   7   12   12   6 12

Lesson 18

Part 3 (page 211)

1. <u>Why</u> did he <u>buy</u> a <u>white</u> <u>tie</u>?

2. Please <u>buy</u> <u>nine</u> <u>pies</u>.

3. <u>I</u> can't <u>find</u> the <u>right</u> <u>knife</u>.

4. <u>I</u> saw a <u>bright</u> <u>light</u> in the <u>sky</u> <u>tonight</u>.

Part 4 (page 212)

1. A cat has <u>nine</u> <u>lives</u>.

2. They <u>climbed</u> the <u>highest</u> mountain.

3. <u>I'm</u> <u>flying</u> to <u>Miami</u> on <u>Friday</u>.

4. <u>I'd</u> <u>like</u> to <u>buy</u> a <u>kite</u>.

Part 5 (page 212)

1. find   climb   Friday   high   bright

2. like   time   smile   drive   arrive

3. cry   my   why   spy   fry

Lesson 19

Part 3 (page 216)

1. The <u>mouse</u> ran <u>around</u> the <u>house</u>.

2. We <u>found</u> a <u>brown</u> <u>cow</u> on the <u>mountain</u>.

3. I waited <u>down</u> <u>town</u> for an <u>hour</u>.

4. <u>Pronounce</u> the <u>vowel</u> <u>sounds</u>.

Part 4 (page 217)

1. A <u>loud</u> <u>crowd</u> was <u>shouting</u>.

2. I learned a <u>thousand</u> <u>nouns</u>.

3. The <u>mouse</u> ran around the <u>house</u>.

4. He was <u>about</u> an <u>hour</u> late.

Part 5 (page 217)

1. shout   loud   south   found
2. crowd   now   down   vowel
3. route   house   mouse
4. ounce   pronounce   announce

Lesson 20

Part 3 (page 220)

1. The <u>boys</u> <u>enjoyed</u> their <u>noisy</u> <u>toys</u>.
2. Their loud <u>voices</u> made too much <u>noise</u>!
3. The <u>boiling</u> <u>oil</u> was <u>destroyed</u>.
4. His <u>loyal</u> friends were <u>appointed</u>.

Part 4 (page 221)

1. He <u>appointed</u> his <u>loyal</u> friend.
2. The <u>boys</u> were <u>noisy</u>.
3. The <u>oil</u> was <u>boiling</u>.
4. He <u>pointed</u> to the <u>noisy</u> <u>toys</u>.

Part 5 (page 221)

1. join   noisy   point
2. boy   enjoy   annoy
3. noise   voice

Lesson 21

Part 1 (page 224)

1. He loves to eat Hawaiian (pie — (poi))!   13 15
6. Is it time to go ((dine) — down)?   13 14

2. She bought some new ((tiles) — towels).   13 14
7. That's a terrible ((voice) — vice)!   15 13

3. The ((boy) — bough) fell down.   15 14
8. What a good ((buy) — boy — bow)!   13 15 14

4. They're afraid of the ((mouse) — mice)!   14 13
9. Did you find the (oil — (owl) — aisle)?   15 14 13

5. It's a steel (file — (foil)).   13 15
10. Spell the word (tile — towel — (toil)).   13 14 15

Part 2 (pages 224–25)

Vowel 13	*Vowel 14*	*Vowel 15*
my	cow	boy
try	*crowd*	*join*
bright	*south*	*voice*
dime	*noun*	*annoy*
find	*hour*	*appoint*
climb	*mountain*	*destroy*

331

Part 3 (page 225)

1. It took five hours ~~to~~ climb ~~the~~ mountain.
           13   14   13   14

2. Write ~~the~~ vowel numbers on ~~the~~ lines as you pronounce them.
     13   14   13   14

3. I heard loud noisy voices outside my house!
    13   14   15   15   14 13   13 14

4. ~~The~~ nine noisy boys spilled ~~the~~ oil ~~in the~~ aisle!
       13   15   15   15   13

5. ~~The~~ boy went ~~to~~ buy ~~some~~ ties, ~~some~~ toys, ~~and some~~ flowers.
      15   13   13   15   14

6. ~~There's an~~ oily owl in ~~the~~ aisle!
       15 14   13

Lesson 22 No dictation in this lesson.

Lesson 23

Front Vowels Part 3

Test 1 (page 233)

1. I bought another (sheep — ship).
                      1   2

2. Do you have a (pain — pen)?
                   3   4

3. Who borrowed my (pan — pen)?
                     5   4

4. She has a new (pen — pin).
                  4   2

5. She's (sleeping — slipping)?
         1   2

6. He (tasted — tested) it.
       3   4

7. I can smell the (leather — lather).
                 4   5

8. The waiter gave me the (bill — bell).
                        2   4

9. Do you have a (pin — pain — pen — pan)?
                 2   3   4   5

10. Spell the word (seat — sit — set — sat).
                    1   2   4   5

Test 2 (page 234)

Vowel 1	Vowel 2	Vowel 3	Vowel 4	Vowel 5
s_ee_	_i_t	sa_y_	_ye_s	f_a_t
these	little	table	test	cat
easy	big	rain	red	black
green	fish	may	get	last
she	six	gate	letter	sang

Test 3 (page 234)

1. The teacher gave us a special reading test.
       1   3   4   1   4

2. His little cat chased the big rat.
     2   2   5   3   2   5

3. I think we'll take a vacation in November.
     2   1   3   3 3   2   4

4. The last question on the test was easy to answer.
      5   4   4   1   5

5. I guess he'll wait until Wednesday.
     4 1   3   2 4   3

6. Many lands have a celebration on the first day of May.
     4   5   5   4   3   3   3

Central Vowels Part 3

Test 1 (page 236)

1. The (**bird** — bud) is beautiful!
        12   6

2. Was it (hot — hurt)?
           7   12

3. My (lock — luck) was good!
        7   6

4. The (**cub** — curb) was black.
       6   12

5. Who (shut — **shot**) it?
      6   7

6. That was a good (**shirt** — shot)!
             12   7

7. Which (curlers — collars — **colors**) did she buy?
            12   7   6

8. Where are the (ducks — **docks**)?
              6   7

9. I didn't see the (cub — **curb** — cob).
              6   12   7

10. Spell the word (lock — lurk — **luck**).
              7   12   6

Test 2 (page 237)

Vowel 12 bird	*Vowel 6* bus	*Vowel 7* stop
shirt	duck	cot
hurt	fun	lock
work	luck	drop
her	sun	not
nurse	shut	shot
church	cut	top
word	lunch	clock

Test 3 (page 237)

1. Her husband got her another fur coat.
   12 6   7   12 6   12 12

2. The girls were studying the problems on Sunday and Monday.
       12   12 6   7   6   6

3. The doctor and the nurse left the hospital at six o'clock.
    7   12   12   7   7

4. My uncle and my cousin hurried home from work.
    6   6   12   12

5. I got a new cotton shirt with a colorful collar.
    7   7   12   6 12   7   12

Lesson 24

Back Vowels Part 3

Test 1 (page 240)

1. It was a golden (hawk — (hook))!
   11   9

2. He's in the (low — (law)) school.
   10   11

3. It was a long ((pull) — pool).
   9   8

4. Who paid for the (wool — (wall))?
   9   11

5. Mr. White is very ((bold) — bald)!
   10   11

6. The ((suit) — soot) was black.
   8   9

7. It isn't ((Fall) — full) yet!
   11   9

8. Whose ((bowl) — ball) is this?
   10   11

9. It looks (fullish — (foolish))!
   9   8

10. Spell the word (pool — pull — pole — (Paul)).
    8   9   10   11

11. Spell the word (cooed — could — (code) — cawed).
    8   9   10   11

12. Spell the word (bull — (bowl) — ball).
    9   10   11

Test 2 (page 240)

Vowel 8	*Vowel 9*	*Vowel 10*	*Vowel 11*
tw**o**	b**oo**ks	n**o**	l**aw**
school	*bull*	*cold*	*ball*
food	*could*	*code*	*caught*
rule	*push*	*pole*	*talk*
you	*pull*	*rose*	*long*
do	*would*	*bold*	*taught*

Test 3 (page 241)

1. Who put the sugar in my orange juice?
   8   9   9   11   8

2. It shouldn't snow in June, July, or August.
   9   10   8   8   11

3. By November the woods ought to be full of snow.
   10   9   11   9   10

4. She put the small blue coat in the lower drawer.
   9   11   8   10   10   11

5. You were gone so long we thought you were lost.
   8   11   10 11   11   8   11

6. He taught football at the local high school.
   11   9   11   10   8

Diphthongs Part 3

Test 1 (page 243)

1. He loves to eat Hawaiian ((pie) — poi)!
   13   15

2. She bought some new (tiles — (towels)).
   13   14

3. The ((boy) — bough) fell down.
   15   14

4. They're afraid of the (mouse — (mice))!
   14   13

5. It's a steel ((file) — foil).
   13   15

6. Is it time to go (dine — (down))?
   13   14

7. That's a terrible (voice — vice)!
                  15   13

8. What a good (buy — boy — bow)!
                13   15   14

9. Did you find the (oil — owl — aisle)?
                    15   14   13

10. Spell the word (tile — towel — toil).
                  13   14   15

Test 2 (page 244)

Vowel 13	Vowel 14	Vowel 15
m<u>y</u>	c<u>ow</u>	b<u>oy</u>
try	crowd	join
bright	south	voice
dime	noun	annoy
find	hour	appoint
climb	mountain	destroy

Test 3 (page 244)

1. The cowboys found a brown and white cow.
     14 15   14   14   13   14

2. We invited the clown to join the crowd inside the house.
     13   14   15   14   13   14

3. About midnight we decided to drive down town.
     14   13   13   13   14 14

4. We enjoyed flying through the white clouds high in the sky.
     15   13   13   14   13   13

5. His voice is surprisingly loud.
     15   13   14

6. I counted five royal crowns in the happy crowd.
     14   13 15   14   14

Supplement C

Contrast 1

Practice 4 (page 279)

1. He's sitting in my seat!
   1　2 2　2　　1

2. She didn't finish the cleaning?
   1 2　　2 2　　1 2

3. He put his sheep on the ship.
   1　2　1　　2

4. I have a feeling these shoes won't fit my big feet!
   1 2　1　　2　2　1

Test 1 (page 280)

1. seat　seat　S
2. itch　itch　S
3. peel　pill　D
4. Was it steel?　Was it still?　D
5. He's living here.　He's living here.　S
6. There's the hill.　There's the heel.　D
7. When did he live here?　When did he live here?　S
8. She's sleeping.　She's slipping.　D

Test 2 (page 280)

1. dip　dip　deep　3
2. each　itch　each　2
3. living　living　leaving　3
4. I'll feel it.　I'll fill it.　I'll feel it.　2
5. He's living here.　He's living here.　He's leaving here.　3
6. I need another sheep.　I need another ship.　I need another ship.　1
7. She's slipping.　She's slipping.　She's sleeping.　3
8. Was it steel?　Was it still?　Was it steel?　2

Test 3 (page 280)

1. Vowel 2　slip
2. Vowel 1　easy
3. Vowel 2　sit
4. Vowel 1　He's leaving here.
5. Vowel 2　I need another ship.
6. Vowel 2　I'll fill it.

Contrast 2

Practice 4 (page 281)

1. April weather is wet and rainy.
   3　　4　　4　　3

2. The lady set the pepper on the paper.
   3　4　　4　　3

3. When it gets late, I wait by the gate.
   4　　4 3　　3　　3

4. The red lace dress was on sale.
   4　3　4　　3

Test 1 (page 282)

1. fail   fell   D
2. get   get   S
3. less   lace   D
4. wait   wait   S

5. I have a debt.   I have a debt.   S
6. I have a pain.   I have a pen.   D
7. He tested it.   He tested it.   S
8. I need some paper.   I need some pepper.   D

Test 2 (page 282)

1. main   main   men   3
2. tell   tale   tale   1
3. gate   get   gate   2
4. pepper   pepper   paper   3
5. He tested it.   He tasted it.   He tested it.   2
6. I bought some more paper.   I bought some more pepper.   I bought some more pepper.   1
7. Do you have a pen?   Do you have a pen?   Do you have a pain?   3
8. edge   edge   age   3

Test 3 (page 282)

1. Vowel 4   edge
2. Vowel 3   sale
3. Vowel 4   pepper

4. Vowel 4   Do you have a pen?
5. Vowel 3   Who bought the paper?
6. Vowel 4   He tested it.

Contrast 3

Practice 4 (page 283)

1. Who dropped the cat into the black box?
        7   5   5   7
2. Put the bottle on the black block in the lab.
     7   5   7   5
3. Grandfather put my new socks in the sack.
    5 7   7   5
4. The black cat sat on top of the rock.
    5 5 5 7   7

Test 1 (page 284)

1. black   black   S
2. box   backs   D
3. sock   sock   S
4. top   tap   D

5. battle   bottle   D
6. cap   cap   S
7. cots   cats   D
8. sock   sock   S

Test 2 (page 284)

1. box   box   backs   3
2. cab   cob   cab   2
3. add   add   odd   3
4. tap   top   top   1
5. She dropped the sack.   She dropped the sock.   She dropped the sack.   2

6. cap   cap   cop   3

7. cots   cots   cats   3

8. battle   bottle   bottle   1

Test 3 (page 284)

1. Vowel 5   b<u>a</u>ttle

2. Vowel 7   s<u>o</u>ck

3. Vowel 5   bl<u>a</u>ck

4. Vowel 7   It was a big b<u>o</u>ttle.

5. Vowel 7   I have two little c<u>o</u>ts.

6. Vowel 5   I have two little c<u>a</u>ts.

Contrast 4

Practice 4 (page 285)

1. He won a watch and a lot of money.
    6   7   7   6

2. My brother is studying at another college.
    6   6   6   7

3. The summer months are too hot for comfort.
     6   6   7   6

4. The doctor promised to come on Sunday or Monday.
    7   7   6   6

Test 1 (page 286)

1. shut   shot   D

2. robber   robber   S

3. hut   hot   D

4. cop   cup   D

5. Which color did you want?   Which color did you want?   S

6. Where's the duck?   Where's the dock?   D

7. My lock was good.   My lock was good.   S

8. Who shut it?   Who shot it?   D

Test 2 (page 286)

1. color   color   collar   3

2. robber   rubber   robber   2

3. cut   cot   cut   2

4. nut   nut   not   3

5. My lock was good.   My luck was good.   My lock was good.   2

6. It's a wooden duck.   It's a wooden dock.   It's a wooden duck.   2

7. Who shot it?   Who shot it?   Who shut it?   3

8. Which color do you like?   Which collar do you like?   Which color do you like?   2

Test 3 (page 286)

1. Vowel 6   r<u>u</u>bber

2. Vowel 6   sh<u>u</u>t

3. Vowel 7   l<u>o</u>ck

4. Vowel 6   Which c<u>o</u>lor do you like?

5. Vowel 6   Who sh<u>u</u>t it?

6. Vowel 7   Where is the d<u>o</u>ck?

Contrast 5

Practice 4 (page 287)

    1. Curt shut his shirt in the door!
         12 6   12

    2. Worst luck! Someone burned the buns!
         12 6   6 6   12   6

    3. Uncle Burt! Can you come to supper?
         6   12   6   6 12

    4. Lunch will be served in the other room.
         6   12   6 12

Test 1 (page 288)

    1. bird   bird   S

    2. bun   bun   S

    3. shirt   shut   D

    4. lurk   lurk   S

    5. The bud was yellow.   The bird was yellow.   D

    6. Come and see the buds!   Come and see the buds!   S

    7. I didn't see the cub!   I didn't see the curb!   D

    8. It was fun!   It was fun!   S

Test 2 (page 288)

    1. shut   shut   shirt   3

    2. cut   curt   cut   2

    3. lurk   lurk   luck   3

    4. bun   burn   bun   2

    5. ton   ton   turn   3

    6. Come and see the buds!   Come and see the birds!   Come and see the buds!   2

    7. The cub was black.   The curb was black.   The curb was black.   1

    8. He took a turn.   He took a ton.   He took a ton.   1

Test 3 (page 288)

    1. Vowel 12   shi<u>r</u>t   4. Vowel 12   Come and see the bi<u>r</u>ds!

    2. Vowel 6   l<u>u</u>ck   5. Vowel 12   It was Fe<u>r</u>n!

    3. Vowel 6   The c<u>u</u>b was black.   6. Vowel 6   He took a t<u>o</u>n.

Contrast 6

Practice 4 (page 289)

    1. I should buy some sugar, some soup, some cookies, and some fruit.
         9   9   8   9   8

    2. Ruthy! Don't put your foot on the new blue cushion!
         8   9   9   8 8   9

    3. Woody pushed Louie into the pool! Who did it? Woody did it!
         9 9   8   8   8   8   9

    4. Who took my good new cookbook? Suzy took it.
         8 9   9   8   9   9   8   9

Test 1 (page 290)

1. pull   pull   S
2. full   fool   D
3. pool   pool   S
4. suit   soot   D

5. look   look   S
6. full   full   S
7. It was a long pool.   It was a long pull.   D
8. The suit was black.   The soot was black.   D

Test 2 (page 290)

1. pull   pull   pool   3
2. Luke   look   Luke   2
3. suit   soot   soot   1
4. fool   full   fool   2
5. look   Luke   Luke   1
6. The suit was black.   The suit was black.   The soot was black.   3
7. It was a long pool.   It was a long pull.   It was a long pull.   1
8. It looks foolish.   It looks fullish.   It looks foolish.   2

Test 3 (page 290)

1. Vowel 9   look
2. Vowel 8   fool
3. Vowel 9   good

4. Vowel 8   It was a long pool.
5. Vowel 9   It looks fullish.
6. Vowel 8   The suit was black.

Contrast 7

Practice 4 (page 291)

1. Moe and Joe taught us the wrong song!
   10   10 11   11   11
2. Don't go 'til the lawyer calls!
   10   10   11   11
3. I thought Paul was going home!
   11   11   10   10
4. We won't know the cost 'til we talk to Mr. Shaw.
   10   10   11   11   11

Test 1 (page 292)

1. low   law   D
2. pole   pole   S
3. toast   tossed   D
4. jaw   Joe   D

5. He's getting balder!   He's getting bolder!   D
6. Where's my red ball!   Where's my red bowl?   D
7. I'm in the law school.   I'm in the law school   S
8. Mr. Lewis is bald.   Mr. Lewis is bold.   D

Test 2 (page 292)

1. caught   coat   caught   2
2. whole   hall   hall   1
3. bold   bald   bold   2

4. pole   pole   Paul   3

5. saw   'so   so   1

6. I'm in the law school.   I'm in the law school.   I'm in the low school.   3

7. Mr. Lewis is bold.   Mr. Lewis is bold.   Mr. Lewis is bald.   3

8. Where's my red ball?   Where's my red bowl?   Where's my red ball?   2

Test 3 (page 292)

1. Vowel 11   jaw

2. Vowel 11   Paul

3. Vowel 10   coat

4. Vowel 11   Mr. Lewis is bald.

5. Vowel 10   Where's my red bowl?

6. Vowel 11   I'm in the law school.

Contrast 8

Practice 4 (page 293)

1. Doctor Shaw gave my father a dog.
   7   11   7   11

2. Paul bought a new collar for this dog.
   11   11   7   11

3. The caller caught his collar in the car door!
   11   11   7   7   11

Test 1 (page 294)

1. caught   caught   S

2. cot   cot   S

3. Don   dawn   D

4. yon   yon   S

5. collar   caller   D

6. sod   sawed   D

7. It's dawn.   It's dawn.   S

8. Where's the collar?   Where's the caller?   D

Test 2 (page 294)

1. caught   caught   cot   3

2. Don   dawn   Don   2

3. sawed   sod   sod   1

4. car   car   core   3

5. collar   caller   collar   2

6. Is it far?   Is it four?   Is it four?   1

7. It's Don.   It's Don.   It's dawn.   3

8. Where's the collar?   Where's the caller?   Where's the collar?   2

341

Test 3 (page 294)

1. Vowel 11   t<u>au</u>ght
2. Vowel 7   c<u>o</u>llar
3. Vowel 11   y<u>aw</u>n
4. Vowel 11   Where's the c<u>a</u>ller?
5. Vowel 11   It's d<u>aw</u>n.
6. Vowel 7   It's just an old c<u>a</u>r.

Contrast 9

Practice 4 (page 295)

1. My cousin has gone abroad to study law.
        6   11   11   6   11
2. Paul wants a cup of coffee and a doughnut.
     11   11   6   11   6
3. His daughter taught us a dozen songs.
      11   11   6   11
4. I called the bus company, but I got a wrong number!
    11   6 6   6   11   6

Test 1 (page 296)

1. gone   gun   D
2. song   sung   D
3. bus   bus   S
4. boss   boss   S
5. He caught it.   He cut it.   D
6. Here comes my boss.   Here comes my bus.   D
7. That color is beautiful!   That color is beautiful!   S
8. I need Chuck.   I need chalk.   D

Test 2 (page 296)

1. bought   but   bought   2
2. wrong   wrong   rung   3
3. boss   bus   bus   1
4. cough   cuff   cough   2
5. He caught it.   He caught it.   He cut it.   3
6. My boss is never late!   My bus is never late!   My boss is never late!   2
7. I'll get chalk.   I'll get Chuck.   I'll get Chuck.   1
8. She cut the apple.   She caught the apple.   She cut the apple.   2

Test 3 (page 296)

1. Vowel 11   wr<u>o</u>ng
2. Vowel 6   c<u>u</u>ff
3. Vowel 11   My b<u>o</u>ss is never late!

4. Vowel 6 Which color did you like?

5. Vowel 6 I'll get Chuck.

6. Vowel 6 She cut the apple.

Contrast 10

Practice 4 (page 297)

1. We said, "Goodbye and good luck!" when the judge left the country.
   9   9   6   6   6

2. Next month the woods will be full of hunters.
   6   9   ·9   6

3. Would you put the money in my bus?
   9   9   6   6

4. My brother put a new roof on his study.
   6   9   9   6

Test 1 (page 298)

1. could   could   S

2. luck   look   D

3. took   tuck   D

4. buck   book   D

5. roof   rough   D

6. stood   stood   S

7. I need two bucks.   I need two books.   D

8. How do you spell "rough"?   How do you spell "rough"?   S

Test 2 (page 298)

1. roof   rough   rough   1

2. huff   huff   hoof   3

3. took   tuck   tuck   1

4. stood   stood   stud   3

5. luck   look   luck   2

6. book   book   buck   3

7. I need two bucks.   I need two bucks.   I need two books.   3

8. How do you spell "rough"?   How do you spell "roof"?   How do you spell "rough"?   2

Test 3 (page 298)

1. Vowel 9 stood

2. Vowel 6 luck

3. Vowel 9 put

4. Vowel 9 I need two books.

5. Vowel 9 Where did he put the ball?

6. Vowel 6 I need two bucks.

Contrast 11

Practice 4 (page 299)

1. The woman put the birdbook in her purse.
   9   9   12 9   12 12

2. The cook should return to work on Thursday.
   9   9   12   12   12

3. If Burt would push it and Curt would pull it, they could move it!
   12 9   9   12 9   9   9

Test 1 (page 300)

1. herd   hood   D
2. cook   cook   S
3. shook   shook   S
4. stirred   stood   D
5. He sold his herd.   He sold his hood.   D
6. Can you see the words?   Can you see the woods?   D
7. My last name is Cook.   My last name is Cook.   S
8. The Burkes are coming tomorrow.   The books are coming tomorrow.   D

Test 2 (page 300)

1. shook   shirk   shirk   1
2. purse   purse   puss   3
3. herd   hood   herd   2
4. look   lurk   lurk   1
5. Can you see the words?   Can you see the words?   Can you see the woods?   3
6. My last name is Cook.   My last name is Kirk.   My last name is Kirk.   1
7. He sold his herd.   He sold his herd.   He sold his hood.   3
8. The books are coming tomorrow.   The Burkes are coming tomorrow.   The books are coming tomorrow.   2

Test 3 (page 300)

1. Vowel 12   lurk
2. Vowel 9   shook
3. Vowel 12   He sold his herd.
4. Vowel 9   My last name is Cook.
5. Vowel 9   The books will be there today.
6. Vowel 12   Can you see the words?

Contrast 12

Practice 4 (page 301)

1. Before it snows, we must close our summer home in the country.
   10   6   10   6   10   6

2. Chuck cut his elbow when he shut the broken window.
   6   6   10   6   10   10

344

3. I don't know, and I won't know until the judges vote on Monday.
   10   10   10   10 6   6   10   6

4. Joe sold one boat to his uncle and the other boat to his brother.
   10 10 6   10   6   6   10   6

Test 1 (page 302)

    1. cut   coat   D

    2. comb   comb   S

    3. none   none   S

    4. struck   stroke   D

    5. The dog was chewing a bone.   The dog was chewing a bun.   D

    6. He wants a nut.   He wants a note.   D

    7. It was a little cut.   It was a little cut.   S

    8. He bought a two-ton truck.   He bought a two-tone truck.   D

Test 2 (page 302)

    1. most   must   must   1

    2. rub   rub   robe   3

    3. come   comb   come   2

    4. none   known   known   1

    5. He bought a two-tone truck.   He bought a two-tone truck.   He bought a two-ton truck.   3

    6. She gave him some nuts.   She gave him some notes.   She gave him some nuts.   2

    7. The hum was very quiet.   The home was very quiet.   The home was very quiet.   1

    8. The cut was black and blue.   The coat was black and blue.   The cut was black and blue.   2

Test 3 (page 302)

    1. Vowel 6   Ch<u>u</u>ck

    2. Vowel 6   m<u>u</u>st

    3. Vowel 10   She gave him some n<u>o</u>tes.

    4. Vowel 6   The dog was chewing a b<u>u</u>n.

    5. Vowel 6   He bought a two-t<u>o</u>n truck.

    6. Vowel 10   The c<u>oa</u>t was black and blue.

Contrast 13

Practice 4 (page 303)

    1. Paul pulled the hook out of the dog's paw.
       11 9   9   11   11

    2. My lawyer's daughter is a good cook!
       11   11   9   9

    3. The boss took a strong cup of coffee and two sugar cookies.
       11 9   11   11   9   9

    4. We took a long walk in the woods.
       9   11   11   9

Test 1 (page 304)

    1. foot   fought   D

    2. took   took   S

    3. ball   ball   S

    4. wall   wool   D

    5. It isn't full yet.   It isn't Fall yet.   D

    6. It was a golden hawk.   It was a golden hawk.   S

    7. Who paid for the wall?   Who paid for the wool?   D

    8. The new bull was black.   The new bull was black.   S

Test 2 (page 304)

    1. took   talk   took   2

    2. wool   wool   wall   3

    3. pull   Paul   Paul   1

    4. It was a golden hook.   It was a golden hawk.   It was a golden hook.   2

    5. Who paid for the wall?   Who paid for the wall?   Who paid for the wool?   3

    6. It was full.   It was Fall.   It was Fall.   1

    7. The new bull was black.   The new ball was black.   The new ball was black.   1

    8. The wool was yellow.   The wall was yellow.   The wool was yellow.   2

Test 3 (page 304)

    1. Vowel 11   h<u>aw</u>k

    2. Vowel 9   w<u>oo</u>l

    3. Vowel 11   It was F<u>a</u>ll.

    4. Vowel 11   The w<u>a</u>ll was yellow.

    5. Vowel 9   It was a golden h<u>oo</u>k.

    6. Vowel 11   It was a golden h<u>aw</u>k.

Contrast 14

Practice 4 (page 305)

    1. I met six French singers.
        4   2   4   2

    2. Which letter did Ted write?
        2   4   2   4

    3. Ken wrote six checks on the fifth of September.
        4   2   4   2   4 4

    4. Six friendly children were sitting next to the president.
        2   4   2   2 2   4   4

Test 1 (page 306)

    1. spell   spell   S

    2. wrist   wrist   S

    3. big   beg   D

    4. ten   tin   D

5. Is it better? Is it better? S

6. That's a big check. That's a big chick. D

7. It tastes bitter. It tastes bitter. S

8. He spilled it. He spelled it. D

Test 2 (page 306)

1. tin tin ten 3

2. beg big beg 2

3. fill fell fell 1

4. did dead did 2

5. I like your pen. I like your pen. I like your pin. 3

6. Does it taste better? Does it taste bitter? Does it taste better? 2

7. She spilled it. She spelled it. She spelled it. 1

8. Is that a pen? Is that a new pen? Is that a new pin? 3

Test 3 (page 306)

1. Vowel 2   wr<u>i</u>st

2. Vowel 4   sp<u>e</u>ll

3. Vowel 2   Does it taste b<u>i</u>tter?

4. Vowel 4   That's a big ch<u>e</u>ck.

5. Vowel 2   I like your new p<u>i</u>n.

6. Vowel 4   She sp<u>e</u>lled it.

Contrast 15

Practice 4 (page 307)

1. Let's ask Edna to lend us a pan.
      4 5 4   4   5

2. I have to move ten heavy leather saddles.
    5   4 4   4   5

3. The weather will be better after January.
      4   4 5   5

4. He asked for ten sandwiches and eleven apples.
    5   4 5   4   5

Test 1 (page 308)

1. add add S

2. led led S

3. cattle kettle D

4. leather lather D

5. He broke the pedal. He broke the pedal. S

6. Did the men come yet? Did the man come yet? D

7. New lather smells good. New leather smells good. D

8. I found an old pan. I found an old pan. S

Test 2 (page 308)

1. paddle   paddle   pedal   3
2. Ed   add   add   1
3. ten   tan   ten   2
4. kettle   cattle   kettle   2
5. New lather smells good.   New lather smells good.   New leather smells good.   3
6. Who bought the kettle?   Who bought the cattle?   Who bought the cattle?   1
7. I found an old pan.   I found an old pen.   I found an old pan.   2
8. I found the band.   I found the band.   I found the bend.   3

Test 3 (page 308)

1. Vowel 4   Ed
2. Vowel 4   pedal
3. Vowel 5   Who bought the cattle?
4. Vowel 4   Which men got the job?
5. Vowel 4   New leather smells good.
6. Vowel 5   I found an old pan.

Contrast 16

Practice 4 (page 309)

1. The class had lunch at half past one.
    5   5   6   5   5   5   6
2. Someone ordered a dozen hamburgers and a dozen apples.
    6   6   6   5   5   6   5
3. My aunt and uncle will leave for the country on Saturday, Sunday, or Monday.
    5   5   6   6   5   6   6
4. My young cousin had a bad accident.
    6   6   5   5   5

Test 1 (page 310)

1. match   much   D
2. cat   cat   S
3. sung   sung   S
4. Someone hurt my uncle!   Someone hurt my ankle!   D
5. I saw a beautiful gal!   I saw a beautiful gull!   D
6. It was Dan on the phone.   It was done on the phone.   D
7. The cab was black and white.   The cab was black and white.   S
8. I bought a little green hut.   I bought a little green hat.   D

Test 2 (page 310)

1. ran   run   ran   2
2. much   match   match   1
3. Dan   Dan   done   3

4. Someone hurt my ankle!   Someone hurt my uncle!   Someone hurt my uncle!   1
5. I saw a beautiful gull!   I saw a beautiful gull!   I saw a beautiful gal!   3
6. I bought a little green hat.   I bought a little green hat.   I bought a little green hut.   3
7. The cub was black and white.   The cab was black and white.   The cub was black and white.   2
8. She had a little cut on her arm.   She had a little cut on her arm.   She had a little cat on her arm.   3

Test 3 (page 310)
1. Vowel 6   much
2. Vowel 5   sang
3. Vowel 5   I bought a little green hat.
4. Vowel 6   Someone hurt my uncle!
5. Vowel 6   She had a little cut on her arm.
6. Vowel 6   I saw a beautiful gull!